THE SOVIETS AS NAVAL OPPONENTS
1941-1945

Friedrich Ruge
Vice Admiral, Federal German Navy (Retired)

NAVAL INSTITUTE PRESS

Library of Congress Catalog Card Number: 78-69952
ISBN: 0-87021-676-7

Printed in the United States of America

Contents

Introduction

The purpose of this book is to represent Soviet naval activities from 1941 to 1945 as they appeared to the German side, particularly to those men who were directly concerned. The Soviet versions of the events are given when available. Both versions are subjective. Consequently, where possible, the best existing evaluations of the actual facts are added. Accordingly, three types of sources have been used: the German war diaries, Soviet publications, and works by Western historians.

The German war diaries were evaluated for the U.S. Navy by a team of former German naval officers in the years 1949 to 1952. Then funds ran out although the work was not yet finished. It was resumed on a smaller scale in 1955, but after two years was again brought to a halt, this time for good. The material collected by this Naval Historical Team contains much detailed information, which has been used here to recreate a considerable number of incidents. Many of them are not particularly important in themselves, but they are instructive, especially for younger officers who have no war experience of their own.

The Soviet publications are mainly the personal stories of officers who took part in the naval war, and popular descriptions of naval operations. There are also some official compilations, such as *The Great Patriotic War*, a six-volume work which was published in Russian early in the sixties in Moscow and was soon translated into German in East Berlin, where many Soviet books appear in German. It is referred to hereafter as the Official History.

All these Soviet publications are stronger in "heroic deeds" and "blows smashing the enemy" than in facts. So far, no Soviet war diaries have been published or made accessible to Western historians. Therefore, it is fortunate that in a thoroughgoing effort, Professor J. Rohwer and Dr. G. Hümmelchen have extracted all the available facts from Russian and Western literature and incorporated them in their most useful work, *Chronology of the War at Sea 1939–1945*. There are quite a number of good books by Western authors on the Soviet naval operations, but for facts, Rohwer/Hümmelchen is the most reliable reference book.

A combination of the three types of sources, as attempted here, makes it possible to describe and evaluate the main events in the three theaters of war, Baltic, Black Sea, and Barents Sea, at the same time leaving ample scope to the reader for forming his own conclusions.

I would like to express my indebtedness for the idea of preparing this study to Mr. A. D. Baker III, who had read the original three-volume compilation of the material gathered by the Naval Historical Team mentioned above and translated into English by Mr. Thomas Koines. The author also wishes to thank those who have assisted him, particularly Mrs. Christine Ulrich and Mr. Jan Snouck-Hurgronje of the U. S. Naval Institute, as well as Mrs. Erika Köhler and Professor Dr. Erich Born, of the University of Tübingen, and he will welcome constructive criticism, corrections and supplementary information.

F. Ruge

THE
SOVIETS
AS
NAVAL
OPPONENTS
1941-1945

Historical Background

The name "Rus" or "Ros" for the men of Slavonic tribes living in the center of what is now European Russia first appeared in the ninth century A.D. It derived from the Finnish "ruotsi," which meant either "oarsmen" or "the men from Roslagen," that is, the Swedish coast opposite the west coast of Finland. In any case it denoted the Varangians, Swedish Norsemen, who crossed the Baltic and followed the trade routes along the big rivers through central Russia. About the year 860 A. D., Rurik founded the "empire" of Novgorod, Askold that of Kiev. Oleg united them soon afterwards. The objective of these Swedish Vikings was to reach the Near East for trade and plunder. As early as 860 A. D. they attacked Constantinople, but were beaten off. In 907 A. D. a massive attack seems almost to have succeeded. In any case, they were granted a trading agreement with very favorable conditions, which in later treaties were not repeated. Their traders also reached the Caucasus area and traded, via the Volga River and the Caspian Sea, with the Caliphate of Baghdad.

In this first Russia the Varangian warriors ruled over a number of local Slavonic tribes, but were assimilated by them in the course of two centuries. Their empire decayed and dissolved into several principalities, which in their turn were subjugated by the Mongols in the thirteenth century. By that time, long-range trading and shipping had greatly declined, and now it ceased altogether for about 300 years. In the fifteenth century, the Grand Dukedom of Moscow gained liberty from the rule of the Tatars. It reestablished connection with the sea by reaching the White Sea. In 1553, trade with England started, and in 1584 Arkhangelsk was founded as the first Russian seaport.

In honor of the maritime exploits of the Varangians, ships of the Imperial Russian Navy bore names like Rurik, Askold, Oleg, and Variag. The Soviet Navy continues to use them. Moreover, there is a tendency today to advance Russian naval history by about 600 years. In 1976 Admiral Gorshkov, Commander-in-Chief of the Soviet Navy since 1956, wrote in his book *Morskaya Moshch' Gosudarstva* (The Sea Power of the State):

As a matter of fact, our ancestors, beginning in the third century, waged war in the Black, Mediterranean, and Caspian Seas. History tells us that even then the ancient Slavic tribes were making extended sea voyages, which gives us reason to believe that navigation by our Slavic forbears in the northern part of the Black Sea, in the Dniepr River areas, and in other parts of eastern Europe had been developed in much earlier times. The fact that in the year 269 A. D. these tribes sailed a large fleet and defeated Athens, Corinth, Sparta and had reached the shores of Crete and Cyprus clearly demonstrates that navigation and a knowledge of sea routes in the Black, Aegean, Marmora, and Mediterranean Seas was anything but a new experience for the ancient Slavic tribes who populated the southern regions of our country.[1]

Actually, beginning in the year 150 A. D., Germanic tribes, mainly Goths, migrated from the coasts of the Baltic to the Black Sea. Around 230 A. D., they settled near the mouth of the Dniestr River. About 20 years later, another tribe, the Heruleans, were driven out of Scandinavia by the Danes and followed the Goths to the Black Sea. In the Greek towns here these tribes found enough ships and shipbuilding facilities to build up fleets quickly. They took advantage of the grave disorders in the Roman Empire between 260 and 270 A. D. to break through the Roman defenses repeatedly and to reach the Mediterranean. Here they sacked a number of coastal towns and even reached Crete and Cyprus. Then they were defeated by the Romans. The Heruleans disappeared from history; the Goths later moved westwards. Their raids between 260 and 270 A. D. had no lasting consequences.

There is no proof that any Slavs took part. If they did, they certainly did not play a prominent role. The fact that these raids into the Mediterranean started from places conquered by the Russians about 1,500 years later would hardly seem evidence enough for Admiral Gorshkov's claim of extensive Slav navigation in the eastern

Mediterranean in antiquity. One is inclined to smile at his story, but it should be realized that the Soviets are rewriting history to support their imperialistic claims. Among other things they claim the right to access to the Mediterranean and to a firm foothold there. They use stories like this as grounds for their claims, and that is why these fairytales have to be contradicted.

THE BEGINNINGS OF RUSSIAN SEA POWER

All through the first half of the seventeenth century the Russians explored Siberia by land, until they reached the Pacific at Okhotsk in 1645. In the few summer months they also proceeded along the north coast by ship and gained the Bering Strait in 1671, Kamchatka in 1679. Expansion to the west and naval history began with Peter the Great (1689–1725). He had a sense for power as well as for sea power, whereas his great opponent, Charles XII of Sweden (1697–1718), did not fully grasp the importance of Swedish control of the Baltic. Peter took energetic steps to secure access to the (comparatively) open sea for his country. He had prepared himself thoroughly by studying naval construction in the Netherlands, navigation in England, and gunnery in Germany. On the Black Sea, he won the port of Azov, but lost it again to the Turks, so that he could not carry out his plans for a fleet of 40 ships-of-the-line. In the Baltic he was luckier. First he gained access to the innermost part of the Gulf of Finland where, significantly, he founded St. Petersburg (now Leningrad) as the capital of Russia, and built the naval base of Kronstadt. Then he secured Estonia, with several ports, and began to build a fleet which was soon strong enough to defeat the Swedes. In 1716 he went to his ally Denmark with his fleet and an army, but instead of attacking southern Sweden, as had been agreed upon, he stayed on Zealand not far from Copenhagen. At the same time, another Russian army occupied the German dukedom of Mecklenburg opposite the Danish islands, although the Swedes had been driven out of all the territories south of the Baltic.

The diplomatic correspondence of that year gives a good picture of Western consternation over Peter's obvious intention to secure for Russia a firm position near the entrances to the Baltic. His continental allies—Prussia, Denmark, and Saxony—did not feel strong enough to force him out. Eventually, the British government sent a powerful squadron to the Baltic. Peter took this broad hint and returned to his own bases. In the following years his fleet dev-

3

astated large parts of the countryside along the extended Swedish coast, burning villages and manors, killing off cattle, even setting fire to the woods.

After Peter's death (1725) the Russian Navy was neglected, but it remained strong enough to send a squadron to the Mediterranean during the war against Turkey (1768–1774). There it destroyed a Turkish squadron at Cesme on the coast of Asia Minor. During the Napoleonic Wars, the Russians again sent warships and troops to the Mediterranean, where they occupied the Ionian Islands (Corfu) in 1800. Nelson wrote to his government that in his opinion the Russian fleet had come to the Mediterranean not to fight the French but to acquire bases for Russia. Consequently, England ejected these forces in 1807 when Russia had allied herself temporarily with France. Twenty years later a Russian fleet again operated in the Mediterranean, this time to support the Greeks in their war of liberation. At Navarino, a fleet composed of a British, a French, and a Russian squadron destroyed the Turkish-Egyptian fleet.

In the eighteenth and nineteenth centuries in several wars against Turkey, Russia enlarged her territory in the Black Sea area. Her fleet conducted a number of successful operations, but other powers, especially Great Britain, prevented the tsars from reaching their main goal, direct access to the Mediterranean by gaining control over the Bosporus and Dardanelles. In the Crimean War (1854–1857) a strong Anglo-French fleet entered the Black Sea and landed a large army on the Crimea for the siege of Sevastopol, the main naval base. The Russian Black Sea Fleet was not considered strong enough for a naval battle and therefore was sacrificed in the defense of the fortress. The crews were put ashore with their guns; ships were scuttled to block the entrances to the port. Another war against Turkey (1877–1878) increased Russia's influence in the Balkans but did not bring her nearer to possession of the Turkish Narrows.

The Soviets have not given up this aim. In July 1945 when the war in Europe was just ended, Stalin demanded positions on the Narrows from Turkey, "for the common defense." This was strictly refused, and no more was heard of it for the time being. But in a series of articles written in 1972 (published by the U. S. Naval Institute *Proceedings* in 1974) Admiral Gorshkov again took up this subject. He wrote:

. . . historically, it has turned out that when a threat arises of enemy encroachment on the territory of Russia from the southwest, the Russian

4

Navy has been moved into the Mediterranean Sea where it has successfully executed major strategic missions in defending the country's borders from aggression. In other words, our Navy has shown the whole world that the Mediterranean Sea is not anyone's preserve or a closed lake and that Russia is a Mediterranean power. The location of her forces in these waters is based not only on geographical conditions (the proximity of the Black Sea to the Mediterranean theater), but also the age-old need for the Russian Navy to stay there.[2]

Again, Gorshkov's historical reasoning is somewhat doubtful, to say the least, and probably he would not like it if Mediterranean powers applied the same reasoning to the Black Sea. However, it is interesting because it shows the tenacity of the Russians in the pursuance of political aims that at first seem far beyond their possibilities. In the Baltic, the First World War left them only the eastern end of the Gulf of Finland, but they have since annexed the Baltic States and the northern part of East Prussia, and through the Warsaw Pact, they dominate the coast to the Bay of Lübeck. On the Black Sea, where at the time of Peter the Great not a single Russian lived, they now dominate more than half the coast, and they aim at targets beyond the Turkish Narrows. There is no difference between the aims of the tsars and those of the Bolshevist leaders. Now as then, the Navy is one of their tools. Sometimes, it seems forgotten, but it is always remembered again. Getting a picture of its operations during the last war is important for understanding its role today.

THE RUSSO-JAPANESE WAR (1904–1905)

In the Far East during the second half of the nineteenth century, the Russians wrested vast territories from China. On the Pacific coast they established the big naval bases of Vladivostok and Port Arthur and stationed naval forces there as strong as the Japanese Fleet. Yet the Japanese attacked when Russia made preparations to advance into northern Korea. (Incidentally, in a diplomatic note the Russian government suggested the 39th parallel as dividing line between Russian and Japanese interests.) The success of the Japanese campaign in Manchuria and of the siege of Port Arthur depended entirely on sea power.

The Japanese won because training and leadership in their navy proved better than in the Russian. Admiral Makarov, probably the only man who might have changed that, was killed early in the war when his flagship *Petropavlovsk* blew up and sank with all hands after striking a Japanese mine. The Baltic Fleet, sent to relieve Port Arthur, arrived too late to prevent the fall of the fortress and suffered total defeat at Tsushima. (A Russian landing detachment occupied this island in 1861 but was compelled by a British warship to reembark).

In reaction against mismanagement and defeat on land and at sea, revolution broke out in many places in Russia, and led to mutiny in the Black Sea Fleet (whose ships were prevented by international treaties from passing the Turkish Narrows) and to the cruise of the "armored cruiser" *Potemkin* (actually a battleship) made famous by Eisenstein's film.

WORLD WAR I–BALTIC

However, order was restored, reforms were initiated, and under the able Admiral von Essen the reconstruction of the Russian Navy was taken in hand. In the Baltic, the aim was to reach sixty percent of the strength of the German High Seas Fleet. At first, help from the outside was utilized to a considerable extent. The armored cruiser *Rurik* (15,400 tons, 4 254-mm. guns, 8 203-mm. guns) was built in England by Vickers, turbines for large destroyers in Germany. At the same time, the creation of an efficient armaments industry was begun; large shipyards were built. In June 1909 the keels of four fast battleships (23,400 tons, 12 305-mm. guns) were laid in shipyards in St. Petersburg. The ships were commissioned in 1914–1915. Three similar battleships, slightly slower, but better protected, were finished in Black Sea shipyards between 1915 and 1917, but four very large battle cruisers (32,400 tons, 12 356-mm. guns) for the Baltic were never completed. A high-quality product of the new Russian shipyards was a series of 36 large destroyers, excellently suited for minelaying.

When war broke out, both sides considered the Baltic a secondary theater of operations. The Germans had to be more active because they were more vulnerable to Russian naval operations. They generally used their old ships in the Baltic but had the advantage of being able to send ships from the High Seas Fleet as reinforcements on short notice. This possibility made the Russians very cautious. They were well prepared for minelaying, and in the first winter of the war undertook a number of cleverly planned operations of this kind in the eastern and central Baltic. Several German warships and merchant steamers were sunk or damaged by Russian mines; operations were considerably hampered. On the other hand, German submarines, as well as mines, proved dangerous to the Russians. After the death of Admiral von Essen in the spring of 1915 Russian naval activity decreased noticeably.

In the spring and summer of 1915 a massive German-Austrian land offensive forced back the Russian armies several hundred kilometers. When German land forces approached the large naval base of Libau (Liepaja) a squadron of Russian armored cruisers tried to interfere but retreated after a short fight with German light cruisers, in which no ship was seriously damaged. The only other encounter between surface forces in the open Baltic happened on 2 July 1915. A squadron of five Russian armored cruisers intercepted the minelayer *Albatross* (2,200 tons, 8 88-mm. guns), which was protected by the light cruiser *Augsburg* (4,300 tons, 12 105-mm. guns). The *Albatross* was soon damaged and beached herself at Östergarne on the Swedish island of Gotland. Then the German armored cruiser *Roon* (9,500 tons, 4 210-mm. guns) and the light cruiser *Lübeck* joined in the fight. With 4 254-mm. and 20 203-mm. guns the Russians were still far superior but they did not succeed in seriously damaging the German cruisers. They received some hits, too, and finally retreated although no other German forces were near.

In August 1915, a German squadron, reinforced from the North Sea, made two attempts to break into the Gulf of Riga. In the first, the mine barriers proved impenetrable. The second succeeded, in spite of considerable losses to mines, but had no lasting consequences because the German Army did not participate, although its flank on the Gulf of Riga was being continuously harrassed by bombardments from the sea and even raids by parties landed from the sea.

In the summer of 1915, the number of British submarines in the Baltic was increased. The larger E-boats again passed the Sound (between Denmark and Sweden) as in the fall of 1914; the smaller C-class arrived via canals from the White Sea. They proved distinctly more effective than the Russian submarines. For two years neither side undertook any large naval operations. The Germans suffered losses to mines and submarines, but their domination of the Baltic was never challenged. Sea power worked unobtrusively.

For Germany it was vital to have absolute control of the central and western Baltic: she received most of her iron ore from Sweden, most of the grain from her eastern provinces and coal from the Ruhr district was carried by ship, the supplies for the northern wing of the army fighting Russia went by sea, and—last but not least—sea power relieved the army from the necessity of defending the long coasts in the Baltic. Lord Fisher, for many years the British First Sea Lord, strongly advocated large-scale operations in the Baltic. He was of the opinion that this would compel the Germans to station one million men along their coasts. His estimate was probably too high, but it indicates the size of the potential problem for the German armed forces. Early in 1915 the Royal Navy ordered the *Courageous* class (19,000 tons, 4 381-mm. guns, 32 knots, draft only 6.8 m.) for Baltic operations. However, the outcome of the Battle of Jutland (31 May/1 June 1916) clearly showed that such an undertaking would be too risky even for the Grand Fleet. The battle did not change the over-all strategic situation and therefore in some quarters is considered of little importance. True, the blockade of Germany continued but so did that of Russia, since the British had to abandon their plans for directly supporting her through the Baltic.

As early as January 1915 the Russian government had asked the Western allies to open the sea routes to European Russia again. This request led to the well-conceived, but clumsily executed attack on the Dardanelles in the spring of 1915. In the land campaign of that year the Russian armies suffered disproportionately heavy losses in men as a result of lack of ammunition. According to Minister of War Suchomlinov, field batteries received no more than four rounds per gun for a whole day of fighting. When the Black Sea and the Baltic remained closed the situation in Russia deteriorated steadily. Construction of the Murmansk railway had only just begun; from Arkhangelsk 900 kilometers of narrow-gauge rail led to the main railway system. Nine thousand kilometers of single-track railway crossed Siberia to the Far East. In the winter of 1916–17 food in the larger towns was in such short supply that four meatless days per week had to be instituted. The revolution in February 1917 was the consequence of starvation at home and decimation and defeat in the field. When the Kerensky government tried to continue the fight, the Central Powers put pressure on with three limited offensives. The last was an amphibious operation to take the Baltic Islands of Ösel, Moon (Muhu), and Dagö. Russian ships still fought well but without luck. The old battleship *Slava* was damaged by German battleships and had to be blown up by her own crew. The destroyer

Grom was taken. The Germans lost a number of smaller vessels to mines.

In this context it is amusing to read another fairytale of Gorshkov's: "The Moon Sound operation (12 to 20 October 1917) . . . had the far-reaching goal of uniting the Central Powers, Britain, the U.S.A., and France in the struggle against the Russian Revolution."[3] When he quotes Lenin to support this strange idea he only shows that this paragon of political wisdom knew very little of sea power and its consequences. He should have been grateful to the Central Powers, for the loss of the Baltic Islands further weakened the Kerensky government and helped make the Bolshevist October Revolution possible. Figures and facts are distorted in Gorshkov's short description of the operation, which practically ended the naval war in the Baltic.

World War I–Black Sea

In the Black Sea the Russian naval forces were more active than in the Baltic. After the German battle cruiser *Goeben* joined the Turkish fleet in August 1914 neither side had a marked superiority until the new Russian battleships appeared. There were quite a number of engagements, but no conclusive results. When their allies attacked the Dardanelles the Russians repeatedly bombarded the fortifications at the entrance to the Bosporus but did not attempt any landing operations. By this abstention they may have missed the best opportunity for radically improving their supply situation.

The Turkish army in East Anatolia depended on sea transport for a great part of its supplies. When the first new Russian battleship was commissioned in the winter of 1915–16, Admiral Kolchak, formerly chief-of-staff to Admiral von Essen, made good use of her, and soon the Russians had the upper hand. Well-supported from the sea, their army advanced deep into Turkish territory. At the same time naval forces attacked and nearly stopped the vital transport of coal from Zunguldak on the Black Sea to the Bosporus. With a British army advancing on Palestine, Turkey's situation soon became critical, but then the October Revolution put an end to Russian operations in Anatolia. The Germans occupied the Ukraine and the Black Sea ports. After the German capitulation, French forces entered Sevastopol temporarily. The best ships of the Russian Black Sea Fleet left with them and rusted for many years at the French base of Bizerta in Algeria.

After foreign war, two revolutions, and a long civil war, the remnants of the Russian Navy were in bad shape. Its reconstruction had to take second place behind that of the Army. The experts disagreed on the type of navy needed by the Soviet Union. The Communist Party decided for a kind of "jeune école" fleet, a navy for coastal defense with torpedo craft and submarines. Then Stalin assumed command. With his acute sense for politics and power he saw the possibilities of a strong navy for furthering his plans. He also saw the technical difficulties and therefore did not precipitate matters. The second Five-Year Plan (1933–1937) provided for construction of six heavy cruisers, a number of large destroyers and a minimum of 50 submarines. Then, in the Party Congress of 1934, Stalin launched his campaign for capital ships—through a prominent submarine officer. For the construction of battleships and carriers, begun in the third Five-Year Plan, he tried to get help from the USA, but his request was turned down. After the treaty with Hitler in 1939 he received a half-finished heavy cruiser (the *Seydlitz*), fire-control gear, and other equipment. In the Supreme Soviet, Premier Molotov declared that in the third Five-Year Plan the Navy had first priority. *Pravda* declared: "Only the biggest High Seas Fleet will meet Soviet demands."[4] When the Germans attacked in 1941, the big ships were not yet ready, but 291 submarines of the target number of 325 were in service or nearing completion.

10

The Baltic

In the fall of 1939 the Soviets took advantage of the war between Germany and Poland to occupy the eastern part of Poland, as well as Latvia and Estonia. Then they attacked Finland. At first they met with reverses, but the difference in manpower and means was so great that in March 1940 Finland had to give in. She ceded Vyborg and the naval base of Hangö on the Gulf of Finland and had to permit the Russians use of Petsamo on the Barents Sea. Here the Russians had already developed the port of Murmansk and the naval base of Polyarnyy on Kola Bay.

German planning did not make any use of the possibilities of the Baltic as a main road for attack and supply. Certainly, the submarine war against Great Britain had to be continued in full force but this did not preclude naval participation in the attack against the Soviet Union. Moscow was a main objective, and a look at the map will show that from the inner part of the Gulf of Finland the distance is 600 kilometers, as against 1,000 kilometers from the frontier in Poland. But the German General Staff did not take that look. Neither did it realize that complete elimination of the Soviet Baltic Fleet would save considerable forces later on. As a consequence, the error of 1914 was repeated. There was no combined plan. The Navy remained on the defensive whilst the Army conducted rapid offensive operations over vast areas and great distances with barely sufficient forces and inadequate logistic capabilities.

In June 1941, the Soviet Fleet in the Baltic (under Vice Admiral Tribuc) was composed of:

    2 battleships (23,300 tons, 12 305-mm. guns)
    2 heavy cruisers (8,000 tons, 9 180-mm. guns)
    2 flotilla leaders (2,900 tons, 5 130-mm. guns)
   12 new destroyers
    7 old destroyers
    7 torpedo boats
   65 submarines of different types
    6 minelayers
   33 minesweepers
    1 gunboat
   48 motor torpedo boats and slower craft with torpedoes.

The Fleet had its own Naval Air Arm with 656 planes stationed on airfields near the coast.

On the German side the following ships took part:

   10 minelayers
    5 submarines (from the training squadron)
   28 motor torpedo boats (MTB)
    3 ships for sweeping magnetic mines (*Sperrbrecher*)
    3 squadrons of modern minesweepers (about 20 boats)
    5 squadrons of trawlers for minesweeping and antisubmarine warfare (30 boats)
    2 squadrons of motor minesweepers (16 boats)
    2 ships with motor launches for sweeping shallow mines.

The German Navy had no naval air arm and had to rely on the general Air Force, which had units for cooperation with the Navy but had not done enough in that direction.

The Finnish Navy had two coastal defense ships (3,900 tons), six motor torpedo boats, five submarines and some minesweepers and patrol craft.

When on 21 June 1941 the German armies crossed the frontier and entered Russia, German naval forces had already begun to lay large minefields in accordance with the naval defensive planning. One group of fields extended from Memel (now Klaipeda), the northernmost port in East Prussia, to the vicinity of the Swedish island of Öland. Another group was laid far back, off the Pomeranian coast in the Kolberg area. Defensive minefields against surface ships have a decided attraction for one's own shipping. These mines were no exception and accounted for a number of German ships.

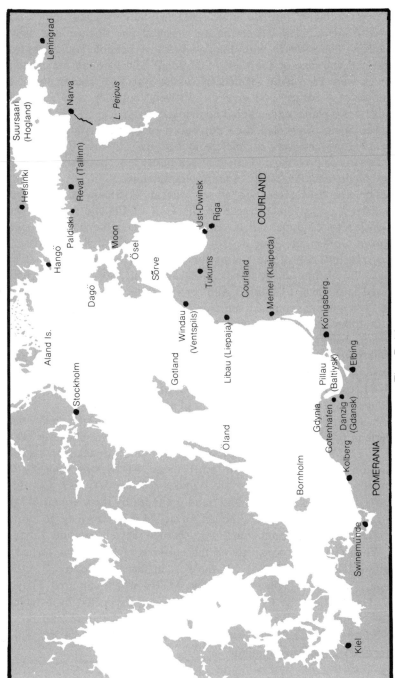

The Baltic

German motor torpedo boats (MTBs) laid magnetic mines off several Soviet ports and entrances, captured one steamer and sank another. The alliance with Finland made it possible to lay mines near the entrance of the Gulf of Finland. The German minelaying forces were repeatedly sighted by Soviet warships, among them a battleship, a cruiser, and several destroyers, but they were attacked only by two planes and suffered no damage.

The Soviet Navy had been put into a preliminary state of alarm on 19 June and was completely alerted on 21 June. Their strict orders not to provoke a German attack under any circumstances may explain the initial inactivity of the Soviet warships.

The first Soviet reaction at sea was an operation to lay large minefields across the entrance to the Gulf of Finland in the night from 22 to 23 June. To cover the minelayers, the heavy cruiser *Maxim Gorky* and three destroyers left the Gulf of Riga. Outside, they ran into one of the German minefields. The destroyer *Gnevny* sank; the *Maxim Gorky* lost her forecastle, but was kept afloat and towed into Reval (Tallinn). Another destroyer suffered minor damages when her paravane cut mines which exploded.

In Libau, their most advanced Baltic base, the Soviets had stationed their 1st Submarine Brigade with 15 submarines, besides some patrol and minesweeping craft. When the Germans could not be stopped, five submarines, which were under repair (S–1, M–71, M–81, ex-Latvian *Ronis* and *Spidola*), were scuttled, as well as the old destroyer *Lenin*, an icebreaker and some smaller ships.

A minesweeper laid several small minefields, which sank the German minesweepers M–3134 and M–1706 and the subchaser UJ–113. The Russian submarines put to sea, some to take up patrol positions, the rest bound for other bases. M–78 was sunk by a torpedo of German U–144 off Windau (Ventspils); S–3 was destroyed with depth charges and hand grenades by the German MTB S–35 off Steinort on the Latvian coast. M–83, returning to port, possibly in a damaged condition, scuttled herself outside Libau.

When German troops entered the outskirts of Libau, five torpedo cutters (similar to MTBs) left the port in the night from 27 to 28 June. They had a fight with German MTBs, which captured TKA–47. On 29 June the German 291st Division, supported by a naval close combat detachment, was in possession of the town and port, where the Russians had destroyed as much as possible of the military and technical installations.

14

The destroyer *Lenin* was among the Soviet ships scuttled in the port of Libau in June 1941.

In the first days of the war, up to 20 Soviet submarines were at sea in the Baltic. L–3 laid mines near Memel, S–4 reconnoitered near the Pomeranian coast, S–10 in the Gulf of Danzig. The others took up waiting positions against a possible German attack by sea. At the end of June these submarines were recalled, apparently without having attacked any German ships. M–101 was lost, probably torpedoed by the German U–149.

Cruisers and destroyers based at Ust-Dwinsk, the outer port of Riga, laid mines in the western part of the Irbe Strait, the entrance to the Gulf of Riga, on the nights of 24 and 26 June. During the second operation they met German MTBs, which were also laying mines. In the ensuing fight the destroyer *Storozevny* was damaged; another vessel was sunk, possibly the Soviet submarine S–10, which was returning to port. Russian mines sank the German mine-sweepers M–201 and R–205. Four R-class motor minesweepers were damaged.

All through the 1941 campaign, the Baltic Red Banner Fleet, as it was officially named, was active only with submarines and mine-laying. At the beginning it had at its disposal at least 65 submarines (some sources give 75). In the first weeks, 11 were lost at sea, mostly on mines; five more were put out of action in Libau. The remaining boats had so little effect that as early as 12 July German commercial and supply shipping was resumed. Soon permission was given to proceed without any escorts. By December 1941, when ice conditions made it impossible for the Soviet submarines to leave their bases on the Gulf of Finland, they had sunk not more than one steamer and one submarine (U–144 by ShCh–307 on 27 July outside the Gulf of Finland). Their mines accounted for two more steamers. Twenty-seven Soviet submarines were lost in the Baltic or destroyed in port before the end of 1941.

The Gulf of Riga

The defensive attitude of the German Navy led to a peculiar military situation in the Baltic countries of Latvia and Estonia. German troops soon occupied the southern shore of the Gulf of Riga, as in 1915, but now including the town of Riga and its port Ust-Dwinsk. Northeast of Riga, the front then stabilized in such a way that Soviet naval forces could continue to operate in the Gulf of Riga and to use the dredged channel in Moon Sound to reach the Gulf of Finland. The German Army already suffered from lack of supplies; the possibilities of sea transport were rediscovered; the Navy was asked to escort ships with army supplies to Ust-Dwinsk. It was to be assumed that the Russians had mined the approaches to that port and also the Irbe Strait, the entrance to the Gulf of Riga. Therefore MR–11 (*Minenräumschiff*–11, a mine-clearing ship) received orders to proceed to Ust-Dwinsk. She was a former merchant ship of 5,100 GRT, armed with three 105-mm. guns and carrying 12 motor launches for sweeping shallow mines. Escorted by minesweepers M–23 and M–31 (600 tons, 2 105-mm. guns), she arrived off the Irbe Strait on the morning of 6 July 1941. During her approach she was unsuccessfully attacked by Soviet planes. The situation which now developed is described in the war diary of MR–11 as follows (abbreviated):

On 6 July at 1026 hrs the Commanding Officer of MR–11 received a radio message ordering him to wait at the entrance of Irbe Strait for a convoy of 4 motor barges with army supplies destined for Riga. It was escorted by trawlers of the 31st Minesweeping Flotilla. As more air attacks were to be expected the Commanding Officer came to the resolution to leave only M–23 for the convoy and to proceed at once with MR–11 behind M–31 (minesweeping gear out).

At 1045 hrs the two ships were attacked by 3 planes which dropped 8 bombs near them. No hits.

At 1200 hrs 4 vessels sighted almost due north. When they approach they are made out as two larger and two smaller destroyers (*Grossny* and *Lenin* classes). Course of MR–11 east-north-east, 3 destroyers steer east, one southwest, probably to cut off our retreat.

At a distance of about 18,000 meters the three destroyers open fire. Their first salvoes straddle MR–11, but when the fire is returned at a distance of 15,000 meters (the utmost range of the 105-mm guns) the Russian fire soon becomes less accurate.

M–31 receives orders to lay a smoke screen. To do so it takes up a position on the port bow of MR–11. The apparatus for making artificial smoke does not work but the Russian destroyers turn away, possibly because they take the maneuvers of M–31 as an attempt to attack with torpedoes (which the M-boats actually did not carry). The fourth destroyer now turns up to a parallel course. The other destroyers reopen fire without hitting the German ships whereas MR–11 observes at least one hit on one of them.

They lay a smoke screen; there is an interval in the engagement from 1255 to 1330 hrs, in which MR–11 rounds Kolka Lighthouse, enters the Gulf of Riga and changes course to the south. At 1330 hrs five planes attack with 14 bombs, no hits, one plane shot down.

At 1335 hrs the two larger destroyers approach from the starboard quarter and attempt to fire at the two German ships across Cape Kolkas. Distance about 25,000 meters, salvoes very short. Enemy proceeding at high speed, salvoes come nearer. Fire returned although distance still too great. At 1415 hrs the destroyers break off the fight and disappear in a northwesterly direction.

At 1430 hrs another attack by 3 planes, 6 bombs, no hit. At 1900 hrs dropped anchor off Ust-Dwinsk, protected by patrolling MTBs.

The fact that the large and unhandy ship was not hit by any bomb is due to the strong and well-directed antiaircraft fire. The planes which at the first attack on the evening of 5 July approached lower than 2,000 meters, kept heights between 3,000 and 4,000 meters in the continuous attacks of the following day. Expenditure of ammunition: 96 rounds 105-mm, 850 rounds 37-mm, 3,730 rounds 20-mm.

Fighting the four destroyers 198 rounds of 105-mm shells were fired, 120 fall of shot were observed near MR–11.

It is my opinion that the enemy had no clear picture of the type of ship he was confronted with. Probably he was deceived by the quick succession of our salvoes.

Rossow (Commanding Officer)[1]

The official Soviet history, *The Great Patriotic War*, mentions this action as follows:

When laying mines in the Gulf of Riga on 6 July 1941, Soviet destroyers under the command of Commander G. S. Abaschwili had an engagement with a group of German ships. Several ships of the enemy were damaged and forced to turn away.[2]

One wonders what the Soviet battle report looks like. In any case, the convoy escorted by M–23 reached Ust-Dwinsk unmolested but five days later M–23 had to be beached after hitting a mine near Pernau (Pärnu) (northeastern part of the Gulf of Riga) where she had escorted MR–11.

The Soviet High Command quickly recognized the importance of the supply traffic to Riga and Pernau and formed a special unit of destroyers, motor torpedo boats, and patrol boats under Rear Admiral W. P. Drozd to operate against it. Between 12 July and 2 September Soviet destroyers, MTBs, and planes repeatedly tried to intercept the slow German convoys, which were protected only by minesweepers (heaviest caliber: 105-mm.), motor minesweepers (37-mm.) and sometimes by MTBs (20-mm. or 37-mm.). Under the Soviet threat the supply traffic had to be suspended repeatedly, but never for more than a few days. Large convoys passed through the Irbe Strait on 12 and 13 July, on 18 July, on 26 July, on 1 August, etc. Fifty thousand tons of supplies reached the German Army in Riga and Pernau within six weeks. Soviet destroyers attacked for the last time on 21 August, MTBs (torpedo cutters) on 2 September.

The Soviets reported German losses after most attacks, for example the sinking of 12 transports on 18 July and of two minelayers and one destroyer on 1 August. Actually, quite a number of transports and warships were slightly damaged by fragments and near misses, but not a single transport was sunk or put out of action. One small army assault boat (for the attack on the islands) was sunk by a shell or a bomb. Ten minesweepers of different types were lost on mines. There is no doubt that had they been more aggressive, the Soviets could have interrupted the supply traffic completely. For this phase of the naval war it is typical that in at least one case (on 18 July) the motor minesweepers, escorting a convoy of motor barges, simulated a torpedo attack when Soviet destroyers approached. The destroyers turned away; the convoy reached port without any damage. The Russians lost their destroyer *Steregushchy* to bombs and one destroyer (probably *Smely*) to a torpedo launched by MTB S–54 on 26 July.

Retreat from Reval

Against stubborn resistance the German 18th Army slowly advanced into northern Estonia and on 7 August reached the shore

The old Soviet destroyer *Karl Marx* was sunk by a German dive-bomber in Loksa Bay in the Gulf of Finland on 8 August 1941.

of the Gulf of Finland at Kunda and Juminda Cape about 30 miles east of Reval, cutting the land connection between Reval and Narva, viz. Leningrad. The Soviets had assembled a great fleet of warships and transports at their large naval base at Reval, and there was extensive traffic all along the coast between the northern exit of Moon Sound and the port of Kronstadt. To hamper it the Finnish Navy had laid a minefield off Juminda at the end of June. During July and in the first days of August, Finns and Germans laid more minefields. When the Soviets began to evacuate Reval by sea in the middle of August, minelaying was resumed.

At first, some small convoys succeeded in passing the mined area with tolerable losses. Evidently, the Russians swept channels during the night, for during the day the German army batteries in position near Cape Juminda did not see any ships. Then a convoy which left Reval in the evening of 24 August lost three of its nine transports on mines, as well as the destroyer *Engels* and three minesweepers. Two more transports were sunk by air attack.

On 27 August the German 42nd Army Corps reached the outskirts of Reval. On the following day, four large convoys and about 120 warships, from heavy cruiser down to motor minesweeper and torpedo cutter, left the port for Kronstadt. In the afternoon they

19

were attacked from the air; during the night they attempted to pass the Juminda minefields but had to anchor because losses were too heavy. During the following day they proceeded under heavy air attacks.

For once, there are detailed Russian reports on this operation but they disagree about the losses. The Official History says:

Almost immediately after leaving the port of Tallinn [Reval] the Soviet warships and transports were attacked from the air, taken under fire by land artillery and some time later attacked by MTBs. Thanks to the heroic efforts and the skillful maneuvering of the crews of the warships the blows of the German Air Force were unsuccessful, not a single ship was lost to air attack . . .
With nightfall there came a new great danger, the mines. The Fleet had not enough minesweepers to escort a large number of ships through the minefields simultaneously. Therefore in the attempt to break through these fields, several destroyers, patrol ships, and minesweepers were lost on mines.[3]

Actually, four ships (three transports, one icebreaker) are known to have been lost to air attack before crossing the minefields. Five destroyers, three submarines, ten smaller warships, and thirteen transports sank in the minefields; more were damaged (names of all these ships as well as the four lost to air attack are known). On the following day, at least four more transports were sunk by air attack; three had to be beached. Only one reached Kronstadt, in a damaged condition. In the following days small Russian warships rescued more than 12,000 men who had saved themselves on islands or rocky beaches in the Gulf of Finland. The Soviet submarine ShCh–322, which had orders to cover this retreat, did not return to port, and was probably lost on a mine.

Leningrad

While the Baltic Islands Moon, Ösel, and Dagö, as well as the base at Hangö in southwestern Finland, were held by strong Soviet forces, German armor advancing on Leningrad first came under the effective fire of battleships and cruisers, either moored in the mercantile port of Leningrad or moving in the shipping canal from Leningrad to Kronstadt and to the Gulf of Finland, on 7 September. Ten days later these ships were attacked by dive-bombers. Several were damaged; the battleship *Marat* sank in the shallow water of the mercantile port. However, her heavy turrets were soon in order again, and she was a mainstay of the Soviet defense all through the war. The German army artillery was not capable of putting the Soviet ships out of action. They greatly helped the Red Army to defend Leningrad and to hold a beachhead around Oranienbaum southwest of Kronstadt. As a consequence, the innermost part of the Gulf of Finland with the islands of Lavansaari and Seiskari remained in Russian hands throughout the war. The ships of the Fleet could even train there to some extent.

Occupation of the Baltic Islands

The Russian garrison on the Baltic Islands still hampered traffic in the Irbe Strait with heavy artillery fire from Sõrve Peninsula, and traffic in the Baltic with MTBs. Therefore the German armed forces undertook a combined operation to occupy the islands. To keep losses low the operation started on 13 September with simultaneous feints against the island of Ösel from the northwest, from the west, and from the south (from the Irbe Strait, against the fortified peninsula of Sõrve). Small fleets, composed mainly of auxiliaries, minesweepers, and patrol boats, appeared, took the beaches under fire and pretended to start minesweeping and disembarkation. The only heavier ships which took part were two Finnish coastal defense vessels (3,900 tons, 4 254-mm. guns). On the way back one of them (*Ilmarinen*) struck a mine and sank. The only other loss was that of M–1707, a minesweeping trawler which struck a mine during the second demonstration off Sõrve, undertaken at the request of the Army.

The Russians took all these movements as serious landing attempts and reported a great number of German ships destroyed, namely eight transports, twelve landing craft, two patrol boats, one torpedo boat, three destroyers, one auxiliary, and numerous motorboats. Actually, besides the *Ilmarinen* and M–1707, only some small assault boats were lost on rocks or because of mistakes in navigation.

The German Supreme Command thought it possible that under the growing pressure the Soviets would try to send their larger ships to Sweden for internment before the Gulf of Finland was closed. To counter such a move, a "Baltic Fleet" was formed around the battleship *Tirpitz* (42,000 tons, 8 380-mm. guns). Light cruisers bombarded Sõrve and were attacked in vain by submarines and MTBs. Formed somewhat earlier, this "Baltic Fleet" could have taken a hand at preventing the Soviet convoys from leaving Reval. Now it was dissolved after a few days because it was evident that the Russian ships were all headed for Kronstadt-Leningrad.

The feints against the Baltic Islands were successful: the Russians rushed reinforcements to the places that seemed threatened. The real attack came "from the rear," from Estonia. Infantry crossed the Moon Sound in numerous small boats. The island of Moon was quickly taken against strong resistance, and the dam to Ösel and a beachhead there were secured before reinforcements arrived from the western part of the island. Fighting stubbornly, the Russians retreated to Sõrve Peninsula. There the last resistance ceased on 5 October. One week later, German troops crossed the Soela Sound to the island of Dagö. Again a feint had successfully diverted the attention of the defenders; on 21 October the last surrendered after minesweepers prevented them from leaving the island in fishing boats for Hangö. On the islands about 15,000 Russians were taken prisoners; the Germans lost 3,000 dead and wounded.

Evacuation of Hangö

In the Leningrad area, the Soviets counterattacked furiously and, beginning on 5 October, even undertook a series of desperate amphibious operations on a small scale to enlarge the Oranienbaum beachhead. Admiral Wurmbach, stationed at Reval in command of the coastal defenses on the Gulf of Finland, writes in his evaluation:

At the beginning of October, the Russians carried out minor landing operations. In the first night they sent about 150 men, mostly young men, who had been soldiers for only a few days. They landed from small boats near Strelnya between Leningrad and Oranienbaum. As soon as the boats were near the shore the soldiers were forced to jump overboard and to wade to the shore. As the coast was manned by observation posts only at that time (there were not yet any batteries there) they reached dry land; in view of their insufficient fighting qualities, which were further greatly decreased by the very cold weather and their wet clothes, they were either killed or taken prisoner. In the following night the operation was repeated with 300 men and in the third night with about 800 men. As the defense forces had been strengthened in the meantime, the results were also negative, and many of the men did not reach the shore. On the fourth day tanks attempted to break through from Leningrad to Oranienbaum but they were also repulsed. Had the Russians landed 1,000 men at the very first attempt, and attacked simultaneously along the coast from Leningrad and Oranienbaum, they certainly could have taken the coast and established temporary contact at least. This shows the inadequate planning and lack of cooperation between the Navy (the landings were carried out by Navy personnel) and the Army.

The last sentence is not quite conclusive, for the Command of the Baltic Fleet had formed seven naval brigades and some other units for the defense of Leningrad. In the fall of 1941, 80,000 naval personnel fought under the High Command set up for the Leningrad area.

At the entrance of the Gulf of Finland the great base of Hangö still held out. The garrison of about 25,000 men did not attempt an all-out attack on the rather weak Finnish forces which kept the fortress loosely encircled from the land side. The reason probably was that the Soviet main army was too far away. But there was all the more activity in the skerries, small rocky islands outside the port. The Russians landed forces on several of these islands and took some of them. On others, their attempts failed against strong Finnish resistance.

Hangö was supplied by sea, partly by submarines, but the difficulty of getting through the minefields and the impossiblity of getting through the ice to be expected from December till April made it necessary to evacuate the garrison. This was carried out by four large and some smaller convoys between the end of October and the first days of December, with Vice Admiral Drozd in charge. Losses in ships and men were heavy: three destroyers and at least ten smaller warships and transports sank. On 3 December, during the last operation, the transport *Josef Stalin* (7,500 GRT), a passenger steamer packed with men, struck several mines. Ammunition detonated inside the ship: 4,000 men were killed; many hundreds were taken off by the escorts. The wreck drifted on and was finally taken in tow and beached by German patrols. They found 2,000 men still alive on board.

Soon afterwards, ice set in; the large Soviet submarine K–51 had to give up her attempt to reach the central Baltic for a three-month cruise.

How surprised the Red Banner Fleet was by the outbreak of the war is difficult to say. It was soon compelled to give up its advanced base at Libau, but then it was able to continue to operate almost unrestricted in the eastern Baltic and particularly in the gulfs of Riga and Finland, because the German Navy confined its activities mainly to minelaying and escorting convoys and kept its larger ships back.

In his book on the naval war in East-European waters Jürg Meister says:

In the summer of 1941 the Red Fleet still was in full reconstruction, many of the new ships' crews were not yet completely trained and in the submarine fleet especially, neither the boats nor their crews were ready for war. But the complete tactical failure of modern destroyers in several fights with German auxiliaries, minesweepers, and motor mine-sweepers cannot be explained. The Soviet mine and submarine war also fell far short of what the Germans expected.[4]

On the other hand, the Red Banner Fleet greatly assisted in the defense of Leningrad and Oranienbaum as well as in the evacuation of Reval and Hangö. As has happened repeatedly in Russian naval history, personal heroism and failure to exploit favorable situations often coincided. In the years following 1941 the Baltic Fleet made full use of the possibilities still left to it in the Gulf of Finland, until in 1944 the situation changed completely in favor of the Soviets.

BALTIC 1942

In early spring, 1942, the fact that the Red Banner Fleet had not been put completely out of action set off two operations in the Gulf of Finland. The first was a Finnish attack across the ice to take the island of Suursaari, and then, supported by German troops, that of Suur-Tytersaari nearby. Both moves succeeded, and the islands were held against massive counterattacks. On the other hand, the islands of Lavansaari, Peninsaari, and Seiskari remained in Soviet hands. This gave the Red Fleet a minimum of space for training purposes and facilitated the attacks on the Finnish and German ships guarding the minefields.

The second operation, undertaken at the request of the Supreme Command of the German Navy, was a series of air attacks on the battleships and cruisers of the Baltic Fleet at Leningrad and Kronstadt. Bombers and dive-bombers made about 600 sorties and hit most of the larger ships, without putting them out of action, however. Quite a number of planes were lost.

After both operations the Soviet naval forces were still able to support the Leningrad front and the Oranienbaum beachhead, and to keep the three islands mentioned above fully supplied and well-defended. As a consequence, the danger from Russian mines and submarines continued in the Gulf of Finland and in the eastern Baltic. The Finnish Navy was for closing the Gulf of Finland com-

The Soviet passenger steamer *Josef Stalin* was used for evacuating troops from Hangö in November 1941. Left behind by the Soviet escort ships after being damaged by mines, the ship was beached by German patrols and the troops taken prisoner.

pletely with a net barrier, but the necessary material was available neither in Finland nor in Germany. As a second-best measure, extensive minefields were laid by Finnish and German ships, but the fact that the Russians held the islands of Lavansaari and Seiskari made it impossible to go as deeply into the Gulf of Finland as the situation on the mainland would otherwise have permitted. The German Navy wanted to take Lavansaari, but Soviet counterattacks had created difficult situations along large parts of the German front. No forces could be spared during the period when the operation could have been carried out over the ice. On 6 April, it was definitely canceled.

This decision had far-reaching consequences. All through the campaigns of 1942 to 1944, the Red Fleet, which had its own air arm, used Lavansaari as a stationary carrier from which planes supported the minesweepers when they worked at clearing passages for their submarines through the Finnish-German minefields. Batteries on the island protected their own small craft and, together with the planes, hampered the movements of the German patrols, which had to be kept up all the time. In contrast, the German Air Force, after the attacks on the Russian ships in Leningrad and Kronstadt, could hardly ever spare even a few planes to assist the Navy in the Gulf of Finland. In the long run, omitting to take Leningrad and in this way to eliminate the Baltic Red Banner Fleet completely, cost dear. For minesweeping and submarine hunting alone, nine squadrons had to be transferred to the eastern Baltic. These together with the mine-layers numbered over 100 vessels. This was about one third the number of corresponding forces operating in the offshore waters along the coasts of the Netherlands, Belgium, and France as far as the Spanish frontier.

Inland, the Finnish troops had reached the northern bank of Lake Ladoga, but the Soviets had a fleet of small ships there and maintained traffic across the lake between their canals. This enabled them to supply Leningrad better than the besieging German army could be provisioned. Finns, Italians, and Germans sent small craft by motor transport to Lake Ladoga but they were not suited to the conditions there. In this way, seapower played an important part even inland.

Soviet submarines in 1942

Besides supporting the front, the main task of the Soviet Fleet now was to get submarines through the Finnish-German mines and patrols to the open Baltic where a considerable traffic was running all the time. The submarines were carefully prepared for their mission. They were given a thick coat of paint, probably as protection against hydro-electric mines (first used by the U.S. Navy in 1918 for the big system of minefields across the northern exit of the North Sea where most of the German submarines passed). The paint may have been a primitive anticipation of "Alberich," a special plastic skin that absorbed sonar waves and was used by German submarines in 1944–45.

In addition, wooden frames were arranged in such a way that the mooring ropes of mines, which might be encountered when proceeding at great depth, would not foul horizontal rudders, bilge keels, or other parts of the hull.

The minefields nearest to Lavansaari were to be crossed on the surface in places where Russian minesweepers had swept channels. The enemy patrols were to be harassed from the island, from the sea, and from the air in every possible way. Farther out the submarines were to try to get around the minefields in shallow water or to pass under them by diving as deeply as circumstances allowed. When the noise of a mooring rope scraping along the hull was heard, the engines were to be stopped until the sound ceased, showing that the mine had been passed. Meanwhile, the enemy patrols and sub-chasers were to be kept busy from the air to divert their attention and to prevent them from using their hydrophones.

Between 12 and 19 June 1942, the Russians succeeded in getting a first wave of eight submarines through the minefields west of Lavansaari, one or two a night. M–95 was lost on a mine. The others were first employed to reconnoiter the Finnish-German mine and patrol system as well as the routes used by enemy shipping. Then they operated in various parts of the eastern Baltic, mainly in the western part of the Gulf of Finland, but also along the Swedish coast and even to the coast of Pomerania. S–7 sank four steamers totalling 9,164 GRT, ShCh–317 four ships with 8,283 GRT, the others no more than one ship each. Among their victims were three Swedish ships torpedoed without warning and without declaration of a zone of blockade by the Soviet government.

The Soviet High Command gave orders to the submarine captains to respect Swedish territorial waters and Swedish ships, but did not make any official announcement of these instructions. They first came to light after submarine S–7 was sunk on 21 October 1942 by a Finnish submarine and her captain picked up. As far as can be ascertained, in 1942 Soviet submarines attacked Swedish merchant ships in 17 incidents, sinking five ships altogether. After the experi-ence with the first wave of Soviet submarines the Swedish govern-ment introduced compulsory convoys protected by Swedish warships. These repeatedly used depth-charges against attacking submarines.

The Soviet captains had a noticeable tendency to overestimate their successes. ShCh–317 reported five ships with 46,000 GRT torpedoed and sunk whereas the actual figure was four ships with 8,000 GRT. This case is particularly interesting because Captain 2nd Rank V. A. Jegorov, Commanding Officer of the Submarine Division, took part in the cruise to assist the young captain. Returning to base this boat was damaged by a mine and then sunk by subchasers.

Commenting on the Soviet historian Piterski's report of this phase of the Soviet submarine war, Dr. J. Rohwer states:

On 15 June 1942 ShCh–304 reported the sinking of a transport of 10,000 GRT, but actually her torpedoes missed magnetic minesweeping ship MR–12 (7,500 GRT). ShCh–320 assumed she had sunk 3 ships with 22,000 GRT, among them submarine tender *Mosel*. Actually she missed minelayer *Kaiser* in the entrance of the Gulf of Finland, then sank the German steamer *Anna Katrin Fritzen* (676 GRT) off Nidden (East Prussian coast) and missed steamer *Gudrun* which she took for the *Mosel*. S–4 was out of luck and in a cruise of 48 days succeeded only in missing the steamer *Fritz Schoop* off Rixhöft (Pomeranian coast). ShCh–303 had the impression she had sunk a steamer of 7,000 GRT on 12 July near Porkkala (Finland), but this attack was not even observed. On 20 July, the same boat torpedoed steamer *Aldebaran* (7,891 GRT) near Utoe (entrance of Gulf of Finland) but the ship could be brought into port. In this case, it was supposed that a steamer of 10,000 GRT had been sunk.[5]

These exaggerations may be explained partly at least by the insufficient training conditions in the narrow waters that could be used by the Soviet submarines. Moreover, their practice seemed to be to dive at once after launching torpedoes, and apparently they took each detonation as a hit. Similar mistakes were not uncommon in other navies (including the German Navy, particularly after the introduction of the acoustic homing torpedo), but generally they were somewhat more limited.

The second wave started in two parts: seven submarines attempted the passage between 11 and 21 August, followed by three submarines between 5 and 8 September, energetically supported from the air and by different types of patrol craft. The German motor minesweeper R–106 was sunk by close-combat planes, subchaser UJ–1216 by MTBs. Three submarines struck mines—M–97 and ShCh–405 sank, and ShCh–323 was severely damaged but returned to base.

This second group reported 14 merchantmen with 100,000 GRT sunk. The actual result was seven ships with 14,000 GRT torpedoed, of which five with 10,000 GRT sank.

The third wave also passed the minefields in two echelons, the first of seven submarines between 18 and 30 September, the second of ten submarines between 5 and 27 October, with one boat following in early November. The minefields had been reinforced in the meantime: submarines ShCh–302, ShCh–304, ShCh–311, and ShCh–320 were lost outwardbound. ShCh–305, ShCh–306, and S–7 were sunk by Finnish submarines. At least two were damaged by mines when they returned.

The third wave claimed to have sunk 18 ships with 150,00 GRT. The actual result was ten ships with 34,000 GRT torpedoed, of

The most successful submarines in the Baltic Fleet were the ShCh class. ShCh–406 was lost in late summer 1943, while trying to pass through the German minefields in the Gulf of Finland.

which six with 12,000 GRT sank. Three more with 12,000 GRT were lost to mines probably laid by Soviet submarine L–3. Added up, the result of the Soviet submarine campaign in the Baltic in 1942 was: 23 ships with 52,000 GRT sunk, eight ships with 32,000 GRT damaged. The Soviet Official History gives exaggerated figures for the individual boats, but as the total result, 29 ships sunk and two more damaged, without mentioning the tonnage.

Ten Soviet submarines were lost, and at least seven damaged. In addition, at least 18 patrol boats, minesweepers, subchasers, and MTBs were lost as they assisted their submarines to pass the minefields.

The last submarine returned in the middle of December. Then ice conditions in the Gulf of Finland made operations impossible. There can be no doubt about the perseverance of the Soviet submarines and their ability to operate in the Baltic. However, an evaluation of the experiences laid down in the German war diaries indicates that their operational and tactical training was insufficient. It is probable that lack of adequate training facilities was one of the causes. However, the submarine captains did not seem flexible enough to take advantage of the opportunities present before the German antisubmarine measures were strengthened. The boats of the first wave, in particular, preferred to attack small steamers proceeding independently. Later in the summer, they also attacked convoys but generally lacked the tenacity needed for that type of fighting. They neither repeated unsuccessful attacks nor did they make any effort to destroy damaged ships completely. (The magnification of their successes may have prevented the captains as well as the Soviet Submarine Command from getting a reliable picture of the true state of affairs. Even the Soviet Official History still maintains, for example, that "ShCh–303 under Commander J. W. Trawkin sank a transport with 1,500 soldiers and officers, and submarine D–2 a ship with 3,000 German soldiers."[6] The names of the ships are not given, and these events simply did not happen.)

It is a slight exaggeration, therefore, when Admiral Isakov writes that "the Soviet submarines put terror into the heart of the enemy."[7] However, they developed into more than a mere nuisance, mainly because the antisubmarine forces on the Finnish-German side were too weak to protect the large amount of traffic that became vulnerable once the Soviet submarines made it through the minefields to the open Baltic.

To improve the situation three Finnish submarines were employed for hunting Soviet submarines. Within a few weeks at the end of October and beginning of November, they succeeded in sinking three of them. As a consequence, Soviet submarine activity shifted to the central Baltic, without much success, because there, too, the submarines usually selected as their targets small ships which sailed independently.

The general development was summed up by the German Commander of Minesweepers and Patrols. In his war diary, he wrote at the end of the year 1942:

In contrast to the summer of 1941 the enemy demonstrated activity at sea which had not been observed among the Russians up to that time. They made ready and committed a large number of patrol boats and motor minesweepers, many minesweepers as well as PT boats (MTBs) and a few gunboats. They have 2 to 3 submarines in constant operation in the Baltic. The Russian MTBs were likewise very active and frequently sought out suitable targets among our antisubmarine patrol forces near Hogland [Suursaari], and they even scored one success in torpedoing submarine chaser UJ–1214.

Russian patrol boats primarily protected the convoys between Leningrad and Kronstadt and along the coastal area and the islands occupied by the Russians. They also protected the motor minesweepers in the course of their work at the minefields.

Russian MTBs laid moored mines on the supply route between Kotka and Hogland and at the entrance to Koivisto. These two operations were the only enemy minelaying activities which were discovered. The fear that the enemy might lay moored mines in the submarine hunting area fortunately proved unfounded. The use of mines there would have restricted, if not occasionally paralyzed, submarine hunting operations.

Several times in this year the Russians attacked trawlers and minesweepers in the submarine hunting area with aerial torpedoes. The attacks were poorly executed and remained unsuccessful.

Someri Island

By utilizing Lavansaari Island as a forward base, the Russians succeeded in tying down considerable Finnish-German forces. They even tried to improve their position by an attempt to take Someri Island, off the Finnish coast north of Lavansaari, on 8 July 1942. The Finnish report on this operation is interesting to read. It says:

The Russians apparently underestimated the strength of the island fortress and . . . were too weak to complete their mission. An air attack in the night of 7/8 July was more disadvantageous to the operation than advantageous, for it had only little effect, but the garrison was warned in time so that the element of surprise was lost. The Russian artillery fire was poorly controlled and was quite often directed at targets of secondary importance. Cooperation of the Russian forces on land, at sea, and in the air was bad, and the tactics seemed unsatisfactory. The most surprising fact was that the Russians employed no cruisers or destroyers, which they had at Kronstadt and Leningrad at that very moment. The presence of a couple of destroyers would probably have prevented the Finns from bringing reinforcements to the island. The complete lack of proper landing craft was also noteworthy (a deficiency which the Russians could not overcome during the entire war, even though some improvements were evident in 1944 and 1945). This lack compelled the Russian infantry to lie unprotected on the decks of the motor torpedo boats which were little suited for this mission. Heavy equipment could not be carried by these boats nor could it be landed.

The operation against Someri was one of the first landing attempts on a somewhat larger scale in the Gulf of Finland, and at the same time it was one of the most disastrous Russian landing operations in the Second World War.

This Finnish evaluation explains why the Russian attack failed. Since the manner in which it was undertaken is illuminating in other respects, too, a description of the entire engagement seems appropriate.

The island of Someri is situated about ten nautical miles north of Lavansaari, and the Russian batteries stationed there could reach it.

The distance from Someri to the Finnish coast is slightly greater. The island is about 950 meters long, 450 wide, entirely rocky, but not higher than 15 meters. The Finnish garrison consisted of 92 men, one Lotta (a member of the female auxiliary service), and one horse. There were four strong points with two 75-mm. guns, three 45-mm. guns, about 20 20-mm. and machine guns, and two 81-mm. mortars.

Around midnight of 7 July (no real darkness in that high latitude), Soviet planes dropped about 100 bombs. Then patrol boats took strong point Itaepaeaea under fire, and MTBs approached the coast to put soldiers ashore. One blew up in the Finnish fire, but about 80 men landed, encircled the strong point and took it after three hours. Three of the 26 defenders broke through to another strong point. The Russians now tried to land more men and to take the other positions but were beaten back and lost several MTBs.

Two Finnish gunboats and five small patrol boats had been alerted and arrived one by one from 0200 hours on. They succeeded in dodging repeated attacks of the numerous MTBs (one report mentions 27) and in preventing them from reaching the island.

At 0630 hours the German minesweeper M–18 arrived; at 1100 hours a Finnish infantry company (109 men) was brought from the mainland, and the gunboats, which had expended all their ammunition, received a new supply.

The Finnish infantry made slow progress, although supported by naval gunfire. In the afternoon, a Soviet gunboat, two torpedo boats, and some minesweepers took the Finnish ships under fire, but did not hit them because they kept at a distance of about 13,000 meters. The Finns again ran out of ammunition, and two Russian MTBs succeeded in landing more men. Three German ships (artillery carrier SAT–28, tender *Nettelbeck*, M–37) reinforced the defense. The Russians did not reach the island again. In the evening some Russian soldiers surrendered; in the early morning of 9 July a final attempt to land more men was beaten off; shortly after noon the last 53 men gave up. But till the evening of 11 July the Russian vessels repeatedly tried to approach, evidently under the impression that the fighting was not yet ended.

In numerous engagements the Russians did not put a single ship out of action. In 14 air attacks the two Finnish gunboats and M–18 were damaged. Finnish planes sank gunboat *Kama* and probably two MTBs. On Someri the Russians lost 128 dead and 149 prisoners;

the Finns reported sinking about 15 MTBs and patrol boats; Russian figures are not available. The Finns lost 21 dead and 63 wounded.

This operation was characteristic in several respects. The planning and the initial attack were bold, and men were used ruthlessly, but after partial success at the beginning the enterprise bogged down. The larger ships, which could have made the difference, were held back. There can be no doubt that one or two destroyers could have put out of action all the small ships that supported the defense.

BALTIC 1943

During the winter of 1942 to 1943 the Russians managed to repair some of the larger ships of the Red Banner Fleet. When the ice disappeared at the end of April the following ships were ready: 2 battleships (one damaged and aground but with artillery functioning), 2 heavy cruisers, 11 destroyers, 6 coastal defense ships, 33 submarines, 57 minesweepers, 29 MTBs, 75 subchasers and other small craft. There were 280 planes, which in the following months were increased to 940. This gave the Russians a clear superiority in the air.

According to official Soviet statements, by the middle of 1943 nine naval rifle brigades and some independent battalions had been formed of naval personnel, numbering 130,000 men. They fought on land in the defense of Leningrad. Nothing is known about the selection and the training of these forces, and the effect of this measure on the combat readiness of the Fleet can only be surmised.

As before, the tasks of the Red Navy were supporting the Army, and attacking enemy shipping in the Baltic. The larger ships down to the destroyers were used exclusively against land targets in the Leningrad-Kronstadt area, and for supporting and reinforcing the large Oranienbaum beachhead. German plans to take it were never executed because sufficient forces could not be made available. It is somewhat surprising that the German artillery did not succeed in putting out of action the ships that often shelled German positions.

For the Finnish and the German navies, the main task was to prevent the Soviet submarines from attacking their vital traffic outside the Gulf of Finland. In 1942 the Germans alone had escorted nearly 1,900 merchant ships with a tonnage of 5.6 million GRT, and over 400,000 soldiers had been transported by sea. As soon as the ice situation permitted, Germans and Finns laid extensive minefields, practically in the same positions as in 1942. There had been proof

33

The *Storozhevoy*-class destroyers, one of which is shown here in company with two Fugas-class minesweepers and a Beriyev MBR–2 flyingboat, were the most modern Soviet destroyers of the period.

enough, however, that mines were no impenetrable obstruction for the submarines. Those that got through had not caused too much damage, but they were a permanent threat and tied down a great number of antisubmarine and escort vessels. Therefore preparations were made to close the western part of the Gulf of Finland completely by a net barrier which extended from the Estonian coast west of Reval to the Finnish coast near Porkkala. It was laid in several sections all through April, at times in very bad weather, but the operation was undisturbed by the Soviet Navy (which probably was still icebound).

As in the previous year, Soviet submarines succeeded in passing the area of the minefields, again supported energetically by their light forces and from the air. In the second half of May, at least three Soviet submarines appeared between the mines and the nets and tried tenaciously to gain the open Baltic, but not a single one succeeded. ShCh–406 and ShCh–408 were destroyed after a long chase; ShCh–303 was damaged but managed to get back to her base, in spite of the mines.

During the summer of 1943 the attempts to break through the barriers were repeated. Again light Soviet forces opened a road through the minefields for their submarines. The light vessels guarding the fields suffered some losses under the attacks of Soviet MTBs and planes. On the other hand, the Soviet submarines S–9 and S–12 were hunted and destroyed. The nets proved to be a perfect obstruction; not a single submarine succeeded in breaking through. As a consequence, all through 1943 and spring and summer 1944, not a ship was lost in the Baltic to submarine attack. Rear Admiral N. A. Piterski explains this very modestly as follows:

Owing to the great danger from mines in the Gulf of Finland we could not send our big ships to sea. Without the surface forces of the Fleet, it was very difficult for our submarines to penetrate the strong enemy defense system. Therefore the Baltic remained free from Soviet submarines for some time.[8]

The net barrier held till the German land front had to fall back from the Estonian coast, and Finland was compelled to make peace with the Soviet Union (4 September 1944). Then the net ceased to be an obstacle because it could be bypassed. It was later removed.

The light forces of the Red Banner Fleet were very active in 1943. Minelaying increased, especially between Suursaari and Someri; massive minesweeping west of Lavansaari continued all the time. The sweepers suffered some losses to the German patrols and the battery on Tytersaari but could not be hindered seriously.

In his comprehensive report on the year 1943, Commander Minesweepers said:

The enemy conducted the naval war in a similar manner as in the preceding year, but there was substantially greater activity of surface vessels (minesweepers and MTBs). The number of these small craft had been increased considerably by those which had been employed the year before on the Neva above Leningrad and now were free (because the German front had been forced back). The Russians first built up the airfields on Seiskari and Lavansaari and had to provide rather heavy supply traffic to that end. The supply routes were protected so strongly that our motor minesweepers did not succeed in laying mines on them. They were attacked by stronger patrol boats and had to abandon the attempts.

Several times the Russians endeavored with larger forces—up to 30 boats—to clear a route from Lavansaari via Vigrund in the direction of Aseri (i.e., to the west). The minesweepers were protected by MTBs which gave smoke cover and attacked our patrol boats. The enemy also attacked our patrols behind our minefields with strong air units . . .

Russian MTBs were employed in laying mines in the waters of the Finnish skerries and west of Tyters, in dropping agents on the Finnish and Estonian coasts and in attacking mine and net barrier patrol vessels.

The Russian Submarine Command obviously had found out that the defensive measures were so effective in this year that a breakthrough to the west was impossible. Therefore submarines were sighted only rarely after the end of the summer. But even then their only mission was to drop agents on Hogland Island [Suursaari], on Tytersaari Island, or on the Estonian coast.

The Russian Air Force was employed more actively than in the year before. Right at the beginning of operations aerial mines were dropped in Reval Bay. At the end of November British mines of the ELM-type [*Englishe Luft Mine*] were dropped in the inner channels. Torpedo planes were employed more than in 1942 against merchant shipping north of the latitude of Libau. However, the Russian air forces for minelaying and torpedo missions must have been very small. The bombers operating against our patrols behind our minefields were much more active. They attacked our boats on their positions in favorable flying weather mostly by day, but also on clear nights, finally forcing our units to withdraw during the day.

The attack methods of the Russian planes are well known. New tactical concepts were not observed.

It was not surprising that the large increase in the number of naval planes made itself felt, even though the planes had to direct many of their attacks against targets on land (the Soviet Official History says ninety percent[9]). Torpedo planes were now capable of operating up to 800 kilometers from their bases. The German admiral commanding in the Eastern Baltic summarized in August 1943:

Enemy air activity unusually intensive. No fighter defense from our own Air Force available, Finns supply some fighters. In the week from 18 to 25 August 465 planes counted over the Gulf of Finland while only 93 were counted the week before . . .

Attacks by well-trained pilots especially in the Tuetters [Tyters] area . . .

In June, 46 attacks by 155 planes with 300 bombs dropped, in July 54 attacks by 186 planes with 350 bombs dropped . . .

A considerable number of German and Finnish minesweepers and patrol vessels were damaged; a few (five?) were sunk. From August to November, boats of the 3rd Minesweeping Flotilla on patrol behind the minefields were attacked over 30 times, three minesweepers suffered considerable damage, two were hit by fragments, one sank. They claimed to have shot down nine planes. In 1943 Commander Minesweepers reported 139 men killed, 199 wounded by air attack, and 26 planes shot down.

Attacks on merchant ships became more and more frequent but losses were still light. The Official History still claims that in 1943 Soviet naval planes sank 32 transports with 77,000 GRT as well as

The German forces in the Gulf of Finland had to survive many Soviet air attacks during 1943 and 1944. This minesweeper, the M–15, was heavily damaged and grounded on the southern shore of the Gulf.

39 warships, and that 18 transports and 39 warships suffered heavy damage.[10] This is greatly exaggerated. Professor Rohwer, the best authority, considers Piterski's figures (13 merchant ships with 26,000 GRT sunk and 6 with 16,000 GRT damaged) still too high.

The increase in the range of the Soviet naval air arm was made possible mainly by Boston-type bombing planes that the Soviet Union received from the USA under lend-lease agreements. At that time the importance of their activities lay more in the additional stress they put on the already over-strained German capabilities in men and arms than in the modest losses they caused. Minelaying from the air was increased, too: some steamers were damaged or sunk in the Irbe Strait.

During 1943 the Soviets did not undertake any serious landing operations. A small-scale raid against the port of Ruchi in Luga Bay was easily beaten off. In another raid near Strelnya on the south bank of Kronstadt Bay in October, a small party blew up two army assault boats and fired at a bunker. Several agents with radio transmitters were dropped by parachute or taken in small boats to places where they could observe and report naval movements.

37

On the whole, 1943 was a year of many minor clashes in the Gulf of Finland, without significant military events or changes, a kind of naval trench warfare.

BALTIC 1944

The year 1944 began with a serious setback for the German Army, which initiated a decisive change in the situation around the Gulf of Finland and therefore greatly affected the fighting at sea. Beginning on 14 January 1944, Russian armies attacked all along the Leningrad front. Ice had set in late. In November and December ships of the Red Fleet had transferred the 2nd Attack Army from Leningrad to the Oranienbaum beachhead, a force of 44,000 men, 200 tanks, 600 guns, and 30,000 tons of material. Two battleships (one still aground but guns intact), four cruisers, eight destroyers, and some gunboats supported the January offensive with their fire, expending 24,000 rounds.

The German 18th Army was thrown back and had to leave behind all the heavy guns that had been installed to fight the warships and to bombard the fortifications of Leningrad. With great difficulty the retreating Germans built up a patchy new front from Narva to the west bank of Lake Peipus and to the army farther south.

As the Soviet Army did not at this time attack on the Finnish front to the northwest of Leningrad, the Red Fleet did not gain much more operating space by this change of the land situation, but it became increasingly active. According to the Official History, the following vessels were fully operational: 1 battleship, 2 heavy cruisers, 2 flotilla leaders, 8 destroyers, 28 submarines, 6 coastal defense ships, 13 gunboats, 51 MTBs, 9 mine and netlayers, 55 minesweepers, 169 motor minesweepers, 85 submarine chasers, 9 armored boats and a number of other small craft. The number of planes at the beginning of 1944 is given as 389, which indicates considerable losses in 1943, for the fleet air arm started that year with 280 planes and received 660 new ones in the course of the year. By the end of 1944 it had 700 planes.

On the German-Finnish side, the net barrier was laid in the same place as in 1943, and a system of strong minefields similar to the preceding year's was in place on either side of Suursaari in a wide semi-circle around the Soviet island base of Lavansaari. The ice disappeared early: on 5 March German patrol boats took up positions in the Gulf of Finland. On 9 March, they were attacked by

Soviet planes for the first time. As in the previous years a kind of slow-motion running fight developed, the Russians trying to break through the minefields, the Germans guarding and defending them. For the time being the net barrier was out of reach of the Red Fleet. The submarines were kept back and did not try to break through.

To support the advance of their army on Narva the Soviets undertook some landing operations. They were small and did not seem to have been prepared well. For instance, on 8 February a few hundred men were landed with orders to take a number of bunkers on the shore and then to advance inland to join up with the forces approaching Narva. According to the statement of an officer who was made prisoner, some large units of the Red Fleet stood ready to support the landing. No ships appeared, however.

Another operation somewhat later also remained unsupported. Admiral Burchardi, in command of the German Navy in the Eastern Baltic, wrote in his war diary:

During the heavy fighting for Narva in the spring of 1944 the Soviets carried out a night landing about 10 km behind the German front. There was an ice ledge 1–2 meters high along the shore. About 600 soldiers, among them several women, were taken close to the beach by small craft, then had to wade ashore. They were equipped with rubber suits for that purpose. In a short time they were wiped out or taken prisoners. The position was unfavorable for landing according to the German charts insofar as a bar some 100 meters in length extended from the shore which made the approach to the beach proper longer. Whether the landing had been made at that point unintentionally is not known. In any case, the Russians landed at a place where I never would have ordered a landing. It was unsuccessful, and the troops taking part were annihilated.

As in the previous years the German minefields were kept under constant watch by minesweepers and patrol boats of various types, none armed with more than one or two 105-mm. and some smaller guns. Again and again they were attacked by such large numbers of Russian planes that they ran out of ammunition. For example, on the afternoon of 23 March boats of the 3rd Minesweeping Flotilla had to beat off 21 attacks by a total of 140–150 planes. All through March there were 137 air attacks on the patrols off Narva; nearly 7,000 bombs were dropped, according to the reports of the boats; and there were many strafing attacks. The boats managed to avoid three aerial torpedoes, but four boats were damaged by bombs, and six by the guns of the planes. Casualties were 15 dead, 42 seriously and 39 slightly wounded.

All the reports show that the Russians attacked courageously and stubbornly but that their aim generally was not very good. Of course, the German crews had much experience and knew that a well-directed fire was their best protection. German fighter cover was rare. On 10 April when the German air fields could not be used because of the thaw, M–459 and M–413 were attacked by over 70 planes in continuous waves. M–459 sank after a bomb hit; M–413 took several hits at the waterline but managed to reach port.

On 8 May, 18 planes attacked boats of the 17th Patrol Flotilla (converted trawlers) with bombs and guns. When one plane was damaged it continued to fire its gun and dived into patrol boat Vp–1701, which sank. It goes without saying that this war of attrition used up considerable German forces. It also appeared to suit the Russian temperament.

The Russian surface forces continued to sweep mines west of Lavansaari in order to create a passage through the minefields. This took considerable time and effort because the fields were several miles deep, and new ones were laid when necessary. The Russians covered their sweepers with gunboats and MTBs. There were numerous scraps with the German and Finnish patrols, with losses on both sides.

Collapse of the Finnish front

In the second half of June the Soviet Army began its long-expected offensive against the Finnish front to the north of the Gulf of Finland. After heavy fighting the Russians broke through the fortifications of the Mannerheim Line and took the town of Vyborg. Strong naval forces covered the seaward flank and landed troops on the numerous small, rocky islands off that part of the coast. The large ships supported the initial attack with gunfire but then were held back. The Official History says:

In connection with the attack of the Leningrad Front on the Isthmus of Karelia in June 1944, the Baltic Red Banner Fleet intensified its activities in Vyborg Bay and in the entire area of skerries between Vyborg and Kotka. As a consequence of the great danger from mines and of the threat by the enemy Air Force, the Fleet Command, in accordance with the directives of the Soviet Supreme Command, came to the resolution not to employ the large ships for operations against the maritime connections of the enemy. For the most part, this task was solved by naval air forces and the MTBs.[11]

The Finns asked for help. The German Navy sent torpedo boats, MTBs, minesweepers and other small craft, but they could not change the situation. According to all reports, the Russian MTBs in particular fought courageously and their tactics were good. On 20 June, they succeeded in sinking the torpedo boat T–31 (1300/1750 tons, 4 105-mm. guns). Seaplanes sank artillery ferry AF–32 and mine transport *Otter* (1,250 tons) and damaged several minesweepers.

Some of the battle reports give a good illustration of the fighting. The 1st R-Flotilla (motor minesweepers) put into their war diary that the attacks of 19 and 20 June were carried out with considerable aggressiveness and good tactics, and were much tougher than earlier attacks on the Narva position. There were many low-level air attacks with bombs and machine-gun fire, and sometimes bombs were released simultaneously by another wave flying at medium altitude. Several bomb hits (fortunately duds from the low-flying planes) and several near-misses were scored. R–70 took several hits and suffered two dead and nine wounded. With the exception of the last two, all attacks were combined efforts by MTBs and ground attack planes. They were well conceived but the MTBs could always be repulsed.

In July these attacks were stepped up. Four German minesweepers and patrol craft as well as the antiaircraft cruiser *Niobe* were sunk, 12 minesweepers, etc., were damaged, 148 men were killed, 269 wounded. The case of the *Niobe* is particularly instructive. She was the ex-Dutch *Gelderland* of 3,500 tons, re-armed with eight 105-mm. and many smaller AA guns to serve as a mobile antiair defense vessel. To support the Finns she was sent into the skerries north of Kotka. Here she was sighted by Russian air reconnaissance and then massively attacked. The battle report reads as follows:

16 July 1944. *Niobe* in position north of Kotka between Hallensaari and Hitanen attacked by 52 Pe–3s, 42 Yl–2s, 8 Bostons, and 30 LAGGs from a generally southern direction out of the sun. Attack in consecutive waves at altitudes between 5,000 and 100 meters, from 1545 to 1620 hrs, with bombs, torpedoes, and aircraft weapons.

The German defense started firing against a fighter formation in the northeast, then with all guns against constantly shifting targets until it was no longer possible to fire. Direct hits on bow and stern batteries by second attack greatly hinder fire. Then independent fire controlled by gun captains.

Entire crew fought well and bravely. 9 planes brought down by anti-aircraft fire . . .

At 1608 hrs the captain of the *Niobe* ordered all hands to abandon ship because *Niobe* was capsizing, and also to prevent heavier casualties from the strong fire of the aircraft weapons . . . The last 7 men and the skipper abandoned *Niobe* at 1740 hrs. About 60 men were killed or missing and most probably dead, and 30 men wounded out of the 300 who took part in the fight . . .

And from a supplement to the battle report:

One of the first attacking waves scored a direct hit on the 7th 105-mm. AA gun (astern). The crew were killed, the gun barrel was torn loose and thrown overboard. Fire control failed and was taken over by the control officer using speaking trumpet as best he could. 3 Pe–2s observed shot down. Immediately afterwards 2 or 3 bomb hits on and around 4th 105-mm. gun (bow). Crew and gun and fire control destroyed. All the other guns continued firing calmly despite heavy aircraft weapons fire. A large number of bombs fell into the water around the ship with considerable fragmentation effect . . . 2 bombs fell into the engine shaft and exploded . . . followed by 2 hits amidships . . . on the port side 4 Bostons flew over the woods towards *Niobe*. They were taken under fire at once but could not be prevented from dropping torpedoes or torpedo bombs from a very low altitude. Two of them must have hit, the whole ship shuddered and began to list to starboard . . . more hits . . . Only the quadruple mount at the stern was not yet submerged. Finally the ship lay on the bottom with a list of 50° to starboard. The mast, stack, and bridge protrude out of the water.

After the Anglo-American invasion in Normandy succeeded in June 1944, the Supreme Command of the German Navy decided to send all available cruisers, destroyers, torpedo boats, and even some submarines into the Baltic. The Navy could do nothing to change the events in France, but Grand Admiral Dönitz still hoped the new submarines with high underwater speed, which were nearing completion, would bring decisive success. To train their crews he needed the central Baltic up to the coast of East Prussia. Therefore, the Russian armies had to be held back. The patrols behind the minefields were kept up; new fields were laid. In one of these operations torpedo boats T–22, T–30, and T–32 ran into a German minefield and were lost.

From June to the end of the year 19 German submarines operated in and near the Gulf of Finland. They did not sight any larger ships but sank about ten small naval vessels. Six were lost, four probably on mines, one to patrol boat, one to Soviet submarine.

In the last days of July the Soviet Army resumed its attack on the Narva front and quickly compelled the German Army to fall back again. Soon advance Russian units reached the Gulf of Riga and cut off the retreat along the southern shore. The 2nd Battle Group of the German Navy (heavy cruiser *Prinz Eugen*, four destroyers, two torpedo boats) was sent in on 20 August, and with the help of the naval guns the road was opened again. However, most of Estonia was lost. Reval, the main port, was cut off and could be reached only by sea. This made it imperative to keep up the guard behind the minefields. Air attacks and losses increased.

In September, the situation deteriorated further for the Germans. Finland was compelled to sign an armistice with the Soviet Union and Russian forces entered the country. Light naval forces began to feel their way along the Finnish coast around the minefields. Under the terms of the armistice all Germans were supposed to have left Finland by the middle of September, but this evacuation took longer and led to clashes with the former Finnish allies. The worst was the ill-conceived attempt, made at the order of the Supreme Command of the German Navy, to occupy the island of Suursaari. It miscarried completely and the attacking units were taken prisoner. Even if it had succeeded for the moment, continuing to guard the minefields and the net barrier would have been impossible, with Finland out of the war and most of Estonia in Soviet hands.

In southwestern Finland, there were only a few German soldiers and wounded men, but considerable depots filled with war material. Removing 4,000 soldiers and 3,000 wounded men by sea did not offer any particular difficulties, especially since the Red Fleet did not intervene. Of 150,000 tons of materials, only 40,000 tons could be transported; all the rest had to be destroyed. The German 3rd Torpedo Boat Flotilla (three boats) demonstrated in the vicinity of the Åland Islands from 15 to 17 September. On the return to Reval, T–18 was sunk by Soviet bombers.

Evidently Russian attention was directed to Reval because here the evacuation was inevitable and had just begun. On the same day (17 September) the German garrison of Suur-Tytersaari Island was removed by MTBs. The Soviets occupied the island three days later, bringing to an end German control of the minefields. Within a few days, convoys with an aggregate tonnage of 1.8 million GRT, escorted by minesweepers and patrol boats, carried 91,000 soldiers, 85,000 fugitives and prisoners and 82,000 tons of war material to German ports. The last convoy of four steamers and one hospital

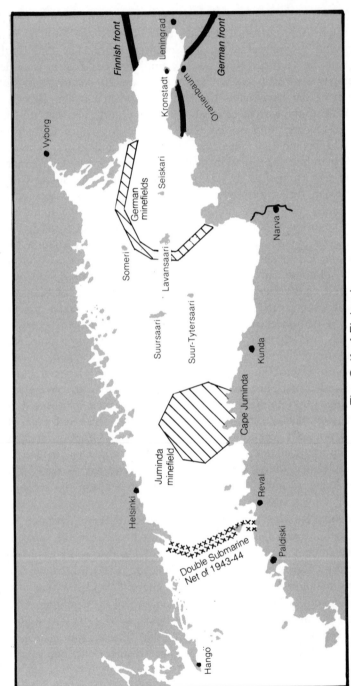

The Gulf of Finland

ship, carrying 9,000 men and escorted by four torpedo boats, left Reval on 23 September. This meant the end of the effectiveness of the net barrier across the western part of the Gulf of Finland. During the whole operation, some transports and small warships were damaged by bombs from the Russian planes, but only a single transport ship was lost.

During the remaining months of the war, the same sequence of events repeated itself several times. Inland, strong Russian armies broke through the thin German lines, cut off large areas and blocked the roads to the west. Evacuation over land was now impossible. The German military units retreated to the coast, accompanied by many thousands of inhabitants fleeing from the Russians. The only road to safety was the sea, but it took time to get all the transport space needed for these masses of men. The beachheads around the ports had to be supported by the fire of cruisers and destroyers to make it possible for them to hold out long enough. At the same time the smaller ships of the German Navy did everything possible to protect the transports, whether they carried troops or wounded, or were crammed with fugitives or full of war material.

The larger Soviet warships could have played havoc with some of these convoys, but the Red Banner Fleet followed the directives of the Soviet Supreme Command, cited above, and did not send its cruisers and destroyers out of the inner part of the Gulf of Finland. Of course, the large minefields were difficult to sweep, but they could easily be bypassed under the Finnish coast. The loss of three destroyers to attack by German dive-bombers in the Black Sea in October 1943 may have been one of the reasons for keeping the ships back. The presence of German submarines in and near the entrance of the Gulf of Finland may also have been a reason. In any case, there was not a single engagement between larger ships, even destroyers, throughout the remainder of the war.

The Baltic Islands

After careful preparations the Soviets began the reconquest of the Baltic Islands on 29 September by landing strong forces on the weakly-held island of Moon. The attackers crossed Moon Sound in a great number of MTBs and other small craft (about 130 according to Russian reports). The defenders, remnants of two battalions, were soon compelled to retreat but were able to cross the dam connecting Moon with Ösel and to destroy it, which delayed the

Russians perceptibly. They now landed on the island of Dagö, but did not succeed in cutting off the retreat of the battalion guarding the island, which gained Ösel with the help of naval ferries.

The Soviets used two army corps for the reconquest of the Baltic Islands. On 5 October the vanguards of the two corps crossed from Moon and Dagö over to Ösel, which was defended by parts of two divisions. After two weeks of fighting most of the island was lost, but Sõrve Peninsula was held against repeated attacks. While the heavy guns there remained intact, the Soviets could not use the Irbe Strait for transports by sea to Riga, which they had taken. They had to supply their armies, which had broken through to the Baltic coast between the ports of Libau and Memel, but they had no port on their stretch of the coast. It was vital for them to open the Irbe Strait quickly, and a battle developed for Sõrve in which both sides made ample use of naval forces.

The Soviet Fleet did not use any of its larger ships to support these operations but relied on its Naval Air Arm and a great number of different types of small combat ships. As before, its High Command overestimated the successes of the air attacks, and it still does. Rear Admiral Piterski writes: "In the area of Moon Sound the Air Force of the 13th Air Army and of the Fleet sank 12 transports, 2 destroyers, 2 guardships, 23 landing craft, 14 cutters, 3 motor minesweepers, 6 tugs, 11 motorboats; in addition it damaged 1 cruiser, 5 destroyers, 7 guardboats, 11 transports, 31 landing craft, 4 MTBs, and a number of other warships and merchant ships."[12] Actually three transports with a tonnage of 5,000 GRT were sunk; two transports and three small warships were damaged by bombs, some more by fragments. Also in October in and near Libau, one tanker and one minesweeper were sunk by air attack; six steamers and seven warships, none larger than a torpedo boat, were damaged, some heavily.

Contrary to Russian expectations two weak German divisions succeeded in holding Sõrve Peninsula for five weeks against repeated strong attacks. This was only possible because the defenders of the primitive trenches hastily dug across the neck of the peninsula were supported by warships on both flanks. Inside the Gulf of Riga, only smaller warships operated, mostly minesweepers, artillery carriers, patrol vessels, and off and on torpedo boats. The Soviet Air Force attacked them almost daily, inflicting some damage, but never putting them out of action completely. At worst they were forced to withdraw a bit to the south when the attacks were carried out by large numbers of aircraft in several waves.

From 2 to 24 October, first two torpedo boats, then the pocket battleship *Lützow* (6 280-mm. guns) with two destroyers and five torpedo boats, shelled the Russian positions from the west, from the open Baltic. On land, several Russian attacks failed to break through, and attempts at landing troops behind the German lines also miscarried because the German warships inside the Gulf could not be put out of action. The Soviets had already transferred a great number of small warships through Moon Sound to the Gulf of Riga. They had many brushes with the German units but they never succeeded in compelling them to withdraw completely. The German ships kept their positions until the peninsula was evacuated on 24 November.

Six days earlier, when the final attack on land began, a group of three artillery carriers, one motor minesweeper, and six armed fishing cutters had an engagement with a considerable number of Russian gunboats east of Sõrve. Two air attacks with bombs and gunfire followed. At the same time, several Fugas-class boats (a cross between gunboat and minesweeper, armed with 130-mm. guns) attacked, but were beaten back. Two of the artillery carriers were damaged but managed to keep their position.

Three days later, M–328, a minesweeper converted into a gunboat, and some patrol boats fought several Fugas boats. One of these was sunk; one of the Russian MTBs, which came to their assistance, was set on fire by gun hits. On the German side Vp–5713 was damaged and had to be towed away. On the following day, Russian MTBs and gunboats attacked the German patrols. These suffered considerable personnel casualties by shell fragments but they continued to keep their positions and to screen the retreat from Sõrve. Russian MTBs succeeded in laying mines near the small port of Montu on Sõrve, which was vital for supplies and for the evacuation, but the mines were swept before they could cause damage.

On 23 November when a large part of the defenders had been carried away by sea, the Russians broke through the trenches. The last German troops retreated, fighting stubbornly, and formed a beachhead, which was evacuated during the night in an orderly fashion. Nineteen landing craft took 4,500 men away, without interference by Russian ships.

In the last days of the fighting, a battle group of one or two cruisers, three destroyers and some torpedo boats stood ready between Sõrve and the Swedish island of Gotland. When visibility permitted, the ships shelled the Russian positions and the troops that were concentrated for the final assault. After the war, Admiral Eastern Baltic wrote:

Finally, the pocket battleship *Admiral Scheer* was ordered into action with her six 280-mm guns. During the day, in navigationally difficult waters, she supported the hard-fighting front on the peninsula with her effective fire. According to my observations, it took the Soviets four days until they were able to react to a new situation or, as in this case, to a novel employment of ships. Thus, the Soviets, here too, did not attack the *Admiral Scheer* until the fourth day, although their jumping-off base was in the immediate vicinity. The ship, however, was able to repel their attacks and to continue firing.

Actually, the battle group was not attacked until the day before the evacuation. The war diary states:

23 November 1944. At dawn, *Scheer* with 4 torpedo boats is shelling target areas designated from Sõrve with good results. 0820 hrs first fighter-bomber attack on battle group, from then on continuous air attacks by smaller units, which are partly turned back by our own fighter protection, which, however, has only flight strength. 1215 hrs own fighter protection absent. Enemy bomber formation attacking battle group. 1335 hrs *Scheer* and torpedo boats attacked by about 30 planes. We managed to outmaneuver all the torpedoes. A small bomb causes minor damage on the foredeck. The torpedo boats also suffer minor damage caused by the mine-like effect of the bombs with time fuzes.

For a detailed report on the last attack, see p. 56.

After it had exhausted nearly all its ammunition the battle group was called back, and the *Lützow* (sistership of *Admiral Scheer*), with three destroyers, was held in readiness.

Admiral Eastern Baltic reported:

The fact that two pocket battleships with only three destroyers are now in the eastern Baltic shows how much the attitude about the enemy threat has changed since the early days after abandoning the Gulf of Finland. The Russian Fleet, as yet untried, is still presumably in the easternmost part of the Gulf of Finland . . .

It is almost incomprehensible that the battle group could stay in the same sea area five days consecutively without sighting a single submarine.

The islands of Moon, Dagö, and Ösel had not been prepared for a longer defense and could not be held against the much stronger Russians. But the attackers did not succeed in cutting off even one of the garrisons: all were taken off by naval forces.

From October 1944 on, German ships, among them the pocket battleship *Lützow* and heavy cruiser *Prinz Eugen*, repeatedly bombarded Soviet Army forces that tried to approach the town of Memel. This support from the sea was instrumental in holding town and port till February 1945. The German ships were repeatedly attacked from the air but did not suffer any serious damage. They were never molested by submarines.

Bombardments from the sea also helped to stop the Russian armies advancing on Courland along the southern shore of the Gulf of Riga and along the Baltic coast from the south towards Libau. Several times one or two of the German pocket battleships and cruisers, with a few destroyers and torpedo boats, shelled large Russian units preparing for attack. In this way, disaster was averted in October 1944 when the German army in Courland was severely shaken. A large beachhead was formed around the ports of Libau and Windau. Twenty-six divisions (600,000 men) held it to the end of the war against all Soviet attacks. They were successfully supplied all the time; four divisions were transported across the sea to Germany.

The bombarding ships were often attacked from the air but never suffered any serious damage. Not a single one was put out of action. It is strange that they were never attacked by Soviet submarines, although these began to operate in the open Baltic soon after Finland left the war.

Soviet submarines in the fall of 1944

After the armistice with Finland had been concluded, the Red Navy, with the help of Finnish pilots, began to bring submarines through the skerries around the minefields to bases in southwest Finland. This took so much time, however, that the first submarines arrived too late to operate against the numerous transports evacuating Reval (18 to 23 September 1944). Not until the beginning of October, when the Soviet offensive cut off the German army group in Courland did they reach their positions off the Irbe Strait, near Windau and Libau, north and south of Memel, off Danzig Bay, and in the central Baltic. Their task was to attack all traffic, but particularly the convoys bringing the supplies to Libau and Windau, which made it possible to hold the Courland beachhead. Some of the submarines laid mines off German ports.

The German "security forces" (minesweepers, escorts, subchasers) had suffered losses and considerable damage in the defense of the mine and net barriers in the Gulf of Finland. Now they were reorganized and the 9th Security Division was set up, but they were too weak to cover the vastly increased area of operations, particularly during the siege of Sõrve Peninsula. The Supreme Command of the German Navy sent reinforcements from the North Sea and the western Baltic but it took time until the situation was in hand again.

Beginning on 5 October 1944, Soviet submarines operated in the shipping lanes from the Courland coast down to Pomerania. Fifteen submarines left their new base. Two of them had to turn back (technical reasons?), and two or three undertook two cruises apiece. By the end of the year they claimed to have sunk with torpedoes 29 transport ships, tugs, and minesweepers, and to have damaged one transport and one torpedo boat. They also reported two transports sunk by artillery, and several ships destroyed by mines. Actually they sank 13 merchant ships (one converted to training ship) with 36,000 GRT, one tug, and minesweeper M–3619 with torpedoes. There were two Swedish steamers and one Dane among the merchant ships, and two of them may have been destroyed by gunfire. Their mines sank torpedo boat T–34, and damaged two steamers and a training ship, which were brought into port.

The volume of German traffic was: 587 ships with 881,000 GRT in October, 764 ships with 1,577,000 GRT in November, 575 ships with 1,112,000 GRT in December.

In December, only one ship was lost to submarine attack, proof of the success of the measures taken to better protect the convoys. On the whole, the Soviet submarines represented an additional threat to German shipping and caused some losses, but were in no way decisive. The loss of France and the retreat from northern Finland set free many escort vessels, minesweepers, and artillery ferries, which were transferred to the Baltic. Not all of them could be sent to protect German shipping from the attacks of Soviet submarines and planes because the Royal Air Force dropped mines in great numbers in the western Baltic, which had to be swept. Enough reinforcements could be sent to the eastern part, however, to keep the Russian successes at a tolerably low level.

The attacks of the Soviet Air Force did more harm than the submarines. The air tactics will be described in context in the following section. Here it may be said that the air staffs greatly overestimated the actual successes of their attacks. For example, Piterski reports that ten heavy attacks were made on the port of Libau, with the result that 21 transports and three guard ships were sunk and 38 vessels (including two docks) were damaged.[13] As far as can be ascertained the actual figures were: one steamer and M–3113 sunk, six ships (five steamers, one submarine) heavily damaged, eight vessels damaged by fragments or near misses. Therefore the official Soviet summary for 1944 is to be taken with a grain of salt: "The combat actions of the Baltic Red Banner Fleet in 1944 were extremely effective. Its actions impeded the German Supreme Command in the use of its warships."[14]

This was exactly what the Soviet Supreme Command was not able to do. In spite of submarines and frequent air attacks the German surface ships were masters of the sea, operating against the flanks of the Soviet Army, and guaranteeing sea transport from and to all Baltic ports still in German hands.

BALTIC 1945

In contrast to the preceding winters there was no interval in the operations at sea in the winter of 1944–1945. The Soviets now had ice-free bases for their submarines and small surface vessels, and their land offensives to the west gained ground and more ice-free ports. In the middle of January most of the German eastern front collapsed under the massive attacks of well-equipped Russian armies, which reached the Oder River inland after a few weeks. East Prussia was cut off. The troops remaining there were compressed in the Samland-Königsberg and Elbing areas. Even the land connection between Königsberg, the capital, and Pillau (Baltiysk), its seaport, was interrupted until the artillery of torpedo boats and gunboats firing from the canal between the two towns forced the Russians to retreat temporarily.

In the last days of February the German front in Pomerania collapsed, but a beachhead around the large ports of Danzig and Gdynia held out for four more weeks. A smaller beachhead was formed around the Pomeranian town of Kolberg. The possession of these ports enabled the German Navy to carry out what probably was the largest evacuation across sea in history. All available ships, including large liners, carried an estimated 2.2 million people westward—wounded, fugitives, soldiers. The Courland beachhead was supplied all the time, and there was never any lack of targets for Soviet submarines and aircraft.

51

Soviet submarines in 1945

At the beginning of 1945 the Soviet Baltic Fleet consisted of the following ships: 1 battleship, 2 heavy cruisers, 12 destroyers, 28 submarines (20 operational), 5 coastal defense ships, 78 MTBs, 73 minesweepers, 204 motor minesweepers, 47 armored boats, 220 small submarine chasers and patrol boats. The number of its planes was 787.[15]

Regarding the tasks of the Fleet, the Official History says:

"A part of the naval forces supported the Red Army in smashing the beleaguered German Courland Group" (they did not succeed at this task until the end of the war) and continues:

"On account of the great danger from mines, and because there were no ports available which were suitable for them, the heavy surface ships remained in Kronstadt and Leningrad."

"It was [the Fleet's] task to employ MTBs, submarines, and ground-attack planes in order to interrupt the traffic for provisioning the German Courland Army. For this purpose 5–6 submarines operated from Windau to the Pomeranian coast, 400 planes were active, heavy railway batteries of the coastal artillery fired at Memel and Libau." In the same context, the significance of "giving correct orders," and strong communistic indoctrination ("individual education effort of particular importance") are mentioned.[16]

The submarines had some spectacular successes but did not inflict any decisive losses. In the second half of January the evacuation of East Prussia began on a big scale.

On 30 January 1945 Soviet submarine S–13 sighted the liner *Wilhelm Gustloff* (25,000 GRT) northwest of the Bay of Danzig. The ship carried 6,000 fugitives and wounded and had been sent to sea without any escort from Pillau by a local authority. Hit by three torpedoes, she sank quickly. Most passengers and crew perished in the icy waters; warships coming to assistance could save only a few.

On 10 February, the same submarine S–13 torpedoed the liner *General Steuben* (14,700 GRT) in spite of an escort. About 3,000 people lost their lives; only a few hundred could be saved. The third catastrophe of a similar kind was the sinking of the transport *Goya* by submarine L–3 in the night of 16/17 April. The ship came from Hela and carried over 6,000 men, although she displaced only 5,200 GRT. Only 165 were saved.

From January to May, 1945, Soviet submarines sank 13 trans-

52

ports with an aggregate tonnage of 63,000 GRT by torpedoes, three transports of 4,000 GRT and four warships by mines. By comparison, the mining offensive of the Royal Air Force in the western part of the Baltic to the mouth of the Oder River was far more successful. In the first three months of 1945 in this area, 67 ships with an aggregate tonnage of 138,000 GRT sank after striking mines, and many more were damaged. The German records of the last phase of the war are incomplete, but experts have since collected all available data, and these figures cannot be far from the actual German losses.

The German supply and evacuation traffic through the central Baltic generally used a swept channel in comparatively shallow water along the Pomeranian coast. When there was danger of mines (dropped from the air or—in a few cases—laid by submarines) the transports had to proceed in deeper water more to the north. Only here did Soviet submarines attack and torpedo the steamers mentioned above and some smaller ones.

All through the spring of 1945 a few submarines were constantly operating against the supply ships going to Courland and the troop transports leaving Libau. Generally, the German ships were well protected, and losses were kept low. In February and March, coordination between Soviet air reconnaissance and submarines was noticed. However, it did not lead to submarine attacks on the German warships, which constantly intervened in the fighting on land in the area of Königsberg-Pillau, off Elbing, at Kolberg, and particularly in the Bay of Danzig. Here, heavy warships remained without interruption for nearly a month (10 March to 8 April), firing at land targets and replenishing fuel and ammunition from ships on the roadsteads. Transports of every kind were also to be found here at any time. The reason they were never attacked by submarines may be that this area was assigned to the Soviet Air Force, which attacked almost daily. In any case, the 22 or so Soviet submarines operating in the central Baltic had some successes but they were less dangerous than the Soviet Air Force or the British mines.

Soviet naval air in 1945

The Soviet Naval Air Arm was the most active branch of the Red Navy in the Baltic. In the course of the war it made great progress in material and training. However, there were wide differences in the performance of the various squadrons. Over-all, their record remained distinctly below the accomplishments of the Anglo-Americans. The minesweeping and patrol squadrons transferred from the West were impartial judges.

The most outstanding trait of the Soviet pilots was their tenacity. They were best at ceaselessly attacking smaller warships, which, of course, were not too well armed. In their operations, they obviously followed strict orders to the letter. Repeatedly it could be observed that quickly adapting to a changed situation was not one of their strengths.

Of thousands of attacks in 1944–1945 only a few typical examples can be given here. During the Russian break-out from the Oranienbaum beachhead and from the Leningrad front, three German destroyers were sent in to shell the flank of the advancing Soviet Army. With their excellent antiaircraft armament they easily beat off the few air attacks made on them. They used Baltic Port/Paldiski as base. There, they were never disturbed, although the port of Reval, only 35 miles to the east, was frequently attacked.

Similarly, the minesweepers and patrol boats guarding the mine and net barriers were persistently attacked when near the barriers, but hardly molested when they retired under the coast. The attacks in the vicinity of the barriers were usually carried out by groups of three to ten planes following each other at short intervals. This forced the patrols to expend their ammunition, but the Russian planes did not follow the German ships when they retreated a few miles.

Shields of armor steel for the antiaircraft guns, developed by the German minesweepers in France, proved valuable here, too. Nevertheless, in the course of time the great number of the air attacks caused considerable losses of personnel. Many boats were damaged by fragments, and some were even sunk. Direct bomb hits were rare.

An exception was the attack by two Soviet fighters on three German torpedo boats on 19 September 1944. These had stopped to search cutters with fugitives bound for Reval. The torpedo boats were caught napping: before they could get up speed, the fighters fired rockets at them. One hit T–18 (850/1,100 tons) amidships; she broke in two and sank.

The almost endless stream of ships of all kinds evacuating Reval was the target of numerous air attacks. But though many ships had little or no armament and escorts were few, only one steamer was sunk. Two more were damaged but were brought into port.

The frequent but not very successful attacks on the small warships on guard east of Sõrve Peninsula have already been mentioned. The following report by a minesweeper gives details:

At first a big plane (Boston-type) used to appear in the distance. Then groups of other planes attacked every 40 minutes, almost exactly to the minute. When we remained on our position, the number of planes was increased from 10 to 20, then to 40. They attacked with bombs, torpedoes, machine guns, and gliding bombs which sailed for about 50 meters. To drop them the planes came so near that it sometimes looked as if they wanted to ram us. Off and on, one of these bombs jumped over our boat. Other bombs were dropped from 3–4,000 meters. They had delayed-action fuzes and were ugly because their detonations made our boilers leak, and we had to retire for repairs. If we left our position they sent a fighter after us to take a look, but we were left in peace. On the day after the evacuation of Sõrve Peninsula not a single plane came into view.

Sometimes they dropped bundles of very small fragmentation bombs around the boat, which detonated on hitting the water. They damaged the outer plating and the bulwark railing very badly. Later on every convoy going east was shadowed by a Soviet plane from the island of Bornholm on. Our escort forces had specialists on board who monitored the Russian radio traffic. They could say exactly when the planes had started, and these generally arrived when expected.

From the wealth of experience gained in these encounters, the following rules, given here in abbreviated form, were developed by the German Supreme Command and distributed to all ships operating in the Baltic in the winter of 1944–1945:

a) Russian planes approach to minimum distance. They drop objects similar to torpedoes, length 3 meters, diameter 40 cm., at a distance of about 50 meters from their targets. During the attack the planes fire with machine guns.

Defense: open fire with all antiaircraft weapons early, maneuver for a good arc of fire.

b) Procedure when attacking convoys (confirmed by statements of prisoners of war and by own battle reports):

By day Soviet naval aviation will attack after reconnaissance run by Air Force. German ships are reported by radio. Attack in several waves, following each other closely. Composition of a typical wave: 4–6 Boston planes, among them 2–3 with torpedoes, protected by 4–6 fighters.

They attack flying low. Course is set first for the position reported by the reconnaissance plane, then following the course of the German ships, at an altitude of 50–60 meters, sometimes rising to 100 meters for a better view, approaching objective at 20–30 meters. Target is the biggest ship of the convoy. Attacking smaller escorts prohibited.

The planes carry one torpedo or two bombs.

ships on Hela roadstead. However, they were mostly outgunned by the German destroyers.

Early in April, the battle group had to be withdrawn, mainly for lack of fuel. There were no German fighters, but enough smaller warships were on hand to protect the transports arriving with supplies and leaving crammed full of fugitives, so that heavy losses did not occur. On 15 April, the hospital ship *Pretoria* was attacked by 20–30 planes although she was clearly marked as a hospital ship. She was damaged, but under the protection of Z–34 succeeded in taking wounded on board and leaving with a convoy. Z–34 then was torpedoed and towed to Swinemünde as mentioned above. Commander Hetz later wrote:

In the last 3 months of the war we did not see a single German fighter.
One should not underestimate the Russian Naval Air Arm, however. On Swinemünde roadstead they flew stubbornly into the immense fire power of the warships there. However, they utilized the panic already mentioned, and the ships were crammed with fugitives.
On 5 May, Z–34 left Swinemünde behind minesweepers at 5 knots. 5 to 6 planes were about to attack. Order: No fire at a distance over 2,000 m, then open fire all at once. (Z–34 had 5 127-mm guns, 4 37-mm, and 16 20-mm, all antiaircraft guns). The result was that the Russian planes flew round the group for 20 minutes in an undecided manner. When they approached again they got the same burst of fire at 2,000 m. Finally they flew back east in formation and dropped all bombs and torpedoes in the water. Evidently, they were fed up.

The almost complete absence of German fighters, the great number of convoys and single ships, often not well protected or armed, the great difficulties in bringing away crowds of fugitives: all this made it easy for the attacker. The Soviet Naval Air Arm was active all the time but it overestimated its successes. For 1945 Piterski gives them as more than 150 freighters with an aggregate tonnage of about 420,000 GRT, 49 warships down to motor minesweeper, and 100 merchant and warships of smaller tonnage.[17] The most probable figures for ships lost to air attack at sea are 41 transports with an aggregate 134,000 GRT and 27 warships.

Soviet surface ships in 1945

After the fall of Sörve in November 1944 the road through the Irbe Strait to the open Baltic was free for smaller surface ships, including large destroyers. The larger warships could have left the Gulf of Finland between the Finnish coast and the island of Dagö at any time. The Soviet Official History stresses the dangers and difficulties caused by mines. Its excuse for keeping the larger ships in Kronstadt-Leningrad is that the Germans had laid so many mines in Reval and Paldiski as to make them unserviceable until spring 1945.[18] It is highly improbable that minesweeping in sheltered waters, without enemy interference, would have taken so long. Besides, there was the former Soviet base at Hangö, which could have been used.

Evidently, a channel for larger ships through the Gulf of Finland was indeed swept in the late fall of 1944. In any case, the Official History reports that more imports arrived from Sweden and Finland, and that the Soviet naval forces protected 1,514 crossings, which served to transport 315,000 tons of material and more than 42,000 men. "The most important task of the Fleet was to eliminate the great danger from mines. Although the Fleet had more than 220 minesweepers at its disposal, they could guarantee completely safe movements of the convoys only under great difficulty."[19] That they could do it was to be expected in view of the experience they had gained in the previous years.

Nothing is said about losses in these Soviet transport movements. Some ships may have struck mines initially, but the road from the Gulf of Finland into the open Baltic was evidently free from mines not later than December 1944 or January 1945. However, the only surface ships of the Red Fleet encountered during the fighting all along the coast from the Courland beachhead to the mouth of the Oder River were MTBs.

Their successes were minimal. Because of the increasing danger from the Soviet air attacks, the ships bringing supplies to Courland entered and left the ports of Libau and Windau only by night, but not a single transport was sunk by an MTB. Neither are any MTB successes claimed by the Russians for the Memel area. In the Bay of Danzig they appeared for the first time on 1 April 1945.

On 26 March Soviet planes attacked a small tanker, escorted by four motor minesweepers, on her way from Pillau to Libau. They succeeded in sinking the tanker and three motor minesweepers with bombs and torpedoes; then German fighters intervened and shot down 11 of the Soviet planes. German MTBs from Libau saved the survivors, took them to Libau and returned to the place where the tanker was still burning. They rightly expected that Russian MTBs would try to pick up survivors, papers, signalbooks, etc. In this way, three German MTBs succeeded in completely surprising nine

Russian MTBs. In a fight lasting two hours, they sank at least two of the Russian boats, boarded another one, and took five officers (among them the senior officer of the 2nd Soviet MTB Squadron) and nine men prisoners.

Although the engagement was fought at ranges of less than 300 meters, only one German sailor was slightly injured. The German senior officer described the group of Soviet MTBs "as a disorderly bunch of craft with stern lights burning and which kept getting in one another's way." The Russian senior officer was wounded and taken to a German hospital. Questioned there he stated that he attributed the failure of his squadron to inadequate training.

At the end of March 1945 the Russians took Gdynia on the Bay of Danzig and then Danzig itself from the land side, which gave them bases for MTBs and other small craft. Piterski says:

From 9 April on the torpedo cutters (MTBs) searched and chased on the enemy shipping lanes in the Pillau area. In the middle of April systematic operations in the Bay of Danzig began from Neufahrwasser, the outer port of Danzig. This base, situated near Hela port and the mouth of the Weichsel River (where German troops were encircled), was extraordinarily well suited to obstruct shipping in this area. Thanks to their surprising appearance and the high art of their commanding officers the first operation of the MTBs from Neufahrwasser led to a success. Two boats under the command of Lieutenant N. L. Korotkevich and Lieutenant Commander V. V. Solodovnikov sank destroyer Z–34 on the roadstead of Hela.[20]

As mentioned above, Z–34 was hit by a torpedo (night of 15/16 April) but did not sink. From 10 April to 6 May, Soviet MTBs undertook ten night operations in the Bay of Danzig. There was no shortage of targets, for in April alone nearly 400,000 men were embarked from Hela and carried to ports of the western Baltic. According to Piterski, the Soviet MTBs "sent 16 German warships and merchantmen to the bottom of the sea."[21] This is exaggerated. Besides Z–34, they torpedoed the steamer Emily Sauber (2,500 GRT) near Hela on 28 April but the ship was beached. A steamer, allegedly torpedoed out of a convoy on 21 April, has never been identified.

Soviet MTBs had several brushes with German warships, but did not sink any. They were no more successful along the Pomeranian coast to Swinemünde. Although Kolberg, the last of several small ports between Danzig and Swinemünde, fell into Russian hands on 17 March, Soviet MTBs did not appear in the waters between the mouth of the Oder River and the Danish island of Bornholm until the last days of the war. On 5 May, they attacked the destroyer Z–34, which was proceeding west on one engine. Their torpedoes missed; they were driven off by gunfire. One MTB was sunk, another damaged. Two days later Soviet and German MTBs met near Rønne on Bornholm. After a short fight, one Soviet torpedo cutter began to burn and was sunk by the German boats, after they had taken off eight men.

On 8 May 1945, immediately before the capitulation of Germany became effective on the eastern front, 126 small ships in six convoys left Libau and Windau in Courland with 25,000 men on board, fleeing the threat of captivity in Russia. Bad weather delayed them but only some of the smallest ships with a few hundred men were captured by the Soviet Navy on 9 May. About the same time the Soviets took over Bornholm. There three of their MTBs attacked the German tender *Rugard*, but their torpedoes missed, the ship took them under gunfire, and they retreated.

Summing up it can be said that the Baltic Red Banner Fleet, though in a state of alert, was surprised by the German attack on Russia. In the first months of the war its attitude was defensive: it concentrated its efforts on minelaying and evacuating threatened bases. Then, for three years, it took an energetic and effective part in the defense of Leningrad/Kronstadt and the Oranienbaum beachhead. In the stationary war around the mine barriers in the Gulf of Finland, its light forces, and later its aviation, were opponents to be reckoned with, which tied down considerable light forces of the German and Finnish navies. In 1942 Soviet submarine crews showed great tenacity and courage in breaking through the minefields, but had little success in their operations against shipping.

They were hardly more successful in 1944–1945 when the road to the Baltic was open again. The Soviet Naval Air Arm and units of the Air Force were more effective, but all three together could not prevent sufficient supplies from reaching the Courland beachhead, nor the evacuation of most of the beachheads from Sõrve to Swinemünde.

The Soviet torpedo cutters were often aggressive and effective, but they exerted little influence on the great shipping movements in the last months of the war even though they had many easy targets. There can be no doubt that the larger surface ships could have been useful, especially in these last months of the war, but they were kept back in the Gulf of Finland, perhaps because they were not trained well enough, perhaps to save them for the peace.

According to official Soviet sources the Baltic Red Banner Fleet caused the loss of 624 transport ships with 1,598,411 GRT from 1941 to 1945.[22] Careful Western compilations reach figures of about half that size. The Official History says:

Since only a limited number of submarines and MTBs were available, and since it was not possible to commit the heavy surface vessels, the Fleet was not able completely to blockade the Courland Group and other encircled beachheads from the sea, and it could not interrupt the sea communications of the enemy in the Baltic for any length of time.[23]

On the preceding page it says:

The figures and facts we have given refute the assertions of the Fascist Admiral Friedrich Ruge that the Soviet Baltic Fleet looked strong only on paper. The members of the Baltic Fleet, who fought under complicated conditions, compelled the enemy to extensive defense measures and inflicted serious losses upon him.

The quotation disapproved by them reads as follows:

. . . the Russian Baltic Fleet, at least on paper, seemed fairly powerful. [Number of ships for 1941 given] Yet no German officer who had fought the Russians in 1914–1917 had any real respect for their fleet. It is true that the ships' crews knew well enough how to fire their guns, and in a tight corner they would fight bravely to the end. But what the Russians had always lacked in the Russo-Japanese War, as well as in 1914–17, was the ability to make quick decisions and to exploit the ever-changing tactical and operational opportunities inherent to a war at sea. The Soviet system of education was by no means likely to rectify these particular shortcomings. . . .[24]

It would seem that these reflections were not contradicted in the course of the naval war in the Baltic.

The
Black
Sea

The plan for the campaign of the Rumanian Army and of the German Army Group South in southern Russia did not consider the possibilities of the Black Sea. Of course, there were no German naval forces there, with the exception of some river guardboats and minesweepers of the Danube Flotilla. The Rumanian Navy consisted of four destroyers (1,400–1,850 tons, with 120-mm. guns), three small torpedo boats, one submarine of 650 tons, two more not yet ready for service, eight small MTBs, four gunboats, and some patrol boats. Constanta was the main naval base. The state of training was quite good, but the fleet had little chance of success in offensive operations, because the Soviet Black Sea Fleet was much stronger.

At the beginning of the war it consisted of:

  1 battleship, 23,000 tons, 23 knots, 12 305-mm. guns
  2 new cruisers, 8,000 tons, 33 knots, 9 180-mm. guns
  1 modernized cruiser, 8,000 tons, 30 knots, 4 180-mm. guns
  2 cruisers, 6,900 tons, 30 knots, 15 130-mm. guns
  3 flotilla leaders, 2,900 tons, 36 knots, 4 (?) 130-mm. guns
 10 destroyers of different types, 130-mm. guns
 47 submarines, 250 to 1,080 tons, mostly new
 84 MTBs
    the Naval Air Arm with 626 airplanes (about half of them fighters)
    numerous smaller warships, among them fast gunboats (20 knots)
       with 76-mm. guns.

63

As far as can be ascertained, no special landing craft existed. For their numerous amphibious operations the Soviets used "fishing vessels, launches, drifters, etc." according to one of their reports.

The Black Sea Fleet was commanded by Vice Admiral F. S. Oktyabrski. Sevastopol on the Crimea was the main naval base, Odessa, on the northwestern shore of the Black Sea, the largest commercial port. On the eastern shore, there were the smaller harbors of Novorossiysk, Tuapse, and Sukhumi. The Soviet merchant navy consisted of comparatively small ships with an aggregate tonnage of about 300,000 GRT.

BLACK SEA 1941

The sudden change of Yugoslavia from siding with Germany to an alliance with the Soviet Union (5 April 1941) touched off the Balkan War, which led to German conquest of Yugoslavia, Greece, and Crete. For these operations German divisions had to be used that stood ready for the attack on Russia. Therefore, the campaign in southern Russia was carried out with much weaker forces than originally planned. After somewhat difficult negotiations the Rumanian government agreed to more active participation by its armed forces. These engaged in the attack on Odessa, but did not close in on that city until 13 August, which meant the campaign took seven weeks to move a distance of about 100 miles. The Russians defended themselves stubbornly, aided by the fact that they had complete control of the sea.

Shortly after the beginning of the hostilities, in the early morning of 26 June 1941, the Soviet flotilla leaders *Moskva* and *Charkov* bombarded the town and port of Constanta, cooperating with naval planes. The purpose of the operation was "to reconnoiter by force the defensive system of the Rumanian naval base and to destroy the supplies of gasoline and oil stored there."[1] The ships' gunfire was well directed and, at 25,000 meters, effective. An ammunition train blew up and considerable damage was done, but the stores of liquid fuel were not destroyed. Soon the German 280-mm. railway battery Tirpitz, placed there in March 1941, opened fire and quickly straddled the destroyers. Trying to evade the artillery fire, the ships ran into a defensive minefield, which had been laid by the Rumanian Navy. A paravane of the *Moskva* caught a mine but did not cut the mooring rope. Paravane and mine hit the destroyer amidships, the mine detonated, the ship broke in two. The *Charkov* retreated, perhaps

Taken from aboard the Soviet cruiser *Voroshilov* during operations in the Black Sea in 1941, this photograph shows the destroyer leader *Charkov* on the left, and the destroyer *Soobrazitelny* on the right.

with slight damage. The Rumanians rescued 66 survivors. The Official History says: "The members of the Black Sea Fleet fulfilled their task boldly and bravely," but forgets to mention the loss of the *Moskva*.

The defense of Odessa

The Soviet government decided to hold Odessa, although it had not been fortified before the war. Its defense was possible only with the help of the Navy. When Rumanian army units approached the outer ring of the quickly constructed field fortifications, they came under heavy fire from the guns of cruisers and destroyers. This delayed their advance considerably and for some time prevented them from gaining positions for taking the port and its facilities under fire. Simultaneously, the Soviets brought at least two divisions and much material across the sea into the city. Among other weapons the reinforcements brought rocket launchers, called "Stalin's organs" by the German troops.

When the pressure on the defenses near the coast northeast of the port became threatening, the Russians countered with a well-executed amphibious operation. On 21 September, a naval force under Captain 1st Rank S. G. Gorshkov embarked 2,000 naval infantrymen in Sevastopol and put to sea. Rear Admiral L. A. Vladimirski, in over-all command, went ahead in the destroyer *Frunse* to coordinate the operation with a group of small warships from Odessa. In the evening the *Frunse* tried to assist gunboat *Krasnaya Gruzya* when she was attacked by German dive-bombers, but both ships and a tug were sunk. Nevertheless, the operation continued. At 0100 hours on 22 September cruisers and destroyers opened fire on the Rumanian trenches northeast of Odessa. Half an hour later, a parachute platoon was dropped behind the Rumanian lines. It destroyed a command post, cut telephone wires and caused quite a disturbance. At 0153 hours the 2,000 naval infantrymen began landing behind the Rumanian lines, which were being attacked from the front by the defenders of Odessa. Evidently the landing came as a complete surprise to the Rumanians. They suffered heavily and retreated several miles, losing the positions for shelling the port.

It is very probable that this undeniable success at a time when the Russian armies were falling back and suffering severe losses had a decisive influence on the career of S. G. Gorshkov and on his development as a military leader. Certainly Odessa was too far behind the retreating Russian armies to hold out much longer, and soon the Soviet government gave orders to evacuate the city. But the evacuation was greatly facilitated by the moral and material success of the amphibious operation. Almost undisturbed, from 1 to 16 October 1941, the fleet brought away 86,000 soldiers, 150,000 civilians, and much valuable material. First, the best division was transported to Sevastopol, then civilians, supply services, etc., while enough troops remained to keep the fortifications occupied. Eventually, on the night of 15/16 October, 35,000 fully armed men were taken off.

The Rumanians discovered the complete evacuation so late that the transports were already near Sevastopol by the time they were attacked from the air. Probably one or two ships were sunk but most reached port safely. There, men and material were of the greatest importance for the defense. In Odessa, no more than 6,000 men were made prisoners.

According to the Official History, from July to the middle of October 1941, Soviet ships undertook 911 trips between Odessa and

Sevastopol in both directions and transported 4,173,000 tons. They carried 80,000 men, 1,000 motor vehicles, 500 guns, 3,500 horses, and 25,000 tons of supplies into Odessa. During the siege, they evacuated 350,000 inhabitants, wounded, and sick, as well as 200,000 tons of material. Only three transports and one floating dock (carrying locomotives) were sunk by enemy planes. The total losses in the northwestern part of the Black Sea from 20 June to 28 October are given as thirteen ships.

In his thorough study *Odessa 1941* the German historian Captain Friedrich Forstmeier, FGN, after quoting a Soviet report about the amphibious operation on 22 September, says:

From the German documents, too, it is evident that the surprise succeeded completely. In cooperation with the troops attacking the front from Odessa, the landing force threw the Rumanian 13th and 15th divisions 5 to 8 kilometers back, to the positions from which they had started in the middle of August. They lost the hills decisive for the bombardment of the port. . . . For the situation in Odessa—which has always to be seen in connection with the German advance against the Crimea—the consequences of the setback were of the utmost importance. . . . In the Rumanian High Command a severe crisis occurred. Marshal Antonescu refused to continue the attack and ordered his army to change over to the defense.

About the evacuation of Odessa, Captain Forstmeier writes:

The Soviet leaders could be satisfied: Their divisions had been able to disengage themselves from the defensive lines and to embark unnoticed by the opposing German and Rumanian troops. Obviously, the efforts for strict secrecy, skillful tactics in the frontline and at sea, as well as clever camouflage and deceptive measures bore ample fruit.

Summing up, Captain Forstmeier says:

It is incontestable that the Soviets gained a success of moral and military importance—military inasmuch as intact units of the Red Army could be ferried over to the Crimea. The Soviets had reason to be satisfied with the performance of their troops: 5 divisions had held their ground against the numerical superiority of an army of 160,000 men, consisting of 5 army corps with 21 divisions, and practically paralyzed the attackers. They had prevented the enemy from using an important port for his supply traffic. The defenses on the land side, which had not been prepared, had been improvised with skill. Apart from a few crises, the tactical command showed an unbroken fighting spirit which repeatedly manifested itself in energetic counterattacks.

In spite of the somewhat clumsy bureaucratic apparatus of the Soviet command organization and its own internal conflicts, and in spite of the (unavoidable) rivalry between the services, the cooperation between Army and Navy and the political authorities was so good on the important issues that from 1 October on the evacuation proceeded without serious losses. Particularly impressive is the uninterrupted activity of the Black Sea Fleet, without which the fight would have been hopeless from the start, and especially its performance in the last night of the evacuation. The most important detail succeeded, the surprise of the enemy, thanks to keeping excellent secrecy as well as to clever camouflage and deception, among other things. The success of the defense on land was made possible thanks to the staying power of the Russian soldier.[2]

"And thanks to the support from the sea by the guns of the Soviet warships" might be added. It protected the flanks of the defenders whereas the attackers felt their own flanks constantly threatened. All in all, the participation of the Red Fleet in the defense and evacuation of Odessa was probably the best Soviet naval operation during World War II.

How much influence these events had on the Soviet Supreme Command's policy of using the Red Navy mainly for the support of the Army and for protecting traffic, is a question which the Soviet publications do not answer. Neither do they evaluate the personalities responsible for the execution of these operations. The pictures of the men involved remain indistinct, without color or contour.

The defense of the Crimea and Sevastopol

The successful evacuation of Odessa saved valuable forces for the defense of the great fortress and naval base of Sevastopol. It is difficult, however, to estimate the effect of the unexpectedly long defense of the city on the operations inland. The Rumanian Army had no plans to advance into Russia, the German forces taking part in the siege were not numerous, and the sea as a supply road did not figure in the plans of the German Supreme Command.

During the siege of Odessa the German Army Group South advanced through southern Russia (the Ukraine) with two aims: to occupy the Crimea, with its great base of Sevastopol and other ports, and to reach the sources of Russian oil between the Black and the Caspian Sea. However, as was the case at Odessa, Russian resistance in the Ukraine was much stronger than expected. It was not until the end of September that the German vanguards reached the shore of the Sea of Azov, east of the Crimea. On 5 October, the Perekop position on the narrow strip of land linking the Crimea with the Ukraine was first attacked, but the army commanded by General

The Soviet cruiser *Krasny Kavkaz* served as Captain Gorshkov's flagship during the evacuation of Odessa in 1941. The ship was heavily damaged by German bombs during the Soviet landing at Feodosiya in 1941, but continued to serve and was used for the last time during the landing operations west of Novorossiysk in early 1943.

von Manstein did not succeed in breaking through the fortifications there until 29 October, shortly after the garrison of Odessa had arrived in Sevastopol. In the following two weeks the Germans occupied most of the Crimea, including its eastern extension, the Kerch Peninsula. The fortress of Sevastopol was stubbornly defended by the Russians, and the Germans had to begin a regular siege. Their Air Force bombed the port and attacked the shipping that continually supplied the fortress, but could not stop it, although some losses were inflicted.

There is a strong possibility that a more rapid advance by a better supplied Army Group South could have broken through the Perekop fortifications much earlier. Whether better logistics would have enabled it to storm Sevastopol will remain an open question. The consequences of success would have been far-reaching: for example, the siege artillery needed for Sevastopol could have been used against Leningrad as had been intended.

As the situation actually developed the small ships of the German Danube Flotilla could be used for minesweeping and convoy duties north of Odessa only after the city had been evacuated. Therefore, only three convoys reached ports near Perekop before the ice set in. The Russian Navy attacked the not inconsiderable traffic along the

Rumanian and Bulgarian coasts, which mainly consisted of steamers proceeding independently and unescorted. About ten Soviet submarines were generally at sea, and the Soviet Naval Air Arm was rather busy. About 29,000 GRT of Rumanian, Bulgarian, and German shipping were lost in the course of the year. This in itself was not much, but ships were difficult to replace even though the big shipyards at Odessa and Nikolayev had fallen into German hands. The Russians had had ample time to destroy most of the important installations there, and it was several months before work could be resumed. Russian surface ships did not participate in the attacks on the traffic along the west coast of the Black Sea, but they did not remain inactive.

The Soviets utilized their naval supremacy on the Black Sea in a number of amphibious operations, which were executed in a rather primitive way but had far-reaching consequences. In the second half of November 1941, Soviet troops tried to cross the Kerch Strait (linking the Sea of Azov with the Black Sea) in small local craft but were beaten off. This operation was probably undertaken in conjunction with the Russian counteroffensive at Rostov (on the Don River just above the Sea of Azov). The Germans took this town on 22 November but had to give it up again a week later under the pressure of strong Russian attacks. After hard fighting the front stabilized 70 miles to the west on the Mius River, which flows into the Sea of Azov.

Evidently, the Soviets were determined to recapture the Crimea. At first they probed with small forces. On the night of 5/6 December three MTBs entered the port of Yevpatoriya on the west coast of the Crimea and landed small detachments of commandoes at various points. Probably assisted by partisans (left behind in many towns by the retreating Russians), they set fire to the town hall, which was being used by the Germans, and to an old sailing vessel. German patrols forced them to retreat. But only four days later, an MTB entered the port again, probably to land agents.

Supported by the fire of a destroyer, MTBs again attempted to land commandoes in the port of Yevpatoriya on the night of 15/16 December. They were received by the fire of German sentries and patrols, which had been reinforced to some extent in the meantime. The Russian boats answered with their machine-guns but withdrew.

At other places agents were landed with the help of small boats from MTBs and even submarines. They usually were equipped with

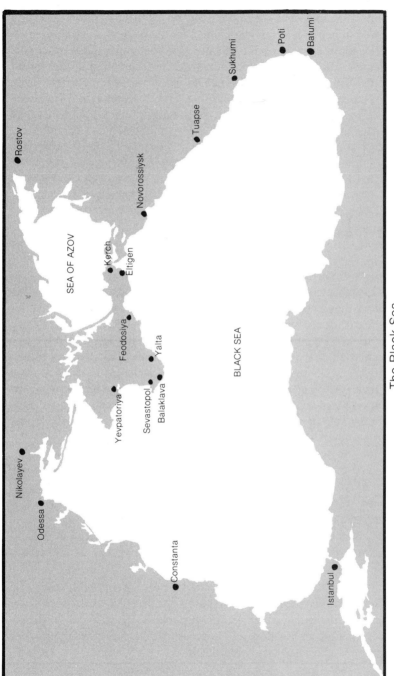

The Black Sea

small radio sets, and they attempted to cut telephone wires and to destroy other means of communication. All these operations gave the Russians a good insight into the weakness of the German coastal defenses. The town of Kerch, important in its situation at the "door" of the Sea of Azov, was occupied by no more than 600 men, Yevpatoriya by 200. For guarding and defending 120 miles of coast between Yalta (near the southern tip of the Crimea) and Kerch, no more than 5,000 men were available. The bulk of Manstein's army was concentrated around Sevastopol, preparing for the final attack.

That attack had to be postponed for six months, however, for in the last week of December 1941 the Soviets undertook a dual amphibious operation on a large scale, probably with the aim of reconquering the Crimea. During the night of 25/26 December infantry units and naval infantry were landed by a great many fishing vessels, tugs, MTBs, and submarine chasers from the Kerch Strait and the Sea of Azov at various points on the eastern part of the Kerch Peninsula. In some places, they were beaten back; in others, they succeeded, particularly where they were supported by the fire of destroyers or gunboats. The Soviet batteries on the Taman Peninsula (which forms the eastern bank of the Kerch Strait) also bombarded the German positions effectively. The Russian forces carried out 25 landings altogether, in ten different areas. From six of them they had to retreat under the pressure of German counterattacks. Four areas could be held, however, and were soon enlarged with the help of newly-landed reinforcements. In Kerch alone, 13,000 Russians were landed.

The Soviets also concentrated considerable air forces in the attacks; a much smaller number of German planes eased the situation to some extent, but could not change it. Because strong Russian forces were also landing in Feodosiya (halfway between Kerch and Yalta) beginning early on the morning of 28 December, General von Sponeck, in command of the division on the Kerch Peninsula, gave orders to his troops on 29 December to retreat to the narrow strip of land joining Kerch Peninsula with the Crimea. He did it without asking Supreme Headquarters and was probably right, for without this concentration his units would have been annihilated one after the other, clearing the way for the Russians to join their forces landed in Feodosiya. However, Hitler was furious and had General von Sponeck court-martialed.

The first wave for Feodosiya consisted of 23,000 men; the convoy carrying them had two cruisers, seven destroyers, six minesweepers, fifteen subchasers, and fourteen transport ships. At dawn on 28 December, at least one cruiser, two destroyers, and about ten smaller vessels entered the port and took the German positions under fire with the help of their searchlights. Here, too, the defending force was weak: a battalion of engineers, in rather a battered condition, and a few naval reservists with four light guns. These were quickly put out of action by the overwhelming fire of the Russian ships, which easily broke through a makeshift barrier of floating timber across the entrance to the port. Most of its installations were in order: the Germans had destroyed nothing because they intended to use the port themselves. Under cover of a smoke screen laid by MTBs, a shock battalion was quickly put ashore. With the help of partisans it took the town and forced the remnants of the German garrison to retreat. More troops and material followed; soon two divisions were ready to move inland.

The Russian Air Force was very active. The German reports stress its good cooperation with the infantry, and they also mention the well-directed antiaircraft fire of the larger Russian ships. All day long these kept moving outside the harbor, supporting the sea flanks of their landing force. German air attacks caused only minor damage; not a single larger ship was put out of action, only a minesweeper and a guardboat.

This amphibious operation had been excellently planned and executed, although a minor landing in Sudak Bay, about 30 miles to the west of Feodosiya, was beaten back by the alerted Germans. The pincer attack first on Kerch and then on Feodosiya was well chosen to put the Germans into a very difficult situation. At the beginning the Russian Air Force made good use of its superiority. At night, it dropped parachute flares to watch the movements of the German troops, who could not find any cover in the steppe country. Reconnaissance was also provided by the partisans and by observers put ashore from the sea or dropped from the air.

Of course, retaking the Kerch Peninsula was a considerable Russian accomplishment. And yet, tactically, the operation was only half a success. It did not accomplish the task now given by Soviet historians as its goal, i.e., to cut off the retreat of the German troops from the Kerch Peninsula. The forces landed on its eastern end succeeded in reconquering the peninsula itself, but the attempt to link up with the Feodosiya beachhead failed, although by 31 December 40,500 men had been landed there.[3] Why these did not advance the few miles east to the neck of the Kerch Peninsula is nowhere explained. This delay gave the Germans time to bring up troops from the siege of Sevastopol, who stopped the Russian advance into the Crimea and then forced them back. Most of the invasion troops evidently embarked again. When Feodosiya was mopped up on 20 January, 4,600 prisoners fell into German hands. Seventy-two tanks, 58 guns, 24 antitank guns, 65 mortars, and 6 rocket launchers were captured. The port installations were almost completely destroyed.

A diversionary landing in the port of Yevpatoriya on the west coast of the Crimea north of Sevastopol on 5 January 1942 was evidently organized from Sevastopol, possibly in the expectation of diverting forces from the siege and from the counterattack in the direction of Feodosiya. The Russian sources do not give any explanation. Two small transports and some MTBs landed a battalion of naval infantry in the port shortly after midnight; destroyers covered them from the sea with their gunfire. As a consequence of the previous landings, the piers had been demolished at their connections with the land. The garrison, about 100 infantry men, 50 navy men, and an army coastal battery, had been forewarned by the dropping of leaflets from the air, by considerable air activity, and finally by the noise of the MTBs' engines.

Therefore, the landing force, led by a lieutenant commander, came under fire very early and suffered heavily. Nevertheless, the attack was continued. The gap in the pier was bridged with the help of partisans; even a tank was brought ashore, as well as a number of mortars and antitank guns. At the foot of the pier, the landing detachment left about 100 dead, among them their commander. The men who got through destroyed the communications center and then occupied buildings near the harbor. They remained there when the ships withdrew after dawn out of range of the German guns, which they had not been able to put out of action. The ships maintained contact with the landing force by light signals. A small minelayer and an MTB ran aground when they attempted to land men to the east of the piers.

The next night a destroyer closed in, evidently to give assistance, but was driven off by gunfire. During the following day MTBs unsuccessfully tried to land more men, and air attacks were made in an attempt to improve the situation. But now German reinforcements and planes arrived: town and port were retaken with the exception of some strong points, which were eliminated in the next three days.

Despite this failure another landing was attempted at Sudak Bay on 26 January, supported by three destroyers and several smaller vessels. Parts of a regiment reached the shore but were soon stopped. After three days, the remnants were taken off by warships.

It seems strange that after the initial success of the double landings little progress was made, since it took the Germans several days to collect forces strong enough for counterattacking. Moreover, the Germans were somewhat hampered by attacks from the garrison against the besieging army. The report of the port captain of Yevpatoriya, Commander von Richthofen, is very illustrative. (Richthofen had served in the German Navy from 1900 to 1920, during World War I as gunnery officer of a battleship. In World War II, he was called up again. Later he was port captain of Sevastopol.) He writes:

Preparation:
Was based primarily on the element of surprise. Planning was generally good, favored by carefully collected intelligence on the German positions. They attempted to destroy the German communications, cut telephone wires, and to overwhelm isolated posts.
Execution:
It began with great vigor and speed. They had taken care of many details. But as soon as they met resistance their vigor turned into hesitation and paralysis, doubt set in, and lack of purpose replaced the initial careful planning. The fact, for instance, that the initial success of the landing at Yevpatoriya by about 1,800 men with all their weapons was not followed up, although the Germans had only 150 men (however, in well-concealed positions and widely dispersed), and that these were able to hold out for four days, cannot be explained otherwise. After the landing, coordination with the air and naval forces was poor.
In Feodosiya, the landing was first successful, favored by fog (which also prevented the German Air Force from taking off) and very strong forces. It proved a complete failure, however, and it permitted the Germans to retake that important port after a relatively short time. The equipment which the Russians had was good, their artillery was good, the MTBs were first-rate and performed well even in a fairly rough sea.
The operation had been prepared long before, but did not result in the intended strategic success because of inadequate tactical coordination with the naval and air forces. It appeared to me that the fault lay with the leadership. Moreover, weather conditions play a very great role in the Black Sea, and appeared not to have been assigned enough importance.
The final execution of the Yevpatoriya operation failed because of the weather (sudden storm). The high Yaila Mountains must have a considerable influence. There are zones a relatively short distance away which have completely different weather.

Defense:

This is where the Russian soldier is at his best. He is unbelievably brave and never gives up even in a completely hopeless situation. Example: The last defenders in Yevpatoriya had to be destroyed by flame throwers in a cellar because they would not give up despite repeated requests. One house had to be blown up because there was no other way to break their resistance.

Summary:

Preparation and planning good, execution not vigorous enough, overall leadership deficient.

German army officers reached similar conclusions. Brigadier-General H. von Ahlfen, commanding the 617th Engineer Regiment, was charged with the engineering preparations for the intended German crossing of the Kerch Strait. After he had directed the defense against the forces which landed in Feodosiya, he wrote:

Final evaluation of the entire Russian operation:

(a) The operation was executed with superior forces correctly from the tactical point of view. Despite its ultimate failure, it caused a substantial delay in the fall of Sevastopol. It tied up the German forces in the Crimea 6 months longer than expected.

(b) Strong points of the Russian operation:

Rapid preparation of the undertaking, 5 weeks after the loss of Kerch Peninsula.

Execution of the landing at Kerch (without special landing craft in a rough sea).

The talent for improvisation, shown by collecting and using non-naval craft.

Excellent coordination in timing and tactics between landing at Kerch and in Feodosiya.

The successful execution proved that, counter to the evaluation by the German Army, the initiative of the Russian Navy was by no means deficient.

(c) Weak points of the Russian operation:

Evident lack of resolution in the leadership of the forces landed in Feodosiya, which were supposed to arrive at their objectives on 31 December at the latest. (The target dates were marked on the Russian maps which were captured in Feodosiya on 15 January 1942).

The medium and lower command echelons of the Soviets had still not been trained to make independent decisions according to the tactical situation.

Failure to exploit their clear air superiority, which was further favored by the weather conditions until 1 January 1942.

Rightly, General von Ahlfen points out the consequences of the amphibious operations on the siege of Sevastopol, for, in spite of their tactical failure, their strategic importance was very great. General von Manstein was compelled to break off the attack which had already begun and which was meant to take the great fortress. The Russians now had time to reinforce it with men and material carried across the Black Sea. In this way, the siege was prolonged by six months, a delay which had not been allowed for in the calculations of the German General Staff. The forces tied up there were urgently needed in other places. Among them were the heaviest siege guns the German Army possessed (caliber up to 600 mm.), which were already designated for the attack on Leningrad. When they were finally available in the summer of 1942 it was too late for an attack on that city. The consequences for the Finnish and Baltic campaigns are evident.

In the Soviet publications no explanation can be found for the varying performance of the Black Sea Fleet, which was excellent in the defense and evacuation of Odessa and then in the great landings, but fell off markedly thereafter. The decline may have been caused by lack of material, for the bases on the east coast of the Black Sea were not equipped with the repair and supply facilities which a large fleet needs. The quality of leadership may have suffered when S.G. Gorshkov, promoted to Rear Admiral, left the main fleet and took command of the flotilla on the Sea of Azov. In this position he carried out the successful landing on the north coast of Kerch Peninsula. Too little is known of the personalities of the other admirals commanding naval units in the Black Sea to evaluate their share in the naval operations. In any case, the exercise of sea power in the closed Black Sea and the Sea of Azov had a considerable effect on the operations on land and may have saved the Soviets from complete defeat.

Black Sea 1942

In the first months of the year Soviet warships repeatedly shelled German positions on the coast of the Crimea, and they often supported the defense of Sevastopol with their gunfire. The main task of the cruisers and destroyers was supplying the fortress, and frequently both assignments were combined. Even the only battleship, *Parishkaya Communa*, shelled German positions and then evacuated wounded from Sevastopol.

A German counterattack in January 1942, meant to regain the Kerch Peninsula, did not succeed in dislodging the Russians from the narrow neck, only 11 miles across, which connects it with the

Crimea proper. The Russians assembled strong forces here and repeatedly attempted to break into the Crimea. Although they were repulsed each time, it seemed advisable to the German Supreme Command to eliminate this threat before the final attack on Sevastopol.

On 5 May, German armor and infantry succeeded in surprising the defenders and quickly broke through their field fortifications. Eight Soviet divisions were rapidly cut off and pressed to the shore. On 10 May, the town of Kerch was taken; two days later the peninsula was in German hands, with the exception of some pockets of resistance on the coast.

From 10 May on, the Soviet cruiser *Voroshilov*, two flotilla leaders and two destroyers tried to assist their troops with gunfire from the Black Sea, but not energetically and without success. At the same time, MTBs tried to take some of the retreating troops off, but in vain. The naval measures came too late: 150,000 men were taken prisoner and 1,150 guns and 260 tanks were captured.

The Soviet sources do not explain why the ships were committed so late. On the night of 4/5 May the flotilla leader *Charkov* and three destroyers bombarded German positions on the southeast coast of the Crimea. The supply traffic to Sevastopol continued without interruption. But the waters off the neck of the Kerch Peninsula were left unguarded. This made it possible for the Germans to carry a battalion in small river motorboats from Feodosiya on the morning of the attack and land it behind the Russian positions.

The Official History blames the command of the "Front," that is, the Army Group, for "wrong organization" and for its "bureaucratic manner of leading its forces."[4] Several officers were degraded. However, the real explanation seems to lie in the frictions at the highest levels which prevented quick decisions. As in the Baltic, it was four days before naval forces came to the assistance of the land forces.

On 14 May during a bombardment off Sevastopol, the destroyer *Dzershinsky* passed over a magnetic mine (laid from the air) and sank.

German warships

When it became evident that the Russian campaign would last much longer than the German General Staff had calculated, the Supreme Command of the Navy decided to send a number of warships to the Black Sea, in addition to the Danube Flotilla. Only small ships could be used, for they had to be carried overland from the Elbe River below Dresden to the Danube below Regensburg. The largest were six submarines of 250 tons. As much weight as possible (including the engines) was taken out before they were lifted by cranes onto special oversize trucks that could carry them only on the autobahn. In the same way, a squadron of ten MTBs and one of 23 motor minesweepers reached the Black Sea, as well as motorboats, fishing cutters, etc.

The shipyard at Nikolayev built "naval ferry barges" (*Marine-Fährprähme*, MFP), flat-bottomed, self-propelled barges of about 200 tons; "artillery carriers" (*Artillerieträger*), the same type of barge, but armed with an 88-mm. gun and some antiaircraft guns; and "war transports" (*Kriegstransporter*) of about 700 tons. Some of these transports were converted into submarine chasers. Their speed was 14 knots. In this way, quite a sizable escort and transport fleet was created, in addition to the Rumanian Navy and small merchant fleet of about 50,000 GRT.

The Italian Navy contributed a squadron of small MTBs (MAS), four midget submarines, and some crashboats. These ships had to be transported by rail; therefore no larger types could be sent. This Axis fleet made it possible to utilize the sea for supply and transport to some extent at least.

The fall of Sevastopol

The final attack on Sevastopol began on 7 June 1942. Seven German and two Rumanian infantry divisions took part, supported by the 8th German Air Corps. Two hundred and eight batteries of all calibers were brought to bear on the Russian fortifications and crushed them one after the other. This took time, and the Black Sea Fleet continued to carry reinforcements and supplies into the fortress, support the defenders with gunfire, and evacuate the wounded. It suffered considerable losses: three destroyers and a number of transports and smaller warships were sunk by bombs.

A few days after the beginning of the German offensive, the Italian midget submarines and MTBs began patrolling outside Sevastopol harbor. A week later the first German MTBs arrived. Although their attacks did not have much success (the MTBs seem to have sunk only one transport), their presence made the situation still more difficult for the Soviet Navy. The last large warship that entered Sevastopol was the flotilla leader *Tashkent* on 27 June 1942. She carried 944 men into the fortress and took 2,300 wounded and civilians back. In numerous air attacks she suffered considerable

In this aerial view of Sevastopol, taken in the first moments of a German air attack, an arrow indicates the cruiser *Chervona Ukraina*.

damage from fragments and near misses. With 1,900 tons of water in her hull she was towed into Novorossiysk where she sank in shallow water.

After that, only MTBs and submarines entered Sevastopol. The submarines undertook 77 trips during the German attack, carried 4,000 tons of material into the fortress and evacuated 1,300 wounded. On 29 June, the attackers succeeded in crossing an inlet, which was half a mile wide, and took the defenders from the rear. Nevertheless, Stalin did not give permission to evacuate the defending troops. Only wounded soldiers and some key personnel, including high-ranking officers, were permitted to leave the fortress. In the last days, Russian MTBs succeeded in taking a few hundred men off. On 5 July the fighting was finished. Nearly 100,000 men were made prisoners, 33,000 were killed, and over 600 guns were captured.

This photograph shows German bombs exploding around the *Chervona Ukraina,* which was sunk during this attack on Sevastopol.

The Black Sea Fleet effectively supported the army defending Sevastopol. It suffered considerable losses, and many ships were damaged. Nothing is said in the Soviet sources about the state of repair of the remaining ships but it cannot have been very good.

The crossing of the Kerch Strait

With the fall of Sevastopol the Germans gained the use of the sea for transport along the coast from the mouth of the Danube to the Kerch Strait. The coastal route was urgently needed because at the end of June the German summer offensive had begun, with two targets, the Volga River on either side of Stalingrad, and the oil fields north and east of the mountains of the Caucasus. In setting these targets, Hitler greatly overestimated the strength of his armies

81

and underrated Russian resilience, as well as the difficulties posed by the large distances, although the previous year had given him a foretaste, when the offensive to take Moscow failed on account of logistic obstacles.

The consequences of his misjudgment, culminating in the catastrophe at Stalingrad, are well known. Here it is of interest that once again on the German side the possibilities of using sea transport were not fully realized. Therefore, taking Taman Peninsula immediately east of the Kerch Strait was considered of secondary importance. Rostov was reached by German forces on 17 July but Russian gunboats and other small craft (under Admiral Gorshkov) still dominated the shallow Sea of Azov. In June and July they undertook several small landing operations and also put sabotage and reconnaissance groups ashore. On the night of 2/3 August, German motor minesweepers finally succeeded in bringing 12 MFPs through the Kerch Strait into the Sea of Azov, losing one MFP to a mine. The motor minesweepers and MFPs put some of the Russian vessels out of action; the Soviet troops began to retreat from Taman Peninsula. Before they could completely withdraw, German forces at last crossed the Kerch Strait.

The crossing had been planned for 15 August 1942 but was delayed by bad weather for two weeks. Even on schedule it would have been rather late, for German vanguards reached Krasnodar on the Kuban River in the first days of August. From there, the distance to the sea between the Soviet bases of Novorossiysk and Tuapse was no more than 50 miles. However, the mountain troops did not succeed in fighting their way through the mountain chains to the sea, although they did send a patrol to the summit of Elbrus, the highest peak of the Caucasus (5,626 meters).

The German army clamored for supplies but the Russians had recognized this difficult logistic situation very well. They bombarded the few ports on the Sea of Azov from the air and mined it so well, also from the air, that only the most vital supplies could be carried across, in wooden boats because of the threat of magnetic mines.

The Taman Peninsula had already been cut off from the mainland to the east by German army forces by the time the weather improved. During the night of 1/2 September strong German units were carried by a great number of ferries, MTBs, and minesweepers

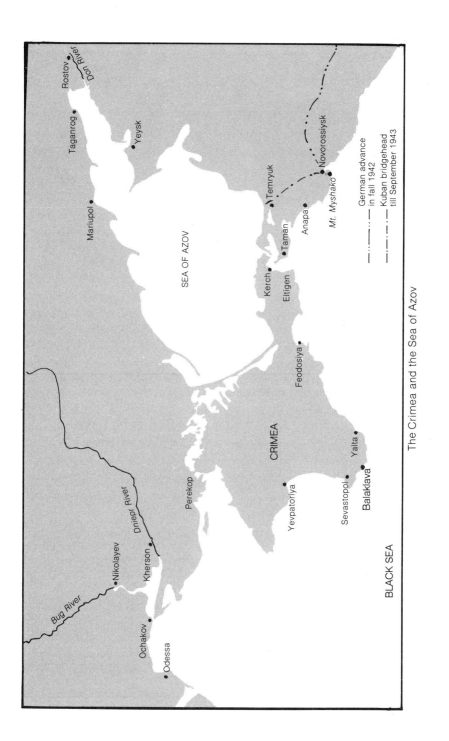

The Crimea and the Sea of Azov

Soviet submarines (top) and surface ships (right) are shown lying in the naval base at Tuapse during a German air attack.

in several groups across the Kerch Strait and the Sea of Azov to land on Taman. Evidently, the Russians were surprised, for they opened fire very late. In particular, a 280-mm. battery, which could have done much harm, did not fire promptly. On 6 September the entire peninsula was in German hands; on the following day, the town and port of Novorossiysk were occupied. Most installations in the port were destroyed, as was the usual Russian practice.

During the Taman operation, about 57,000 soldiers, 26,000 horses, and 8,500 vehicles were ferried over. From now on, a great part of the supplies for the German Caucasus Army crossed the Kerch Strait, mainly by naval ferries, later on also by a cable way. Preparations for building a bridge were made, but the first parts arrived in Genichesk on the western bank of the Sea of Azov in the fall of 1943, just after the Taman Peninsula had been given up by the retreating Germans.

In any case, the Taman operations came too late to assure decisive progress along the eastern shore of the Black Sea, which would have deprived the Soviet fleet of its remaining bases. Halfway to the next port, Tuapse, only 100 miles away, the German offensive petered out. Continued efforts of the mountain troops to gain this place by crossing the mountain ranges from the north also failed. The Black Sea Fleet remained in possession of a minimum of ports and continued its activities.

84

According to German air reconnaissance and monitoring, the strength of the Black Sea Fleet in spring 1942 was probably:

 1 battleship (*Parishkaya Communa*),
 3 heavy cruisers,
 3 light cruisers,
15 flotilla leaders and destroyers,
40 submarines,

and a considerable number of MTBs, patrol vessels, gunboats, mine-sweepers, and subchasers. The transport fleet was estimated at 150,000 GRT in cargo tonnage and 30,000 GRT in tankers.

When, in the middle of June, German and Italian MTBs began to attack the supply traffic to Sevastopol, the Russians quickly countered by switching over to destroyers and submarines, which entered and left the port when light and weather conditions made operating difficult for the MTBs. They could have brought away many more soldiers if Stalin had allowed it.

After the fall of Sevastopol, according to the Official History: "The Black Sea Fleet and the Azov Flotilla had to protect our own sea communications in the Sea of Azov and in the Black Sea along the Caucasian coast, to disturb those of the enemy, to support land forces in defending the coast, and to prevent enemy landings from the sea."[5] The possibilities of sea transport were fully recognized and utilized. In the second half of the year 1942, 213,000 men and 200,000 tons of material were transported by sea for the defense of the Caucasus area.

To disturb the German traffic, the Russians often attacked the bases of the German ships from the air and from the sea. In the early morning of 1 August, two Russian MTBs penetrated into the bay of Ivan Baba (near Feodosiya) where the Germans had installed a base. They launched torpedoes at MFPs lying at anchor: MFP–334 had her stern blown off and sank. The harbor batteries had taken the attackers for their own ships. When they finally opened fire, the MTBs retreated behind a smoke screen.

On the night of 2/3 August the cruiser *Molotov* and the flotilla leader *Charkov* shelled targets in the bay of Feodosiya, using Soviet submarine M–62 as navigation mark. On their way back they were attacked by German torpedo planes and Italian MTBs. The *Molotov* was hit far forward by a torpedo and lost 60 feet of her fo'c'sle.

In the days before Novorossiysk was taken by German troops,

Soviet motor torpedo boats like those shown here frequently attacked German convoys along the Crimean coast.

Soviet cruisers and destroyers evacuated at least 9,000 men and some material. Destroyers also shelled the advancing German forces.

After the Taman operation, the German MTBs and minesweepers used the small port of Anapa, situated immediately east of the Taman Peninsula, as a base. Here they were repeatedly attacked by Soviet MTBs, which sometimes fired torpedoes into the harbor. The German harbor captain reported:

In the months of November and December 1942, Russian MTBs patrolled along the coast almost every night. During that time the enemy made 16 attempts to enter Anapa harbor. Three MTBs were so heavily damaged that it can be assumed that one or two sank. The MTBs fired at the searchlights, the gun positions, and the signal station every time. On three occasions they attempted to torpedo the searchlight control station and two bunkers. However, the torpedoes ran aground in the shallow water and later detonated. The enemy successfully torpedoed the quarters of the enlisted men on the wharf.

On 3 December 1942 an MTB which had run aground north of Anapa was set on fire and destroyed. The harbor captain personally salvaged charts, engine logs, radio instructions, radio transmitter, etc., on the next day.

This naval activity obviously was undertaken in connection with the Russian winter offensive against the over-extended German lines.

Well-equipped with material which they had received mainly from the USA (86,000 trucks alone), the Russian armies began their counterattack on 19 November. A week later, they had already encircled Stalingrad. Here it was Hitler's order to stay in the city which decided the fate of the German 6th Army. Its remnants capitulated on 30 January 1943.

Because of these events far from the sea, no air force units were made available for attacking the few bases where the Russian Fleet was now concentrated, mainly Poti and Batumi. The German Navy had no air arm of its own. Admiral Black Sea repeatedly requested forces to bombard these ports, but nothing came of it.

The Russian warships continued to bring reinforcements and supplies to Tuapse, and to harass the German traffic along the coast from the Bosporus to the Danube, as well as from there to Odessa and round the Crimea along the Kerch and Taman peninsulas to Novorossiysk.

On the night of 2/3 October two destroyers fired 400 shells into Yalta, which was also used as a German base. The night before, a Soviet guardship had bombarded Anapa. Other bombardments had only nuisance value. In the middle of October when strong German land forces approached Tuapse from the north, Soviet cruisers and destroyers, which had already carried 33,000 men and their weapons from Poti to Tuapse, reinforced the garrison with another 12,000 men within three days. The German attack was stopped and could not be resumed.

On 29 November, a squadron under Vice Admiral Vladimirski in the cruiser *Voroshilov* put to sea to attack shipping on the Bulgarian-Rumanian coast for the first time. On 1 December, the flagship and a destroyer bombarded Fidonisi (Rumania), but a mine cut by the paravanes of the destroyer damaged the cruiser, and she had to turn back. Another destroyer of this group did not find any targets under the coast. The second group, two destroyers, launched torpedoes at merchant ships on a roadstead near Rumanian Mangalia, but they detonated on the bottom of the sea. Other units shelled the Bulgarian coast at Galisera. The results of all the bombardments seem to have been negligible, with the exception of damage to the lighthouse at Fidonisi.

The next raid on the shipping along the west coast of the Black Sea was also more spectacular than productive. From 11 to 14

December Rear Admiral V. G. Fedeev in the destroyer *Soobra-zitelny* (1,700/2,100 tons, 4 130-mm. guns) operated with four large minesweepers of the Fugas class (440/540 tons, 18 knots, 1 100-mm. and 2 37-mm. guns) in Rumanian waters. On the morning of 13 December his force sighted a convoy off Sulina and attacked it. It consisted of two steamers, *Oituz* (2,700 GRT, 7 knots) and *Tsar Ferdinand* (? GRT, 10 knots), escorted by the German motor mine-sweepers R–35, R–36, R–165, R–166 (each 125 tons, one 37-mm. and some 20-mm. guns) and the Rumanian torpedo boat *Smeul* (260 tons, 2 66-mm. guns). The situation was rather hopeless but Ensign (*Leutnant*) Glaser, captain of R–165 and senior officer, evidently did not think so. In his report, he wrote (abbreviated):

About 1040 hrs a column of water was sighted about 500 m to port, followed by a faint detonation. Just then the lookout reported sighting the superstructures of two vessels approaching in our direction. Weather: overcast, visibility good, wind force 3–4, sea 2–3. Distance between the two groups about 9,000 to 10,000 m.

The number of rounds hitting the water near the convoy increased. We could make out the muzzle flashes on the vessels which were then identified as enemy ships. I gave the alarm, ordered the steamers to turn away, and began to make smoke. The steamers carried out the order immediately and proceeded on a westerly course at full speed, at first together, later separately because of the higher speed of *Tsar Ferdinand*.

The escort vessels followed my example and laid a smoke screen around the steamers. R–166 and I made for the destroyers which were rapidly closing, and then hauled off in an arc to the south in order to bluff them and to gain time. The fire with 105-mm shrapnel and finally with 37-mm machine guns did not inflict any damage on the two R-boats. The destroyers, which had turned on a parallel course, then turned slightly away. At a distance of about 3,000 meters, they made a 180° turn, zig-zagged and returned to the convoy making smoke. They were on a southerly course, speed about 15 to 18 knots. They continued westward in an arc, then steered practically a parallel course, zig-zagged and continued firing while gradually closing the range. During the whole time they were on the port quarter of our unit.

All the escort vessels were on the windward side, between the steamers and the enemy, and were making a nearly uninterrupted smoke screen. Now and then, they came under shrapnel fire. The fire of the heavy guns was directed exclusively against the steamers. The enemy had zeroed in quickly, many of his salvoes were straddling. The fire was occasionally returned by *Smeul*.

At 1142 hrs, a plane was sighted ahead. It kept at a considerable distance and disappeared after a few minutes. (The convoy had no air cover).

At about 1150 hrs, the destroyers reversed their course. They never separated although the idea of a simultaneous converging attack must have been obvious.

At that time a second plane was sighted at a great distance but it likewise turned away after some time.

At about 1200 hrs, the destroyers appeared from the port quarter at high speed and at about 1220 hrs opened fire again, which they concentrated on *Oituz*. *Tsar Ferdinand* was far away on the port bow.

I was still 1½ to 2 nautical miles from land on a course parallel to the coast. The escort vessels were making smoke screens and dropping "scare" depth charges, moving away from the steamer for a short time to do so. In order not to leave the steamer uncovered, I did not make a feint attack with the R-boats because the range was still too great. The salvoes from the destroyers were very accurate this time, too. The enemy came to within 3,000 to 4,000 meters and then finally sheered off on a course of about 70° (about ENE). The R-boats opened fire with their guns for a short time. The destroyers sheered off at 1242 hrs. At about 1300 hrs, they were out of sight.

Details observed on the destroyers: Two stacks, square bulky bridge, two rod masts, one gun firing. Assume it to be Schtorm class, 700 t, 2 100-mm guns, 29 knots.

(This explains the expression "destroyers." The Schtorm class were torpedo boats of about the same size as the Fugas class.)

There were short lulls in the artillery fire. The conduct of the enemy made an impression of uncertainty. Finally, he shelled the coast at random. The nature of the R-boats was apparently not clear to him. His fire control made a good impression.

Thanks to the smoke screens, no hits were scored on the escort boats and the steamers, and no damage was done.

GLASER, Leutnant.
Commanding officer R–165

Manifestly, the convoy was lucky, for a few hits could have changed the situation much to its disadvantage. On the other hand, in a fight which lasted two hours, the Russians might have found out how weak their enemies were, and how much they were hampered by the steamer *Oituz'* top speed of seven (!) knots.

On the night of 19/20 December, two Russian destroyers bombarded Yalta, a destroyer and a guardboat, Feodosiya. From 26 to 29 December, the same squadron of four large T-class minesweepers (Fugas), supported by two destroyers, again operated on the Bulgarian-Rumanian coast in the vicinity of Burgas and Fidonisi, again without tangible success. Two of the minesweepers fired some shells into Burgas, but did not cause any noticeable damage.

Soviet submarines in 1942

Soviet submarines operated in the western part of the Black Sea all through 1942, except the last weeks of the fight for Sevastopol. As mentioned above, during that time, they carried considerable supplies of ammunition and also fuel into the fortress. The remainder of the year their target was the traffic along the west coast from the Bosporus to the Danube, and, in the second half of the year, the coastal traffic from the Danube to the Crimea and around it as well. A favorite waiting area was the stretch immediately outside Turkish territorial waters from north of the Bosporus to the Bulgarian frontier. Two to three submarines were always stationed there, because a regular traffic had developed between the Mediterranean and the Bulgarian and Rumanian ports.

In February and March 1942 there were as many as 11 Soviet submarines at sea. Some were reported close to the coast, apparently feeling out the German defenses. Occasionally, they even took positions on the coast under fire. Off the Bosporus, they evidently waited for passing Italian and Rumanian tankers, but they were not at all particular in the choice of their targets and considered every ship outside Turkish territorial waters (and in some cases even inside) as enemy. For instance, early on 1 January 1942 Soviet submarine ShCh–214 attacked a schooner sailing off the Turkish coast not far from the Bulgarian frontier. According to P. N. Savateev, the submarine destroyed the small ship by gunfire without ascertaining her nationality or doing anything to save the crew. "The fight lasted exactly 7 minutes. . . . the enemy was kept under fire until the schooner sank."[6] As far as can be ascertained the Soviet government never declared a war zone where submarines would sink ships without warning.

A particularly tragic case followed. On 24 February 1942 the Soviet submarine ShCh–213 (Lieutenant Commander I. V. Isaev) torpedoed the Bulgarian steamer *Struma* about ten miles north of the Bosporus. The ship navigated under the flag of Panama for she had 769 Jewish refugees on board who had been permitted by the Rumanian government to leave the country. The *Struma* had left Constanta on 12 December 1941 bound for Palestine. However, the British authorities there did not give permission to immigrate. The Turkish government allowed only five passengers to leave the ship in Turkey, and compelled the *Struma* to return to Rumania. Shortly after leaving the Bosporus she was hit by the torpedo from ShCh–213 and

Soviet submarine S–209 had a special bow constructed to counter anti-submarine nets.

sank. With the exception of one person, all the refugees and the crew perished. The submarine reported carrying out a submerged attack on a transport, "the name of which was not ascertained," and sinking it with a torpedo.

A few days later, on 27 February, again off the Bosporus, a Soviet submarine destroyed the small Turkish coasting vessel *Cankaya* (164 GRT), which had Jewish refugees on board. Off the west coast on 22 March, a submarine launched a spread of four torpedoes at a group of three naval ferries. None was hit, which was not surprising, because their draft was only six feet. Three torpedoes launched against motor minesweeper R–164 on 24 May were similarly wasted for she drew only five feet. Neither were two river minesweepers harmed when they were attacked on 20 June, for their draft was a little over two feet. Commander Minesweepers remarked: "The fact that Russian submarines fire torpedoes at any type of vessel when they have a chance, has been confirmed over and over again."

Rumanians and Germans laid more protective minefields outside the shipping channels, and in the course of time there were many reports of Soviet submarines destroyed. However, proof was rare, and even now, no completely reliable data are available because the Soviets do not publish them. The patient collection of data from all sources gives a fairly good picture. It is certain that of the submarines carrying supplies to Sevastopol, four were lost through various causes.

According to the German war diaries the operations of the Soviet submarines against the coastal convoys and single ships intensified at the beginning of May 1942, but with moderate results. On 18 May the Soviet submarine ShCh–205 surfaced and attacked the small Turkish steamer *Duatepe* (250 GRT) with gunfire within territorial waters near the Turkish-Bulgarian frontier. After 70 rounds had been fired, the ship was grounded about 200 meters from land. Four days later, the same submarine sank the Turkish steamer *Safak* (400 GRT) three miles from the coast in the same vicinity. Submarine ShCh–214 destroyed three small Turkish sailing ships. On 29 May, submarine A–3 torpedoed and sank the Rumanian *Sulina* (3,500 GRT), proceeding in a convoy near Odessa. On 11 June, on the same route, the Rumanian steamer *Ardeal* (5,700 GRT) was torpedoed by submarine A–5 but was beached and later salvaged.

After these losses, the protective minefields were again strengthened, and a number of MFPs and other small craft were converted to submarine chasers, but it took some time before they could be fitted with sonar. In June, the Italian midget submarines and MTBs (MASs) arrived and soon sank three Soviet submarines. The shipping channels near important ports like Odessa were now patrolled by night to prevent Soviet submarines from recharging their batteries after they had succeeded in passing or bypassing the protective minefields, which sometimes happened.

Minelaying by Soviet submarines was repeatedly confirmed when their mines were swept. But they were of an unsophisticated type and did not cause any difficulties for the German minesweepers, which had already gained considerable experience in the waters from the North Sea to the Bay of Biscay.

In August 1942, five Soviet submarines attacked shipping off the Bosporus and along the coast between Constanta and Odessa. The only success was the sinking of the German tug *Ankara* by submarine M–36 in Odessa Bay. Submarine M–33 was lost in one of the minefields.

In September 1942, 142 Axis ships with an aggregate tonnage of 155,000 GRT, as well as 16 ships of undetermined tonnage (probably very small) and 12 auxiliary vessels, were escorted without any loss. Some attacks were reported, but the great number of submarine alarms may have been partly due to sightings of dolphin tracks.

Out of a similar traffic in October 1942, three steamers totaling 6,500 GRT were sunk, one of them off the mouth of the Danube in only 12 meters of water. Evidently, the captains of the Soviet submarines did not mind operating in very shallow water, for near Odessa attacks in 18 meters were reported.

In November, a tanker of 2,800 GRT was torpedoed by submarine L–23, but was towed in.

Admiral Black Sea noted: "The Russian is committing his submarines not in the open sea but along the coastal convoy routes, mostly in waiting positions at known approach points."

In view of the number of submarines operating the sum total of their successes was not impressive, although the loss of every ship was felt on the other side because of the scant tonnage available.

Soviet naval aviation in 1942

Until the fall of the year Russian air activity generally was insignificant. An exception was a series of attacks on the port of Mariupol on the northern bank of the Sea of Azov. This was in May 1942, when the Germans had retaken the Kerch Peninsula and were beginning to use the shallow waters north of it for transporting supplies. A number of small craft were sunk or damaged by bombs. The Russian planes also dropped a great number of magnetic mines, which accounted for some more of the small ships used for transports.

The war diaries of the German escort forces point out as peculiar the fact that the convoys in the western part of the Black Sea were often shadowed by reconnaissance planes, but never attacked by bombers, although they were the target of the Soviet submarines. In the course of time the German monitoring service gained quite a good picture of the number of submarines at sea, and of the reports the planes made to them.

Another peculiarity was that between May and September, that is, between the taking of Kerch Peninsula and Taman Peninsula, Russian planes attacked Mariupol and dropped many mines to obstruct the increasing supply traffic, but left the German minesweeping planes entirely unmolested. These were unarmed Junkers 52 (transport planes) with a large horizontal magnetic coil on the wings, which made them slower still. They were easy targets, but nothing ever happened.

In September, the air attacks, especially on MTB bases, were stepped up. In Yalta, on 3 September, two Italian MTBs (MASs) were sunk and three damaged by bombs dropped from an altitude of no more than 1,000 meters, because the port was not protected by any antiaircraft artillery. Ivan Baba, Feodosiya, Balaklava, and Kerch were also attacked, but they were better protected, and only one naval ferry was sunk. All the convoys during that month got through without any losses to air attacks. Possibly, the Soviets were using their best planes and pilots inland to stop the German advance. In any case, although they utilized sea transport very efficiently and extensively, they did not make full use of the opportunities that offered themselves almost daily to disrupt the traffic along the coasts held by the enemy, traffic vital to the German armies.

BLACK SEA 1943

From January 1943 on, the course of the war in Eastern Europe was determined by the growing superiority of the Soviet land and air forces. On 14 January, southwest of encircled Stalingrad, strong Russian armies began a new offensive which quickly compelled the Germans and their allies to fall back large distances. With difficulty, the southern wing stabilized along the River Mius, which had formed part of the front during the preceding winter. Most of the German forces that had operated in the area north of the Caucasus (as far as 400 miles to the east) succeeded in passing through the town of Rostov before the Soviets retook it. Strong parts of the southernmost army formed a large bridgehead from north of the small port of Temryuk on the Sea of Azov to Novorossiysk on the Black Sea. The Kuban bridgehead was successfully defended till September 1943 and had to be supplied by sea all the time.

This situation had a strong influence on the naval activities of both sides. Another important factor was that the Russians had access to the Sea of Azov again. The Kerch Strait remained firmly in German hands, but as soon as the ice disappeared the Soviets brought shallow-draft vessels down the River Don. Through inland waterways, some even came from Lake Ladoga far to the north, where they were no longer needed because Germans and Finns had been forced to retreat.

A peculiar situation had developed at Novorossiysk. The German offensive of September 1942 had stopped immediately after passing this town and failed to drive the Russians from positions overlooking the port. Their batteries commanded the entrance, so the port could not be used by the Germans. For the Soviets, possession of Novorossiysk would have improved their base for naval operations considerably. They fully realized this and were active in trying to regain the port.

At the beginning of 1943 their fleet consisted of:

```
  1  battleship,
  4  cruisers,
  1  flotilla leader,
  7  destroyers,
  5  gunboats and guardships,
 31  minesweepers,
 67  motor torpedo boats,
 29  submarines,
260  planes.
```

The Official History says "The Black Sea Fleet conducted active operations on the left wing of the Soviet land front and supported the land forces of the Red Army" and stresses that: "The main task of the Black Sea Fleet was the support of the attacking Soviet troops." In its opinion "the relation of forces at sea was about equal but the enemy had advantages inasmuch as his bases were nearer than those of the Soviets."[7]

By 1943 the German Navy had created quite a sizable "Black Sea Fleet" of small warships. Most of them had come from Germany by overland transport from the Elbe to the Danube, some unarmed from Italy around Greece and through the Bosporus. Shipyards on the Danube had built simply-designed barges and lighters. In this way, the "Fleet" had grown to:

```
 6  submarines (250 tons),
16  large MTBs
23  motor minesweepers,
26  submarine chasers (fishing cutter type),
 1  squadron of Marine-Artillerie-Leichter (MAL), naval artillery lighters,
    armed with two 88-mm. guns and serving as gunboats,
 4  landing squadrons of about 100 naval ferry barges (MFP).
```

In addition, there were local squadrons for the protection of 12 harbors. All these units were under the Admiral Black Sea, who also directed the operations of the Rumanian warships and the movements of all merchant ships and transports.

Of the Rumanian Navy, only the submarine *Delfinul* undertook offensive operations. Four destroyers and all the smaller surface ships were employed for keeping the shipping channels along the west coast of the Black Sea free from mines and submarines, and for escorting merchant ships between the Bosporus and Odessa.

The Kuban bridgehead

Two weeks after the Germans had reached Novorossiysk the Soviets tried to retake it with a landing force supported by MTBs and gunboats, but their surprise attack failed, and heavy fire compelled them to retreat. They now shifted their main efforts to the land front but were beaten back there, too. The troops for these operations and their supplies were brought from rear ports by sea.

The result was that neither side could use the harbor installations of Novorossiysk. For the Germans, the nearest place to unload small ships was Anapa, about 25 miles in the direction of Kerch. The only mole was damaged, but it was repaired and enlarged so that ten naval ferries could use it simultaneously. The army in the bridgehead needed 1,500 to 2,500 tons of supplies daily, which had to be shipped from the west coast of the Black Sea around the Crimea. They were put ashore partly in Kerch, partly in Anapa.

Here, so near the Russians, only MFPs could be used as transport ships. Because of their small tonnage, about 200 GRT (speed ten knots), many trips were required to keep the army in the bridgehead sufficiently supplied. This traffic could not be kept hidden from the Soviets, who generally were much stronger in the air. How well the MFPs could be protected against air attacks remained to be seen. The Official History reports that "in the summer of 1943 the enemy operated 30 convoys per month."[8]

The German troops not needed for the defense of the Kuban bridgehead were ferried across the Kerch Strait and then marched on. As soon as the Russians had some gunboats on the Sea of Azov, they tried to attack the ferries, but they were easily prevented from doing any harm by armed guardboats in the northern entrance of the Strait. Its southern entrance was protected by shallow minefields. From January to March 1943, 105,000 men, 45,000 horses, 7,000 motor vehicles, and 12,000 horse-drawn vehicles crossed the Kerch Strait going west without any losses. Soviet naval forces did not try to intervene from the Black Sea, probably because they were fully occupied with transport duties along the coast, and with operations in the Novorossiysk area. In the first three months of the year 1943 the Soviet Black Sea Fleet transported along the Caucasian coast: 150,000 men, 4,600 horses, 387 tanks, 463 guns, 106 rocket launchers, 3,000 tons of ammunition, 52,000 tons of material and victuals, and 15,000 tons of oil and gasoline.

Any advance of the German forces along the Caucasian coast would have made operations of the Soviet naval forces much more difficult. An energetic concentration of forces against the few remaining naval bases there as part of the German 1942 summer offensive might even have compelled the Black Sea Fleet to self-destruction or internment in Turkey. Although ideas of this kind were foreign to the thinking and planning of the German General Staff, the Soviets were aware of this threat. Their first aim was to retake Novorossiysk or, if this was not possible, at least to prevent the enemy from using it.

On the night of 30/31 January 1943, the cruiser *Voroshilov* and two destroyers bombarded German positions there. Four nights later, a destroyer and four small gunboats bombarded Anapa, probably to create a diversion, since the main operation was undertaken in the vicinity of Novorossiysk. During the dark night a large force crossed Novorossiysk Bay in lighters, tugs, fishing boats, and coastal craft, supported by the fire of the cruisers *Krasny Kavkas* and *Krasny Krym*, destroyers and gunboats. Parts of three brigades were put ashore close to the town under heavy German fire. A smaller force landed at Mount Myshako on a promontory across the bay where there were only a few outposts.

After two days of bitter fighting, the main landing force was wiped out, but the force landed at Mount Myshako, where evidently an attack had not been expected, held on and was quickly reinforced. Within five days 17,000 men were landed there. Counterattacks failed, as did later attempts to crush this beachhead. The Russians installed themselves there for good and built a number of piers for unloading supplies. They were now entrenched in strength on both sides of the bay outside the port, which was of no use at all to the Germans. In April 1943 the Germans tried to take Mount Myshako from the land side, but after some initial successes, they could make no more progress, and after a week, the attempts were abandoned. During this fighting Russian gunboats, MTBs, and lighters carried supplies to their troops in the beachhead, while groups of guardboats screened it against surprise attacks from the sea. Against German and Italian MTBs they showed themselves rather helpless. These sank several small Russian ships and destroyed landing piers with torpedoes. However, the Soviets continued to hold a somewhat smaller area, and this situation did not change till September 1943, when the Germans finally retreated.

Russian cruisers and destroyers sometimes bombarded Anapa, but did not cause much damage. On the night of 30 April/1 May, they also shelled the base at Ivan Baba. The first salvoes landed in the port and the MTB base, in spite of the great distance, estimated at 20,000 to 23,000 meters. The Soviet surface forces left the supply traffic along the coast entirely unmolested. As a consequence, in May 1943, 120,000 GRT were escorted without any loss.

Also in May 1943, the Germans towed a 3,000-ton floating dock from Mariupol through the Kerch Strait and around the Crimea to Odessa without any interference, and even succeeded, in the last days of August, in towing the hull of the unfinished steamer *Feodosia* along the same route, in spite of the bad weather. These slow-motion operations cannot have escaped the notice of Soviet air reconnaissance.

On 17 May 1943, the Soviets again officially formed a Sea of Azov Flotilla, with Rear Admiral S. G. Gorshkov in command. Among its ships were fast motor gunboats, which could do up to 25 knots in these shallow waters, probably by means of tunnel propellers. They had heavier guns than the German motor minesweepers (76-mm. compared to 37-mm.) and were rather active. The German ships could rarely operate by day because the Soviet Air Force was generally too strong. There were a number of night engagements, at first without any losses on either side. In June four MALs (naval artillery lighters) were transported overland to the Danube and then proceeded to the Sea of Azov in order to assist the German boats there with their 88-mm. guns. On the night of 17/18 June 1943, when they approached the base of Mariupol behind motor minesweepers using minesweeping gear, they observed Russian gunboats shelling the coast. The battle report of the minesweepers continues:

Fire was returned from the coast. The RA-boats (a special class of motor minesweepers) took up their gear, and the artillery carriers proceeded in starboard quarterline to take the Russian boats under fire. The RA-boats were on each side of the formation and later on the disengaged side. The artillery carriers opened fire with star shells so that the enemy could be seen clearly in their light. The RA-boats had the moon at their back as had the artillery carriers, so that they were sharply silhouetted in the unusually bright moonlight. Accordingly, the fire of the Russian guns was directly around our boats. Hits could be avoided only by zigzagging at high speed. The first salvoes of the artillery carriers were observed to be right on the target, and the Russians withdrew at top speed.

On 29 June 1943, two boats of the German Harbor Defense Flotilla at Temryuk (northeast of the Taman Peninsula) had an engagement at 0030 hours with some of the motor gunboats operating in large numbers in the Sea of Azov. The attack of the two harbor defense boats with guns and hand grenades at very close range was countered with inaccurate 45-mm. gunfire by the far superior Russians. After a large number of hits and explosions were observed on the Russian boats, they disappeared from view. One harbor defense boat suffered slight damage and had a few wounded.

Also at Temryuk in the same night at about 0500 hours MFP–401 had a duel with a fast gunboat, bringing all her guns to bear at hand grenade range. A number of hits and a loud explosion at the end of the duel were observed. Since the gunboat could no longer be seen after the explosion, and wreckage was found after dawn, it was assumed that the Russian boat was destroyed. The MFP was slightly damaged and had some wounded. The flotilla commander reported on this engagement:

The fight came about because the Russians regularly approached over the same route and could be intercepted. During the fighting, they attempted to board us. They also attempted to come in under the dead angle of our guns, but we were able to avoid this by suitable maneuvering. By our constantly changing course the enemy was forced to turn in wide circles because of his high speed. In this way we could bring our guns better on the target.

The Anapa convoys

Seaborne supplies were carried to the German forces in the Kuban bridgehead from Kerch either by cableway across the Kerch Strait or by naval ferry barges. The capacity of the cableway was limited to 800 tons per day, but 1,500 tons were needed at first, and the need increased to 2,500 and later on even to 4,000 tons. Since the port of Novorossiysk was paralyzed by the Soviets, only Anapa on the Black Sea coast could be used for unloading. Daily service from the Kerch Strait to this port was instituted on 23 February 1943 and ran until 20 September. In 210 days, 190 runs were made, at first by two to four naval ferry barges, later by at least five or six. They left the

Kerch Strait early in the morning and generally were back before dark because the distance was only about 30 miles.

This regular traffic cannot have remained hidden from the Soviets for any length of time. Therefore, it is surprising how few attacks they made, and that they made no attempts to put the cableway out of action. The first 40 convoys reached Anapa and returned to the Kerch Strait without any interference whatsoever. Then a submarine tried to torpedo an MFP of convoy No. 41, but missed. Only two more submarines tried their luck but they were also unsuccessful. Surface vessels kept away completely; only air attacks became more frequent and did some harm. In 27 attacks Soviet planes sank three MFPs and one small landing craft and damaged some MFPs. But they also lost about 45 planes, a few to the antiaircraft fire of the ships, most to German fighters. For once, these were kept in readiness nearby, for everybody in the bridgehead knew that the supply convoys were absolutely vital for a prolonged defense. The fighters' presence was probably the reason why the Soviet command kept the larger surface forces back. The Official History says: "In the fight on the sea routes of the enemy, destroyers and coastal defense ships could be committed in only a few cases, because it was impossible to protect all units with fighters."

A bit later, it continues: "In February and March 1943, the destroyers and coastal defense ships cooperating with air forces struck more than 10 blows against ships in the region of Feodosiya and Anapa."[9] As no details are given these attacks cannot be identified. Probably the writer means the few bombardments of the coast and the ports, which caused very little damage. In any case, the troops in the Kuban brideghead received sufficient supplies to hold out till September 1943.

Soviet submarines in 1943

According to all German observations the Soviet submarines increased their activity in the course of the year. There were still about 30 submarines available, and on an average six of them were operating at any given time, mainly off the Bosporus, against the shipping between Constanta and Odessa, and along the coast of the Crimea, especially near Yevpatoriya. Their attack tactics had improved, and they succeeded in penetrating to the shipping channels close to the coast to make torpedo attacks and lay mines. Sometimes

100

they even attacked installations on land. On 21 April 1943, a submarine fired two torpedoes into the port of Ivan Baba. However, one hit the bottom, and the other was stopped by a torpedo net, which protected the berths of the German MTBs stationed there.

The depth-keeping and the firing mechanisms of the Soviet torpedoes do not seem to have been very reliable. There are numerous reports of torpedoes passing under ships or detonating without hitting anything. For example, a battle report of 9 May 1943 says:

[Off the west coast of the Crimea] submerged torpedo attack on convoy. One torpedo explodes in the wake of the R-boat on the starboard quarter at a distance of about 100 meters. 2 torpedoes pass ahead of steamer *Charkov*. The second torpedo explodes about 1,000 meters behind that boat. The third torpedo expends itself and sinks without exploding.

Another report says that on 22 May 1943, three miles north of the approach buoy of Sevastopol, a submarine attacked the steamer *Celano* with a spread of three torpedoes. The steamer successfully maneuvered to avoid them. One exploded at the end of its run near R–164, which was slightly damaged.

On 29 June 1943, a convoy consisting of six naval ferry barges and two tugs towing barges was attacked with three torpedoes. Two missed, the third hit the stern of MFP–325, but did not detonate.

On 17 July, a submarine attacked a convoy from Feodosiya to Taman with torpedoes. The plainly visible track of one torpedo approached the motor vessel *Adelheid*, the torpedo hit the ship deep down, but did not explode.

Sometimes, submarines attacked on the surface. On 23 January 1943, at 2330 hours, a submarine attacked a convoy near Yevpatoriya, at first with two torpedoes which missed, then with gunfire directed at towed barges. The escorting naval ferry barges replied with their guns, whereupon the submarine dived. On 7 July 1943 off the Bulgarian coast in the vicinity of Varna, a surfaced submarine launched three torpedoes against a convoy, but they missed. The Rumanian destroyer *Marasesti* then attacked the submarine, which quickly dived, and may have damaged her, but could not prevent her from getting away.

On 30 May 1943, a Soviet submarine conducted a regular artillery duel with the naval ferry barges MFP-307 and –329. These claimed three hits on the submarine, but then MFP–329 received a shell in the wheelhouse, which did considerable damage and prevented a systematic pursuit of the submarine. She had dived, apparently damaged.

During the year 1943, 82 attacks by Soviet submarines on convoys and warships were reported. The Soviets claim "that the submarines of the Black Sea Fleet undertook 139 operations against the shipping routes of the enemy and sank 13 transports with an aggregate tonnage of 33,000 GRT. Besides, they sank 10 MFPs and damaged 3 steamers."[10] The actual figures were: five steamers with an aggregate tonnage of 28,000 GRT, one towed lighter (500 GRT), and four MFPs sunk, among them the largest Rumanian transport ship, the *Suceava* of 6,700 GRT.

These losses were small in comparison with the total escorted tonnage, which amounted to 1,300,00 tons during the year. However, losses posed a grave threat in view of the permanently strained supply situation. This threat was underlined by the loss of the steamer *Santa Fe*, torpedoed on 22 November five miles off Varna, while carrying urgently needed ammunition, gasoline, and mines. Two of the MFPs that sank also carried ammunition. On 9 November, MFP–580 blew up in a series of detonations after receiving a torpedo off Cape Tarkhankutski, the westernmost point of the Crimea. On 9 December, MFP–58 blew up here, too, after a torpedo hit.

The German and Rumanian escort and antisubmarine forces probably destroyed five submarines and damaged others.

Soviet naval air in 1943

Though varying in intensity, air activity was more effective and dangerous than submarine activity all through the year. Off the part of the coast held by the Soviets (with the naval bases of Poti and Batumi) it made operating increasingly difficult for the German submarines. Their main task was attacking the Soviet coastal traffic, especially that carrying supplies to the forces at Novorossiysk and Mount Myshako. When the submarines attempted to move close inshore by night, they were picked up by intersecting searchlights stationed on the coast, and then attacked from the air, after the plane had illuminated them with a kind of star shell. They attributed their detection to the noise of their diesel engines, which must have been picked up with listening gear on the shore. By switching over to electric drive, they sometimes escaped the searchlights, but as soon as planes came they had to dive.

In this context, it should be mentioned that contrary to Soviet assertions, not a single one of the six German submarines was lost at sea to enemy action. When the Germans retreated from the coast of the Black Sea in August 1944, one submarine was put out of action by bombs dropped from the air on the naval base at Constanta. Two were scuttled by their crews at Constanta; the last three operated until their fuel was exhausted. Then their crews scuttled them off the Turkish coast.

Soviet air attacks on warships, convoys, and ports were frequent all through the year. The planes used bombs, torpedoes, and often their guns at close range. The impression on the German side was that the Russians carried out naval reconnaissance with torpedo planes for the double purpose of reconnoitering and also attacking when suitable targets were sighted. The convoys had to watch constantly for attacks by single planes with torpedoes. They generally came from the direction of the sun. In most cases, the torpedoes missed, but now and then they hit a target. A war diary (probably Admiral Black Sea) said on 22 January: "The vigorous employment of the Air Force, and particularly of aerial torpedoes, represents a substantial threat to the still inadequately protected convoys."

Besides reconnaissance and torpedo attacks, the third task of the Soviet planes was to drop magnetic mines into the shipping channels. The results of these various activities are illustrated by the events of a few days in January 1943:

20 January: Repeated torpedo attacks by single planes on convoys along the Rumanian and Bessarabian coast. No success reported.

21 January: Air attack on Anapa with 88 bombs (war diary: "The importance of that port for our supplies is recognized").

22 January: Attack by several torpedo planes on a convoy assembling off Sulina. Steamer Kolosvar (1,200 GRT) takes one bomb hit on her stern, is towed to the beach, and later towed into Sulina. Planes flew out of the sun, in misty weather, and launched torpedoes at an altitude of 40 meters, distance 400 meters. One plane fired its guns shortly before dropping false recognition signal (war diary, Naval Special Duty Detachment).

24 January: MFP–323 en route to Feodosiya towing a minesweeping coil (for magnetic mines) struck an ELM (Englische Luft-Mine, a magnetic mine dropped by plane) and sank. Only two men were rescued.

In February 1943, the Soviet landing forces at Novorossiysk were strongly supported from the air. When the bridgehead near the town was cut off from the beach, planes attempted to supply it, but could not save it.

The Kerch area and the German warships there, whether carrying supplies or laying mines, were often attacked from the air. On 25 February, naval ferry barges laying protective minefields south of the entrance to the Kerch Strait were repeatedly bombed and gunned. On the same day, bomb attacks in several waves hit the town and port of Kerch. Two days later near Kerch, MFP–353 was severely damaged by bomb hits. Ten men were killed, five wounded.

Other regions were not neglected. On the same day, Italian MTBs returning from a night operation against the traffic under the coast between Tuapse and Gelendzhik were repeatedly attacked by planes, but suffered no damage. Off the southern tip of the Crimea, a single plane attacked a convoy of towed barges with bombs and guns, but the gunfire of the escorting MFPs prevented it from doing serious damage. On 1 March, the supply traffic across the Kerch Strait was again the target of several attacks. After a direct bomb hit on her stern MFP–176 was a total loss. MFP–273 was severely damaged. On 9 March, MFP–371 (without cargo) struck a mine near Kerch and sank with her entire crew. The necessary minesweeping operations hindered the ferry traffic across the Strait. In the following weeks, bomb attacks and minelaying in the Kerch Strait were continuous. On 22 March, a motor barge carrying ammunition blew up after a bomb hit; MFP–331 and a tug were damaged.

In themselves and in comparison with what was going on in other theaters of war, these events seem no more than mere incidents. However, they added up, and the scale of operations was different here. Except for the few Rumanian destroyers, which never undertook offensive operations, there were no large warships at the disposal of the Axis powers, and very often, no planes for reconnaissance and protection. The Soviet Navy was fully aware of this situation and did its best to damage the supply traffic and the German-held ports. Submarines and particularly airplanes were its weapons.

In the following months, Sevastopol was bombed many times. Some ships were damaged; one used as accommodation for the crews of the MFPs was sunk (not three transports, as the Soviets claimed). At sea, there were so many attacks that only a few examples can be given. Apparently, the tactics differed considerably in quality. On 31 March, in an attack on the escorted minelayer *Grafenau* (a converted steamer), two torpedoes were dropped from a height of 80 to 100 meters, but they expended themselves on the surface. Then in a second pass, two more were dropped, this time from a height of 20 to 30 meters. The torpedoes were outmaneuvered and one plane was shot down. On 10 April a war diary observed: "The fact that no losses occurred in most of the aerial and bombing attacks on supply steamers is to be attributed to the circumstance that those attacks were not carried out vigorously enough, and that the relatively heavy antiaircraft fire forced the attacking planes to turn away too soon."

This was noted after an unsuccessful attack on a convoy with towed barges west of Feodosiya. But it was also noticed that combined attacks of the Soviet planes improved. On the same day an attack of this kind on the tanker *Prodromos* (800 GRT) was carried out with unusual tactical skill. While two bombers came in at an altitude of 2,000 to 3,000 meters, two others attacked from the direction of the sun at a height of only 100 meters. At first, they dropped bombs on an escorting gunboat but missed; then they dropped five bombs close to the bow of the tanker. Just when the ship turned to port to avoid the bombs two torpedo planes made a surprise attack from starboard and dropped three torpedoes at a distance of about 500 meters. All the torpedoes jumped high out of the water: one was a surface runner. Only by skillful maneuvering did the tanker escape bombs and torpedoes. Then the planes attacked again with their guns, in three waves closely following each other.

The German Air Force was very interested in the cargo of the tanker. As a consequence, on her next trip three days later, the *Prodromos* was escorted for the first time not only by gunboats, but also by fighter planes.

All through April attacks continued, most of them unsuccessful. In the first half of May, very low visibility protected the convoys. On 18 May, the 88th Anapa convoy was first attacked near Anapa by a submarine with two torpedoes, which expended themselves on the surface, then three hours later by four bombers and four fighters with bombs and guns. The convoy suffered no serious damage.

On 19 May, the 89th Anapa convoy of four MFPs was attacked by seven or eight planes with bombs and guns when it approached its destination. MFP–309 and MFP–367 with cargoes of ammunition and guns took a number of bomb hits and sank when the ammunition exploded. The survivors were picked up by MFP–126, which was also damaged, and MFP–144, which escaped unhurt. Two of the attacking planes were shot down. But half the convoy was wiped out! This showed clearly how dangerous attacks on this vital supply line could be.

Little is known about the situation of the Soviet Naval Air Arm regarding material and supplies, or personnel, training, and losses. It can be assumed that the number of planes increased considerably in the course of the year, as it did in the Baltic. According to a report of the 1st German MTB Flotilla, new types of planes and equipment were being used by the Russians. From the late fall of 1942 on, Anglo-American convoys traversed the Barents Sea almost without loss and carried great amounts of war material to Murmansk. After the Axis powers lost North Africa in the spring of 1943, the passage through the Mediterranean was free, and supplies went to the Persian Gulf and from there unhampered to the Soviet forces.

1st MTB Flotilla reported:

20 May 1943. Moonlit night. Very fast planes, apparently Mosquitos, attack the flotilla returning from the Caucasus coast (where the MTBs had operated against the coastal traffic), followed by 8–10 bombers.
Attack tactics:
In the approach the planes, firing 2 guns, come to within 25 meters of the boats and drop 15 to 20 fragmentation bombs when pulling up. They also drop 4 to 6 light bombs (about 30 kg) which are suspended under the wings. When withdrawing they fire with 3 or 4 machine guns rigidly mounted in the tail, or in some cases with movable machine guns. MTB S–72 received 15 hits, all of them 20-mm armor-piercing shells. S–49 also hit, developed a big cloud of smoke. Two men slightly wounded, both 20-mm AA guns hit; but remained serviceable. The radio operated only on emergency power. Hits in 2 tanks in compartment No. 6 and holes below the waterline, repaired by damage control group.
A two-engined plane is hit several times by shells from the 20-mm guns of S–72 while making its approach. One landing gear is extended, parts of the other fall into the water beside the MTB. The plane steadily loses altitude and plunges into the water about 1,000 meters away. Fighter protection is requested. One ME–110 (German fighter) does not manage to find the flotilla until the afternoon. S–49 is brought in despite severe damage.

The same unit reported on a day attack:

4 June 1943. No casualties or damage by dive attack out of the sun by 3 YAK–4s, 12 bombs dropped. When defensive fire is opened, one man parachutes out of a plane and is taken prisoner. One hour later two

Douglas Bostons drop bombs from an altitude of about 1,500 meters and fire their guns when withdrawing. MTB S–26 damaged by bomb fragments, 2 men seriously wounded, 3 slightly. One plane shot down. One hour later another attack by 3 Douglas Bostons, which dropped 18 bombs but missed. Aircraft fire again as planes withdrew.

The attacks on the convoys to the port of Anapa continued. On 27 May, the 97th convoy was attacked. MFP–328 was sunk. In the immediate vicinity of the port, MFP–332 with a cargo of 80 tons of gasoline for the Air Force was attacked by 16 bombers and fighters and caught fire. She was beached and burned out; her crew was saved. Six of the attacking planes were shot down by antiaircraft fire and fighters. Three days later, all nine bombers attacking an Anapa convoy were shot down by antiaircraft guns of the ships and by fighters. During the month of May 1943, the Soviet Naval Air Arm undertook about 120 attacks on ships at sea and on ports and unloading places.

On 3 June, a convoy entering Akmechet was attacked by bombers, whose target was evidently the tug *Hamburg*. The ship was damaged and had to be beached, but was able to leave after five days. Immediately afterwards, the port was heavily attacked. According to the war diary of the Naval Special Duty Detachment the reason probably was that the tug looked similar to "Ship 19," a ship specially equipped for submarine hunting, which had had a brush with a submarine a few days earlier.

During the air attacks on the convoys a new kind of aerial torpedo was observed that ran on the surface and detonated after a certain distance. It was supposed that these torpedoes were meant to damage shallow-draft vessels like the MFPs, which were difficult to hit with normal torpedoes (war diary of the 3rd Flotilla of motor minesweepers). There is no proof, however, that they were not simply defective.

Attacks continued all through the summer against the same targets. On 5 June, the MTB base at Ivan Baba suffered heavy casualties and considerable destruction when hit by bombs. On 12 June off Feodosiya five bombers attacked a convoy composed of two steamers protected by two Rumanian gunboats and two MFPs. The planes flew out of the sun and were discovered too late. Three bombs hit the steamer *Birgit* (1,970 GRT) forward—she sank slowly, bow first.

On 17 June, 18 planes attacked a convoy of towed barges near Kerch. One barge was hit and sank after its cargo of ammunition exploded. As it drifted burning, six planes attacked it with 30 bombs.

On 19 June, a group of German artillery carriers and RA-motor minesweepers bombarded the port of Yeysk on the Sea of Azov. Six Russian planes attacked them repeatedly at low altitude. They opened fire at a distance of about 1,000 meters; the motor minesweepers answered with all their guns at 500 meters. According to the Germans' observation the Russian pilots had not the nerve to fly into that hail of fire. Their own gunfire, which at first was well aimed, became inaccurate. One of the Russian planes was shot down.

On 25 June, the 123rd Anapa convoy was attacked just outside the port by twelve bombers covered by six fighters. The defense was prepared: German fighters were in the air and shot down six of the attacking planes. The convoy did not suffer any damage. On its way back, it was attacked again. This time there were no fighters present. MFP–142 was hit and her cargo of old uniforms caught fire. She was towed back and the fire was extinguished.

During June 1943, Soviet planes repeatedly mined the shipping channel at the mouth of the Danube.

On 7 July, Feodosiya and Yalta were attacked from the air. At Feodosiya fourteen planes dropped 50 to 60 bombs. One harbor defense boat was sunk; a slip with a Rumanian gunboat on it was damaged; beyond this only some buildings were hit. Yalta was bombed by five planes. MFP–144 was damaged and had to be beached; a fishing cutter sank. Yalta was attacked again on 19 July —motor minesweeper R–33 sank.

On 13 July, the 140th Anapa convoy was attacked by seven bombers with bombs and guns. The planes evidently were armored, for the 20-mm. antiaircraft shells were deflected. The bombers came in twice, at an altitude of no more than 300 to 400 meters. Nevertheless, they damaged only one MFP slightly. One bomber was shot down.

Three days later, the 142nd Anapa convoy was attacked by nine bombers and three fighters. They came in very low, only 100 to 150 meters high, dropped 80 to 100 small and medium bombs and fired their guns during the approach and the retreat. Some men were killed or wounded by fragments. The only direct hit sank an unmanned landing boat towed by a steamer. The antiaircraft guns of the escorting MFPs brought down two planes; German fighters accounted for another six.

On 26 July, the 152nd Anapa convoy was attacked by 15 bombers with about 80 bombs and the usual gunfire. None of the ships was damaged; one man was killed, one wounded. Then the planes were intercepted by German fighters, which brought down ten of them. This was probably the reason why another group of 21 planes sighted to seaward of the convoy did not attack.

The war diary of the Sea Commandant Caucasus for July 1943 remarked:

The steadily increasing bomb attacks in the last three months on naval ferry barges (MFP) and convoys with tows, bound for Anapa and Temryuk, and in the Kerch Strait, were mainly carried out by armored ground attack planes, against which the 20-mm AA guns were able to score successes only when the planes were in a favorable position and when armor-piercing ammunition was used. The MFPs scored 6 kills, mostly with their 75-mm guns. The fighter cover now available in this area brought down 28 of the attacking planes in July.

In August, there were several attacks on Anapa convoys (Nos. 163, 166, and 167), but they caused only minor damage, and no losses.

On 24 August, 1st MTB Flotilla reported:

Attack by 4 bombers and 6 fighter-bombers in continuous independent passes with aircraft weapons, rocket bombs and fragmentation bombs. One plane fires a type of rocket which explodes at an altitude of 100 to 150 meters and scatters an incendiary composition (not phosphorus), which started some fires on the forecastle of MTB S–46, but they could be extinguished with water.

On the same day, the senior officer of the flotilla reported an unsuccessful night attack on his unit:

Star shells over the boats. One plane fires a green flare, then aircraft weapons. Ten minutes later attack with bombs, at least 10 to 15 drop among the boats. After another ten minutes renewed bombing, 5 hits on MTB S–28. Only the insufficiently shielded exhaust of the airplanes can be made out, at first with the night glass, then with the naked eye against a cloudless starry sky. Estimated altitude between 500 and 800 meters. Half an hour later, again bombs and aircraft weapons fire.

The Russians apparently employ sea reconnaissance planes with locating gear (radar). They fire green flares after identifying the MTBs. These flares home in the bombers, and they maintain contact even after the bombing attack is ended.

On 29 August 1943, the same unit reported:

First wave of planes replaced by new ones so that on an average 10 to 12 planes participate in the attack, which they carry out in close order. Getting in position at an altitude of about 1,000 meters, the enemy dives to about 50 meters over the water. Armament: 20-mm guns, 27-mm guns, and slow-firing 37-mm gun. Result: Maximum speed of the MTBs reduced to 20 knots by hits mostly of 20-mm guns. More or less severe damage on boats. Request for fighter protection, especially urgent since 4 boats are to be employed again on the same day.

These detailed reports are cited to give a picture of Soviet air activity in this theater of war. In the beginning of September 1943, its tempo changed as the over-all situation on the Russian fronts compelled the German armies to fall back here, too. At the same time, the Russians felt strong enough to take the offensive. The German decision to retreat across the Kerch Strait and the Soviet decision to attack along the Black Sea coast coincided.

Evacuation of the Kuban bridgehead

During the summer of 1943, the situation deteriorated steadily for the German land forces in Russia. On 5 July, they started an offensive on the central front with the aim of retaking the town and area of Kursk. The Russians had expected it and stopped it after a few days. At the same time, they launched a strong offensive of their own to the north, in order to cut off the town of Orel. Soon the entire German central and southern fronts were retreating, until in the first days of October they stabilized for a short time along the Dniepr River and down to Melitopol on the westernmost part of the Sea of Azov. The Crimea was threatened, and the Kuban bridgehead was in danger of being cut off. Here the Russian "North Caucasian Front" began to attack on 1 September, at first without much success.

Then on 10 September strong Russian forces tried to take Novorossiysk in a large-scale landing operation. Twenty-five torpedo cutters opened the entrance to the port and destroyed some of the defending positions. Then about 130 small vessels entered the port and, under the command of Rear Admiral Cholostyakov, landed the 255th Marine Brigade, reinforced to nearly 9,000 men, in two waves. The report of the German port captain says (abbreviated):

After a heavy barrage which lasted one hour and a half and which was directed at the city and the port, the enemy began to land troops with about 50 boats at 0315 hours. One torpedo boat, some gunboats, patrol vessels and a few MTBs provided supporting fire. The operation was part of the larger operation aimed at cutting off Novorossiysk and expanding the beachhead.

The Soviets landed about 2,000 men with light and heavy infantry weapons in small detachments on most of the piers. The German port captain directed the defense. He had 240 men (naval personnel), seven

20-mm guns and a number of machine guns to cover a front of 8,000 meters. The defense was thoroughly prepared and vigorously executed. The far superior enemy forces were held up for several hours until an understrength army battalion arrived and was placed under the command of the port captain.

Army and navy then made a combined counterattack. All the positions which had fallen into the hands of the Soviets were retaken, and 130 Russians were made prisoners. The enemy lost several hundred dead, the German naval detachment 30.

More Soviet forces landed at other points. The war diary of the Sea Commandant Caucasus says:

Situation 11 September 1943 at 1200 hrs: 80 men landed at night on the west side of the harbor, according to the statement of a deserter. They were soon taken under fire. After artillery preparation with 210-mm mortars, west mole again in our hands up to the refrigerated storage building. Russians scattered into hinterland. Situation obscure, fighting over entire port area.

Situation 12 September at 0930 hrs: After reestablishing contact with surrounded naval elements, defense against attack by superior forces after artillery preparation and firing of several torpedoes. Several large boats sunk by our naval units. According to the statement of a prisoner of war, about one division was committed, and about half of it succeeded in landing.

The Soviets evidently attached particular importance to this operation for retaking Novorossiysk. The Official History says:

Because the success of the operation depended to a great extent on the accomplishment of the landing forces, the Chief of the Political Administration of the 18th Army, Colonel L. I. Brezhnev, visited the units and detachments with a group of political workers [i.e., party functionaries]. He conferred with the commanding officers and personally handed over membership documents of the Communist Party.[11]

The Russian attacks continued; the Germans mined the port; the town of Novorossiysk was given up after hard fighting on 15 September. By that time, permission had arrived from German Supreme Headquarters to evacuate the entire Kuban bridgehead. This was done slowly and in good order. During this retreat, which lasted nearly one month, the Soviets repeatedly tried to land behind the German lines, usually from the Sea of Azov, but at least once from the Black Sea. Most of the attacks were repelled before the Soviets reached land. In one case, 400 men got ashore but were wiped out by army troops.

On 22 September, the Soviets reached Anapa, but the retreat by land and across the Kerch Strait continued, with the sea flanks protected by MTBs, motor minesweepers, and artillery carriers. These had some brushes with light Soviet forces, but evidently there were no losses on either side, whereas in Novorossiysk at least five Soviet cutters had been sunk. On 30 September, a raid made by three Soviet destroyers on the south coast of the Crimea did not find any convoys or other targets.

The German retreat was harassed by air attacks, which caused some losses. But attempts of Soviet army units to break into the Taman Peninsula and to cut off part of the German forces were beaten back. The bulk of the army that had held the Kuban bridgehead reached the Crimea in good shape and formed a vital part of the defense of that peninsula. The Germans ferried across the Kerch Strait:

240,000 soldiers
 16,000 wounded
 27,000 civilians
115,000 tons of material
 21,000 motor vehicles
 28,000 horse-drawn vehicles
  1,800 guns
     74 tanks
 75,000 horses
  6,500 cattle.

Strong antiaircraft artillery protected the ferries and the cableway against air attacks. Light naval forces, mainly MTBs, motor minesweepers and artillery carriers, closely guarded the entrance to the Kerch Strait. They foiled not very energetic attempts by Soviet forces of the Azov Flotilla to reach the ferries. On the night of 26/27 September, German MTBs fired some torpedoes into the port of Anapa, now used by the Soviets, damaging some ships lying there.

The Official History is of the opinion that the attacking Russian forces prevented an orderly retreat by the Germans.[12] This does not quite correspond with the fact that it took the Soviets four weeks to advance the 40 miles from Novorossiysk to the Kerch Strait. The numbers of men and animals, and the amount of material ferried across also tell a different tale. The attempts to intervene from the sea were not carried out energetically enough to gain a foothold behind the retreating German front or to cut off parts of it.

There were hardly any losses during the crossing itself. The Soviet excuse is that the Germans put women and children on the ferries and therefore the Soviet pilots did not attack them. Women and children were among the non-Russian inhabitants who hoped to escape Soviet rule. The reports fail to explain how attacking bombers could make them out. Strong German antiaircraft fire and fighters were the real reason. It is finally àdmitted "that the enemy succeeded in extricating part of his divisions and in taking them to the Crimea,"[13] but it is alleged that the Germans lost masses of ships, 140 between 9 September and 10 October, half of them in the Kerch Strait. Actually, three MFPs were sunk there by aircraft. In the Sea of Azov five artillery carriers and four MFPs were cut off and destroyed by their own crews. Two hundred forty barges, MFPs, motorboats, etc., which had served as ferries, were transferred from the Kerch Strait to Sevastopol in four large convoys along the coast. They were protected by every available submarine, MTB, MFP, and motor minesweeper. The last reached Sevastopol on 10 October. The losses were one army assault boat to air attack and one MFP (474) to a torpedo launched by a Soviet submarine.

Loss of three Soviet destroyers

On the night of 5/6 October 1943, three Soviet destroyers tried to intercept one of the convoys on the south coast of the Crimea. The flotilla leader *Charkov* bombarded the ports of Yalta and Alushta without causing much damage. The destroyers *Besposhcadny* and *Sposobny* had orders to shell Feodosiya. However, they met five German MTBs, which were at sea in two groups to protect a convoy from Feodosiya to Kerch. The MTBs attacked but were discovered early in the clear night and taken under heavy fire. The tracks of the torpedoes being easily visible, the destroyers avoided them and then chased the MTBs a considerable time. This so delayed their rendezvous with the *Charkov* that the Soviet group was still comparatively near the coast when it became light.

German reconnaissance had already found them in the dark and now directed to them a wing of dive-bombers, which happened to be stationed near Feodosiya temporarily (probably on the move from the Kuban bridgehead to Sevastopol). In their first attack around 0700 hours the *Charkov* was hit and had to stop. The *Sposobny* took her in tow but at 0930 hours the dive-bombers attacked again, after filling up with fuel and ammunition. This time all three ships were hit. The *Besposhcadny* was stopped and the *Sposobny* tried to tow first one, then the other, but was crippled herself by the third attack. The *Charkov* was hit again and foundered. The fourth attack, in the after-

The *Besposhcadny*, a *Gnevny*-class destroyer, was heavily damaged by German bomber attacks during the evacuation of Odessa in 1941. Again in service after being repaired, she was one of three destroyers sunk on 6 October 1943 by German dive-bombers.

noon, finished the other two. Stalin now interdicted all operations of the larger ships without his explicit permission, which explains why they were held back in 1944. The Official History omits mention of this episode, although it reports the previous bombardments of the coast by destroyers.

The Eltigen episode

In the last week of October 1943, the Soviet armies resumed their attacks along a wide front. North of the Sea of Azov, they made rapid progress and reached the isthmus of Perekop in a few days, thus cutting off the land connection of the Crimea. At the same time, Sevastopol was heavily attacked from the air, evidently because the Soviets expected that the Germans would evacuate the peninsula and concentrate ships for that purpose in the ports. From a military point of view this would have been the most sensible solution, and the local Army Command gave corresponding orders. However, Hitler interdicted the retreat and issued the order to defend the Crimea "as a fortress at the enemy's back."[14]

When the Russians perceived this new situation air attacks on Sevastopol slackened but continued against convoys and the smaller bases. About that time the Russian planes began to use a new kind of weapon, about which the German Naval Staff distributed the following information:

In standard air attacks on convoys in the Black Sea torpedoes 2 to 5 meters in length are dropped with a parachute from an altitude of about 2,000 meters. The parachute opens at about 1,000 meters and is disengaged when it strikes the water. Ten seconds after the impact there is an explosion at a depth of about 45 meters with the effect of a depth charge.

Similar torpedo drops were observed in Norway where after hitting the water the torpedoes continued as surface runners on changing courses.[15]

These tactics were very unpleasant for the slow convoys in the western part of the Black Sea, especially when the unpredictable surface runners curved into the middle of a convoy. Then everybody had to try to escape as best he could.

In vain the Soviets attempted to break through the German defenses at Perekop. Several landings, all on a minor scale, were beaten off or forced to re-embark. However, the Russians were left undisturbed in a beachhead they had secured in the middle of the narrow strip of sand, 80 miles long, called Arabat, which separates the Sea of Azov from a swampy lagoon along the east coast of the Crimea. From there, an attack seemed impossible, but the Russians succeeded in building a dam across the swamp undetected by the German reconnaissance. They worked only by night and kept the crown of the dam just below the surface. In the final attack on the Crimea in April 1944, Russian tanks crossed here and joined the fight from an entirely unexpected direction.

During October 1943, the Soviets quickly installed guns and searchlights on the east bank of the Kerch Strait. In the early morning of 1 November, a battalion of marines crossed the northern part of the Strait (not much wider than a mile), surprised and took the battery at Cape Yenikale, and formed a bridgehead. In the following days, they enlarged it until they were stopped by German reserves.

At the same time, the Russians also landed troops at Eltigen, south of Kerch, but here the defense was better prepared, and they were unable to enlarge their beachhead as at Yenikale. Another landing nearby was beaten off at once, as was a similar operation ten days later at Cape Tarkhan on the Sea of Azov.

The German naval forces now tried to interrupt the supply traffic to the two beachheads north and south of Kerch. In the northern part of the Strait the Soviets soon built up an effective defense system of artillery, searchlights, and mines. After a few days, or rather nights—day operations were no longer possible because of

Soviet superiority in the air—the German forces had to give up all attempts at stopping the traffic. A few times they were able to take advantage of a slackening in the Russians' vigilance to lay mines, which caused some losses among the vessels used as ferries.

At Eltigen a different situation developed. Here the Strait is wider. The German coast and army artillery was so strong that by day no ship could reach the beachhead. By night the Germans set up a close and effective blockade of MTBs, motor minesweepers, and artillery carriers. It was probably the only close blockade in World War II and lasted over a month. The Russians tried desperately to get reinforcements and supplies across the Strait. There were fights almost every night, with considerable losses on both sides. For instance, on 7 November German R-boats sank three fully loaded landing boats off Eltigen and put an MTB out of action so that she drifted burning onto the land. Thereupon, a large group of small Russian ships reversed course and returned to the east bank. During the following night, in the heaviest fighting up to that time, German R-boats sank two gunboats and two MTBs off Eltigen and damaged another gunboat severely. But for the time being the Germans had to give up nearby Kamysh Burun roadstead because of incessant low-level attacks by Russian planes during the day.

On 9 November there were several engagements between German MFPs and Russian gunboats and MTBs. Because of the deteriorating situation in their beachhead the Soviets now tried to get supplies across under cover of smoke screens. On 11 November R-boats had seven engagements with Russian ships off Eltigen, while MFPs bombarded the beachhead. During these fights Soviet planes attacked repeatedly. On 18 November low-flying planes succeeded in surprising a column of motorcars near Kamysh Burun. With members of his staff, Vice Admiral G. Kieseritzky, the German Admiral Black Sea, was killed.

All through the rest of November there were daily brushes between German naval forces and Soviet ships trying to break through the blockade. In some cases the German MFPs, which were comparatively sturdy, resorted to ramming. The blockade remained effective; the Soviets began to supply the beachhead by air, dropping up to 80 loads in one day. High level attacks on Kamysh Burun damaged several German ships. All this could not save the beachhead. In the first days of December 1943, the German Army attacked it and slowly crushed it. Frantic Russian attempts to get reinforcements

These two Soviet patrol boats were among the Soviet vessels destroyed during the German blockade of the Eltigen beachhead in November 1943.

and supplies to the defenders failed, with considerable losses. On 11 December everything was over. About 800 Russian soldiers succeeded in breaking through and reaching the northern beachhead; nearly 3,000 were made prisoners of war; 10,000 dead were found in the captured positions.

On the German side, 31 MFPs had taken part as well as six R-boats and five MTBs. Eleven MFPs were lost. Sixteen MFPs, four R-boats, and one MTB were damaged. No exact details have been published by the Soviets about the disposition and numbers of their naval forces. They lost at least twelve guard cutters, three minesweepers, one armored cutter, and a great number of landing craft of various types. On the beach at Eltigen they left stranded three large harbor boats (with deck), one large launch, three gunboats, and 24 landing boats, seven large and seventeen small fishing cutters, all armed, but without engines. These probably had been towed over loaded with supplies.

The success of the close blockade, which for five weeks slowly suffocated the Eltigen beachhead, was made possible by the complete absence of larger Soviet warships. The battleship *Parishkaya Communa* and several cruisers and destroyers were still operational, but the sinking of the three destroyers by German dive-bombers was evidently reason enough for the Soviets to refrain from committing these ships.

The Official History gives a voluble account of this episode but avoids going into tactical details or giving precise facts and figures. It says that the enemy decided to blockade the beachhead of the 18th Soviet Army "from the sea and from the air" and to starve out the Soviet troops. After a discourse on the excellent Soviet morale it states that it was no longer possible to bring supplies into the beachhead. "The Supreme Command ordered evacuation of part of the landing force. The others forced their way through the hinterland to the 56th Soviet Army at Kerch."[16] More generalizations follow, but no figures or explanations. No word is said about the possibility of using the larger ships.

In a comprehensive report on the events of the year 1943, Vice Admiral H. Brinkmann, Admiral Black Sea, wrote:

In the year 1943 the Russian Fleet has in no wise exhausted the capabilities it possessed on the basis of its numerical superiority. Is this a consequence of political considerations, of the poor condition of the ships, or of the presence of our submarines and motor torpedo boats? It is to be assumed that the reasons for the inactivity of the Russian Fleet can be found in each of these points.

And, of course, in the necessity of escorting and protecting the supply traffic along the Caucasian coast. But this mission did not preclude a short-term concentration of forces for a powerful blow at a decisive point.

The end of the year 1943

During the second half of November 1943, Soviet submarines were particularly active against the supply traffic to and along the Crimea. They succeeded in sinking three steamers with a total tonnage of 11,000 GRT. In reaction to this intensified activity the Germans laid a deep minefield between Cape Tarkhankutski, the westernmost point of the Crimea, and Yevpatoriya.

In December, Soviet submarines attacked several convoys between Odessa and the Crimea, but sank only MFP–58, which carried 20 tons of ammunition and blew up. MFP–579 outmaneuvered a surface runner. Despite fog, gales, and submarines, nearly 34,000 tons of supplies were carried to the Crimea during the month. Off the Bosporus, a Soviet submarine sank the Turkish steamer *Kalkavan* (2,000 GRT). Torpedoes fired into the base at Ivan Baba did not cause any losses.

In general, Soviet naval activity seems to have slowed down after the fall of the Eltigen beachhead. There was very little traffic on the Caucasus coast. Four German submarines operated there for 55 days and did not sink a single ship.

In his final report, Admiral Black Sea said that the Soviet submarine arm had made considerable progress in its training during the year 1943, and that it constituted an increased threat to the German supply traffic for which there were not enough ships available. All through the year a total of 82 attacks were made on convoys and warships, but the number of successes was not quite in proportion to the number of attacks.

During November 1943, the Soviet Naval Air Arm sank eight MFPs and damaged 14 more, as well as three R-boats, most of them during the blockade of Eltigen at the temporary base of Kamysh Burun. According to the German reports, 13 planes were shot down.

When the Germans did not evacuate the Crimea but defended the entrances at Perekop and at Kerch, the number of air attacks on the ports there and particularly on Sevastopol greatly decreased. In his war diary the German Sea Commandant of the Crimea remarked on 13 December 1943:

This is remarkable inasmuch as the vital importance of the port of Sevastopol for supplying the Crimea must be known to the Russians. Their restraint, therefore, can only be caused by a shortage of air forces. Apparently, the Soviet Air Force is being committed entirely in the large-scale army operations on the Russian west front and in the fighting on Kerch Peninsula. This also explains the sharp decrease in attacks on convoys.

As far as can be ascertained, all through December 1943 only one MTB (S–49) was damaged by air attack, when she was at anchor near Eltigen. On the shipping channels along the coast of the Crimea some convoys were attacked from the air but not a single transport or warship was sunk or even damaged. This decrease in the submarine and air attacks lessened the tension for the Germans, permitted them to re-equip the rather shaken army which defended the Crimea, and gave them a much-needed breathing spell. The result was that the Crimea held out longer than could be expected in view of the over-all situation.

In his final report on the naval events in the Black Sea during the year 1943, Admiral Black Sea assessed the Soviet air activities as follows:

The enemy air forces demonstrated unusually vigorous activity throughout the year. By reason of his numerical superiority, which permitted him continuous reconnaissance of our bases and gave him complete knowledge of our movements in the northwestern Black Sea as well as in the waters off the shore of the Crimea, the enemy kept himself constantly informed of all German movements at sea and the numbers of the ships in the harbors. He was able to take off at the most favorable times from his conveniently located airfields. Daily attacks on our convoys and naval ferry barge transports along the coast of the Crimea and between Sevastopol and Odessa forced us to carry out these runs in several stages and only during the dark hours. We had to accept this loss of time.

The torpedo planes, which recently have begun to carry out converging attacks simultaneously with bomber units, were a special threat to our steamer convoys in the northwestern part of the Black Sea. This threat has now increased still more because the enemy is closer to our shipping routes after retaking the region north of the Crimea.

According to the same source, there were 311 air attacks at sea and 959 attacks on ports during the year of 1943. The following ships were sunk or destroyed:

Warships:	13 naval ferry barges (MFPs)	
	2 motor minesweepers (R-boats)	
	1 MTB	
	8 guard boats	
	1 tug	
Transport tonnage:	3 steamers	9,000 GRT
	8 lighters	5,600 GRT

Some Rumanian, Bulgarian, and Turkish ships are probably not included. Even taking this into account, these figures remain far below those of Piterski: "In the year 1943, fighter-bombers and

German MFPs carrying supplies along the Crimean coast were the target of Soviet air attacks.

bombers of the Fleet Air Arm sank 65 freighters and a great number of warships, among them a submarine, 3 MTBs, a guard ship, 11 minesweepers, 109 landing and other barges, 40 cutters, and 7 tugs."[17]

Evidently, the reports of the pilots were used to arrive at this exaggeration. Basov in "The actual losses of the German Fleet . . . ," published five years before Piterski, had already reduced the losses of merchant tonnage to 36 ships with 40,000 GRT sunk and 18 ships with 28,000 GRT damaged.[18]

The Germans observed the following improvements in the Russian air tactics:

a) mixed attacks, with bombs, rockets, torpedoes, and guns.

b) combined converging attacks by bomber units together with torpedo planes.

c) heavy air reconnaissance coordinated with units of small warships in the waters of the Caucasus coast, which greatly hindered the German submarines in their movements on the surface. As a consequence by day they could use their torpedoes and guns only under especially favorable circumstances, and generally they were restricted to night-time attacks.

d) frequent flights over guerilla territory in the Yalta hills (observed by German radar). It is certain that arrangements for raids combined with sabotage were transmitted in this way.

Summing up, it may be said that all through the year 1943 the Soviet naval forces played an important part in the fighting in the Black Sea area, with consequences which influenced the operations on land. The Soviet leaders charged the fleet with the support of the armies as its main task. This strategy was facilitated by the fact that the German Supreme Command did not realize the importance of the sea and the shipping routes. On the whole, the Soviets recognized this better but failed to exploit the interrelations of sea and land fully. The exaggerated reports of their submarines and airplanes may have led them to overestimate their successes; the catastrophic loss of the three destroyers obviously prevented the interference of larger warships at Eltigen and elsewhere. This made it possible for the Germans to save their forces from the Kuban bridgehead and to hold the Crimea with supplies transported exclusively by sea.

BLACK SEA 1944

According to the Official History, at the beginning of 1944 the Black Sea Fleet and Azov Flotilla consisted of:

```
  1  battleship (Parishkaya Communa)
  4  cruisers
 29  submarines
 17  coastal defense ships, gunboats, etc.
  6  destroyers
 47  MTBs
 71  minesweepers of several types
 27  armored boats
113  subchasers, guardboats, etc.
```

It comments:

Since the bases did not possess sufficient installations for repairs, many of the warships were not ready for sea. Only 16 of 29 submarines could operate, and only 13 of 47 MTBs. The naval planes, of which 467 were available, were the most important striking force of the Fleet.[19]

It was estimated that the Germans had about 250 planes on the airfields of the Crimea. The Official History adds that the Black Sea Fleet was superior to the enemy but that its operational possibilities were limited because the northwestern part of the Black Sea was too far away from the Soviet airfields, and too many mines had been laid there.

On the land front from Leningrad to the Ukraine, the advance of the Soviet armies continued. By the last days of October 1943 they had reached the east bank of the Dniepr River near the Black Sea. This compelled the Germans to evacuate the town and port of Kherson, which they did without any particular difficulties. The land front near the northwestern part of the Black Sea remained static till the end of February 1944, when successful Russian attacks to the north forced the Germans to retreat quickly here, too. On 31 March 1944, Soviet forces took Nikolayev with its port and shipyard; Odessa was threatened.

With the exception of six small submarines and some MTBs the German navy in the Black Sea had no means for offensive operations. These submarines were active and quite successful on the Caucasus coast but in no way decisive. All the other German naval forces concentrated their efforts on running and protecting sea transport. Admiral Black Sea summed up the situation as follows:

Besides the escort and defense missions going on as before, the main mission of the Navy after the isolation of the Crimea is the safeguarding of the supplies carried there by sea. At present, all available naval forces are being employed in direct and indirect protection of these transports. Defense against air attacks and submarines as well as antisubmarine measures are their primary tasks.

This simple state of affairs could not remain hidden from the Soviet Black Sea Command, and corresponding measures, especially against the supply traffic to the Crimea, were to be expected. However, after the Eltigen blockade Soviet naval activity decreased for several weeks. This may have been a consequence of the exertions during this operation (the MTBs may have found themselves in bad shape), and weather certainly had considerable influence. Admiral Black Sea attributed the caution of the Soviets in committing their fleet primarily to the offensive activity of the German naval forces. He wrote:

By the persistent pursuit of our offensive concept such heavy losses were inflicted on the Russian shipping, especially by our MTBs and submarines on the Caucasus coast, that a large-scale landing on the Crimea, if actually planned, would have been made difficult at least by the lack of transport tonnage.

Moreover, the Soviets suffered heavy losses in war material especially intended for the Kuban front. As a result, our hard-pressed army was afforded perceptible relief.

MTBs and motor minesweepers repeatedly carried out successful attacks on the supply traffic during the fighting for the Myshako beachhead, shelled vessels at the landing beaches and destroyed ammunition dumps on the shore with gunfire and torpedoes. Considerable damage was inflicted on the enemy by artillery carriers and motor minesweepers in numerous offensive operations in the Sea of Azov. He was forced to commit troops and artillery for the defense of the ports of Akhtarsk, Yeysk, and Achuyevo; which were originally intended for the land front.

January to March 1944

The inactivity following the Eltigen reverse lasted well into the year 1944. Besides convoy protection the Soviet Navy did undertake a few offensive operations in the first three months. These were two minor landings in January, and in March the trip of some MTBs around the Crimea to bases retaken from land.

On 10 January 1944 the Russians landed about 2,000 men with 40 landing boats at Cape Tarkhan on the Sea of Azov ten miles west of the entrance to the Kerch Strait, evidently to enlarge the bridgehead at Yenikale. That part of the coast had been neglected by the German Army Command, but a counterattack soon drove the landed force out again. In the second operation, early on the morning of 23 January 1944, about 450 men were landed by 15 boats on the north mole of Kerch in an attempt to enlarge the Yenikale position in this direction. Additional attempts more to the south were repulsed at once. The general situation remained unchanged.

It is interesting to note that the Soviets repeated their amphibious attacks on the Kerch Peninsula at the same places where similar operations had met with limited success in the winter 1941–1942. At that time, they took the peninsula but were unable to exploit this success because the terrain made it easy for the Germans to block the narrow exit to the Crimea proper.

In the late fall of 1943, the Russian armies had advanced so far west that they were able to occupy some small ports and roadsteads along a stretch of the Black Sea coast west of the Crimea, near the German supply route from Odessa to Yevpatoriya and Sevastopol. To exploit this situation the Soviet Black Sea Command sent the 2nd Brigade of torpedo cutters (MTBs) there. From 6 to 8 March 1944, ten MTBs proceeded from the Caucasus coast around the Crimea to the port of Skadovsk. Because of their limited range they had replaced their torpedoes with fuel tanks. One boat lost contact and entered Akmechet, which was still in German hands. She was taken under fire and sunk; some members of the crew were taken prisoners. Nevertheless, the Official History reports that the transfer was not noticed by the Germans.[20] In the first days of April, six more torpedo cutters followed.

As far as can be ascertained these MTBs were used mainly for supporting the Russian advance on Odessa along the coast, where several rivers and inlets had to be crossed. They made hardly any attacks on the supply traffic to the Crimea, and they did not appear during the difficult evacuation of Sevastopol.

All through January 1944, there were only three Soviet submarines in the area of operations. One (L–23) was lost. Admiral Black Sea saw the reason for their absence in the intensified employment of all boats in December 1943 when the Soviets had expected that the Crimea would be evacuated, and in the losses they had suffered. During January 1944, 41,000 GRT (all small ships) carried 33,000 tons of supplies to the Crimea without suffering any loss to submarine attack.

There was also comparatively little air activity during January 1944. The lull was due partly to unfavorable weather and partly to the wear and tear of the previous months. During an attack on the base of Akmechet on 3 January, a barge full of gasoline and rations caught fire and blew up. This remained the only success of the Soviet Naval Air Arm against shipping all through the month, although it carried out several attacks, including two on Ivan Baba on 17 January. On the following day motor minesweepers trying to salvage subchaser UJ–101, which had run aground, were repeatedly attacked by eight Bostons and three fighters. They reported that they "easily beat off the clumsily executed attacks."

About enemy air activity in January 1944 the war diary of Admiral Black Sea said:

Enemy air activity was greatly hindered by ice and poor visibility. The number of attacks was fewer than in the month before. Attacks were concentrated on convoys between Odessa and Sevastopol. According to air reconnaissance, the number of Russian units is undiminished on the air fields in the Nogai steppes, at Skadovsk, and on the Kuban Peninsula. Consequently, we must expect stepped-up operations when the weather improves.

In the same evaluation of the situation, Admiral Black Sea bluntly said: "The Navy is no longer able to provide transportation for all or most of the 200,000 men still in the Crimea. The greater the pressure exerted by the enemy, the more critical the situation will become." However, Hitler's orders were to hold out at any price.

The Soviet armies continued to advance and took Nikolayev on 28 March 1944, but otherwise there was no change in the situation on the Black Sea or in the naval activities there. Soviet submarines attacked convoys a few times, but did not succeed in hitting a single ship. Besides L–23, damaged by antisubmarine forces and then sunk by a plane, ShCh–216 was destroyed by submarine chaser UJ–103 off Yevpatoriya on 16 February.

Air attacks were at a low in February and became more frequent in March. They did not cause any damage to the convoys. In February, Odessa was repeatedly attacked from the air, but shipping was not damaged. In March, several air attacks on Ivan Baba damaged buildings, and attacks on Feodosiya damaged two MTBs. Motor minesweepers working at sea were attacked with bombs, guns, and even torpedoes, but suffered no serious damage. The senior officer of the flotilla commented in his war diary for March 1944: "The most dangerous enemies of the R-boats are not the gunboats with their superior guns, but the Soviet bombers, which are well armed and armored and which appear in ever increasing numbers."

Evidently, the Soviets realized the importance of the motor torpedo boats and the motor minesweepers for the protection of the convoys and the defense of the Crimea, and they attempted to put out of action as many as possible. However, they were not very successful.

In the month of February 1944, 52,455 tons of supplies and 4,053 men were transported to the Crimea. The 17th Army had asked for 49,000 tons of material. Twelve thousand tons and over 10,000 men (soldiers with home leave, wounded, and refugees) were carried out. All the convoys got through without any losses to enemy action. The 73rd Infantry Division was moved into the Crimea, a considerable part of the men by air, all the material by sea.

To prevent surprise attacks and attempts at landing, the southern part of the Kerch Strait was patrolled every night by artillery carriers and by motor minesweepers. Again and again, the Russians tried to put them out of action with artillery fire from batteries on Taman Peninsula and with air attacks, but without success.

The Soviets again began to mine the shipping routes along the coast from the air, but the mines were swept before they could cause losses.

When in March 1944 the port of Nikolayev was evacuated, a number of unfinished ships were towed to Odessa. The 111th Infantry Division was transported to the Crimea, most of the men by air. During the month, 7,000 men, 11,000 horses, and 45,000 tons of supplies went by sea. Another 17,000 tons were transported along the west coast of the Black Sea. The only loss was that of the steamer *Charlotte* (under 2,000 GRT) in an air attack (no details available).

The evacuation of Odessa

After the first comparatively quiet quarter of 1944 the situation in the area around the northwestern part of the Black Sea changed quickly. The Soviet armies had made progress farther inland during the second half of March and now advanced towards the coast south of Odessa to isolate this important port. It is strange that the Red Fleet did not cooperate even when the advancing Soviet troops had cut all the land communications to Odessa. This omission enabled the German naval forces to transport most of the defenders and the ships, and most of the floating material, to Rumanian ports. The seaborne evacuation began on 1 April and was finished ten days later. From 7 April on the city lay under the fire of Russian artillery.

All available shipping space and all operational naval units were employed in this mission; even supply traffic to the Crimea was temporarily suspended. The weather was favorable. Personnel and material were used to the limit. Although the orders for the evacuation arrived so suddenly that no special preparations could be made, the following personnel and material were brought away: 9,300 wounded, 15,000 soldiers and refugees, 54,000 tons of material.

With the exception of one 80-ton barge all the ships were taken away, a total of 81,000 GRT, including:

4 ships, new construction, not quite finished
3 repair ships
27 sea-going barges
13 fuel barges
29 river barges
20 miscellaneous small craft.

To achieve this result 18 steamers undertook 26 trips, 24 tugs and similar craft 60 trips, 25 naval ferry barges 76 trips. Throughout the ten days of evacuation there was never any lack of targets at sea, mostly slow-moving, easy prey for an attacker. Four floating cranes and one floating dock of 6,000 tons were particularly conspicuous. The last units left Odessa on the evening of 9 April after the port installations had been destroyed. Then the port was mined.

The new front was established on the Dniestr River; therefore, Dniestr Liman with the ports of Akkerman and Bugas also had to be evacuated. This was accomplished with naval ferry barges. Consequently, there was considerable traffic on the west coast of the Black Sea, reaching a peak on 8 April. On this day, there were no fewer than 16 convoys moving south, including two tankers, seven steamers, two special ships, 19 tugs, 11 towed barges, and 25 MFPs. All reached their destinations without losses or even attacks.

During this time, five Soviet submarines were operating west of the Crimea. One was a minelayer (L–6). S–31 made several attacks, without hitting anything. Not a single German or allied ship was lost or damaged by submarine attack.

The Russian torpedo cutters (MTBs) stationed in Skadovsk made one or two attempts to approach one of the convoys but were easily beaten off and did not damage any ships. No cruisers or destroyers tried to interfere during the entire operation. The Soviet Air Force evidently concentrated its efforts on the ports of the Crimea. In any case, there are no reports of air attacks during the Odessa evacuation. The result was that considerable tonnage was saved for the evacuation of the Crimea, as well as men and material for the German Army.

The Soviet sources do not give any explanation for the inactivity of the Black Sea Fleet. Piterski says: "Although only a part of the forces of the Black Sea Fleet took part in the Odessa operation, the enemy suffered considerable losses. On the sea and in the ports 16 landing boats, four transport ships, 12 guard boats and MTBs, and other transports and warships were sunk."[21] This is pure invention.

The end on the Crimea

The Russian offensive to retake the Crimea began on 8 April 1944, preceded by heavy air attacks on the naval bases beginning on 1 April. The port of Feodosiya and the antiaircraft batteries there were the first target. Over 30 planes, diving from 2,000 to 100 meters, attacked the port area with about 200 fragmentation bombs and gunfire. The result was only slight damage to naval ferry barges and other small craft, three men dead, six wounded, and six Soviet planes shot down.

On the same day motor minesweepers working off Feodosiya were attacked by about 15 planes with more than 200 fragmentation bombs, 15 heavy bombs (50 kg.) and gunfire. The bow of R–206 was holed by a near miss; R–164 was slightly damaged; one plane was shot down. Port and minesweepers soon were attacked again: 600 fragmentation bombs and 200 heavier bombs fell around the flotilla. At the end of the attacks R–205 received a direct hit and sank; R–204 was damaged but was brought into port. The senior officer of the flotilla noted:

It is astonishing that we did not suffer heavier losses in personnel and material in these day-long attacks. It should be mentioned that the AA batteries on the coast had been withdrawn from Feodosiya only the night before. Again efficient intelligence by the guerillas.

Two days later, Ivan Baba was attacked in a similar way; MTB S–42 was damaged by a bomb.

On 7 April, the MTB base at Ivan Baba was attacked again. According to the war diaries no fewer than 1,500 heavy and medium bombs were dropped from altitudes between 1,500 and 700 meters. The planes also employed many light bombs, rockets, and gunfire. Only two MTBs were damaged by fragments. Six planes were shot down. As it was not possible to have German fighters standing by, no more than four MTBs were allowed to be in the port at the same time.

On 11 April, Feodosiya was hit again. Senior Officer 3rd R-Flotilla reported:

From 0815 to 1745 hrs continuous air raid alarm. In eight attacks, each by about 15 planes of different types, about 1,000 bombs from 200 to 500 kg, 2,500 fragmentation bombs, and a number of incendiary bombs were dropped. During all these attacks, planes of every type fired their machine guns.

R-boats and naval ferry barges shot down 3 planes, R-204 received two bomb hits and sank.

It is surprising that there were no more losses in personnel and material during those attacks which lasted all day long and were certainly aimed at the ships in the harbor, especially the R-boats. The reconnoitering fighters evidently had reported them, and they were well known to the enemy. They had also made the important observation that there was no fire from the well-known AA batteries.

By this time the German 17th Army had given up the defense of the approaches to the Crimea and was in full retreat to the fortress of Sevastopol. Neither the Russian attack on the Perekop field fortifications nor the attempt to enlarge the bridgehead at the Kerch Strait had succeeded at once, but strong forces had crossed the swamps between the Sea of Azov and the Crimea and had taken the defenders from the rear. The Soviets were so strong, especially in armor, that the Germans had no chance of blocking their advance outside the fortress of Sevastopol.

When the attack started, there were about 130,000 German and 70,000 Rumanian troops on the peninsula. Ten thousand were cut off in the Yalta hills but were evacuated by naval ferry barges. On 20 April, the retreat to Sevastopol was completed, and the Soviet attack began. The first attempts were repulsed; the fighting lasted till 13 May.

On 20 April, Hitler again gave strict orders to defend the fortress to the last. Nevertheless, from 14 to 26 April, 80,000 men and 2,500 tons of material were carried to Constanta. Planes of the air arm of the Black Sea Fleet attacked continuously. The steamer *Ossag* (2,800 GRT) was damaged by air attack and later sunk by a submarine. Another steamer was damaged but was towed into port; MFP–565 and 569, as well as a barge, were sunk. In this period there were as many as nine Soviet submarines in the waters between the Crimea and the Rumanian coast, but their other attacks failed. One submarine (L–6) was sunk by depth charges.

Through April and into March, all available ships carried supplies into the fortress and took men out. From 18 to 30 April, 3,000 tons of ammunition, some gasoline, a number of guns and mortars, and even 1,355 soldiers were transported into the fortress. And in the first days of May, 1,000 men, 4,000 tons of ammunition, some more gasoline, vital equipment, and drinking water reached the defenders. These numbered about 70,000 when on 5 May the Russians began their final offensive, with very strong forces and complete air supremacy. Quickly, they penetrated to the harbor and took the main part of the town. On 9 May, Hitler at last gave permission to evacuate the remaining men. These, about 30,000, stubbornly defended Chersonnes Peninsula, from which they could be taken off only over the beach. Admiral Black Sea had already dispatched all available ships, but the retreat, which would have been orderly one or two weeks earlier, now turned into a murderous carnage.

On the German side, 17 steamers and transport ships and at least 50 subchasers, motor minesweepers, and MTBs endeavored to save the remnants of the 17th Army. At sea, the Russians attacked mainly with their Naval Air Arm, estimated by the Germans at about 300 planes. According to the Official History there were 400 planes, among them 12 torpedo planes, 45 bombers, 66 fighter-bombers (ground-attack planes), and 239 fighters.[22] Submarines also closed in, and the torpedo cutters from Skadovsk tried to attack. On 9 May, the few remaining German fighters had to leave the Crimea because the last airfield was threatened. The ships now relied on their AA guns alone. As long as they had enough ammunition, their well-directed fire made such an impression on the Soviet pilots that critical damage to the ships was rare. But losses mounted as they ran out of ammunition.

On 4 May, a convoy of three steamers and five MFPs was attacked with bombs and parachute torpedoes (number of planes not given), but did not suffer any damage. Later in the day, 30 planes attacked the same convoy in several waves. A tug of 400 GRT, carrying 200 tons of ammunition, was sunk by a direct hit. On the same afternoon, 24 planes attacked another convoy of five MFPs with 100 bombs and machine gun fire. Although German planes did not take part, there was no material damage. One man was killed.

On 6 May, a steamer was damaged but could be towed into port. In seven attacks on various convoys only MFP–132 was hit. She had trucks with full tanks on board. These started to burn and she had to be sunk by gunfire after her crew had been taken off.

Admiral Black Sea said in his final report:

Apart from sinkings by artillery bombardment in the port and directly on the coast, the losses of warships and merchant ships were caused almost exclusively by air attacks. The Russians had absolute air supremacy in the Sevastopol area. They attacked our convoys continuously with units composed of bombers, torpedo planes, and fighters.

Under these circumstances, losses were heavy in the last days of the evacuation. Five transport ships with a tonnage of 14,000 GRT, six subchasers and guard ships, five tugs and eleven barges were sunk by air attack; about 8,000 men drowned. Two more transports (1,300 and 700 GRT) were damaged and then sunk by submarines. In other action, the eight submarines operating made many attacks but succeeded in sinking only one lighter, one barge and one small auxiliary-powered sailing vessel, and in damaging a tanker of 7,300 GRT, which was towed to Constanta, however. No success of the torpedo cutters is known.

On 13 May, the last ships left Chersonnes Peninsula. In one month, 130,000 Rumanian and German soldiers had been evacuated by sea, 26,000 soldiers and 6,000 wounded in the last three days (21,500 were evacuated by air). About 78,000 men were killed or made prisoners of war.

The Soviets were greatly assisted by Hitler's obstinacy. They owed their successes against the transport fleet more to persistence than to skill in their attacks. Here is a last example: On 9 May 1944, the tanker *Dresden* (probably around 2,000 GRT), carrying one 75-mm. gun, one 37-mm. gun, and a few 20-mm., left Constanta, escorted by three fishing cutters converted to submarine chasers (one 37-mm. gun). On the following day when the convoy approached the open coast south of Sevastopol, the *Dresden* was attacked by fighters, suffered some damage and had some men wounded. From 1230 to 1520 hours, she embarked troops, then was forced away from the coast by artillery fire. UJ–130, one of her escorts, was hit by a heavy shell that put the engine out of action and had to be scuttled after the crew was taken off. At 1430 hours five bombers attacked and inflicted more damage and casualties. From 1530 to 1830 hours the convoy endured almost uninterrupted attacks by bombers and fighter bombers, which caused more damage and losses. The ammunition was exhausted; the crew defended themselves with light machine guns and small arms. After nightfall the two subchasers escorted the *Dresden* back to the port of Sulina without further incident.

It was the general opinion of the participants on the German side that the losses during the evacuation were to be attributed more to the number and to the tenacity of the Soviet planes than to skill, tactics or aggressiveness. The Soviet planes often broke off their attacks when they met with a determined defense using guns heavier than 20 mm. Generally, they attacked again and again, wave after wave, forcing the enemy to expend all his ammunition and exhaust his energy, in order then to finish him off. There can be no doubt that an intervention by larger Soviet warships in the last days could have turned the evacuation into a catastrophe. The Official History reports that on 11 April 1944 the Supreme Soviet Command ordered that only submarines, MTBs, and planes were to attack the enemy's sea transport.

132

However, such a decision was only justified as long as the enemy could support the evacuation of his troops with planes stationed on the Crimea. In the course of the operations when the enemy had to retreat from the greatest part of the Crimea, fell back to Sevastopol and had only a few planes, an operation of the cruisers and destroyers to block the enemy forces in the Sevastopol area from the sea would have been very appropriate.[23]

This is correct. Criticism of this kind is very rare in the Soviet literature.

End of the Black Sea campaign

If the Supreme Soviet Command did not wish to commit the Fleet's only battleship and its few cruisers, the destroyers alone might have played havoc with the slow convoys, particularly in the last days of the fighting on the Crimea. When it ended, Soviet naval activity slackened. Not a single one of the larger ships appeared in the western part of the Black Sea, although traffic still moved along the Rumanian and Bulgarian coasts and to the Bosporus. There, on 27 July, a Soviet submarine torpedoed the Turkish auxiliary vessel *Semsi-Bari*. On the following day a submarine attacked a convoy between Sulina and Constanta, but both torpedoes missed. On 5 August 1944, submarine ShCh–215 (Captain 3rd Rank A. I. Strizak) sank the Turkish schooner *Mefkure* with gunfire. The ship was transporting 320 Jewish refugees from Constanta to the Bosporus. Only five refugees and some members of the crew were picked up later.

These were the only known attacks by Soviet submarines during the remainder of the naval war in the Black Sea, which ended with the capitulation of Rumania and Bulgaria at the end of August and beginning of September 1944. When the war began the Soviets had about 50 submarines in the Black Sea. In the course of the war about 20 were destroyed, mostly by German antisubmarine forces. These began their work with primitive equipment, but later were well equipped and systematically used.

The Soviet submarines usually operated at important approach points off the west coast of the Crimea and on the shipping routes along the west coast of the Black Sea. They were moderately successful at best. Some of their victims were small Turkish coastal vessels, sunk without warning near or even in Turkish territorial waters. Their respect for Turkish neutrality does not seem to have been great.

The most effective part of the Black Sea Fleet was its air arm. MTBs and similar small ships were aggressive mainly in the Sea of Azov, perhaps because of the leadership of Admiral Gorshkov. As a whole, Soviet naval operations in the Black Sea were not too successful, although Soviet naval forces were far superior to those of their opponents who, at first, had almost nothing. In World War I, the difference was not so great but the Russian Fleet was more active. In World War II, amphibious operations played a special role. They were undertaken to assist the Army, and most were executed with primitive means, with considerable courage, and without regard to losses. But often, initial success was not fully exploited. There seemed to be too little individual initiative when it was necessary to go beyond the operation orders and act independently under changing circumstances. On the defense, as in supplying Sevastopol during the siege in 1942, or in holding Mount Myshako in 1943, the men of the Black Sea Fleet fought with great bravery at sea and on land. Without doubt, their best achievement was the defense and evacuation of Odessa in 1941.

The Northern Theater

The German plans for the campaign from northern Norway via Finnish Petsamo in the direction of Murmansk and Kandalaksha (the westernmost point of the White Sea) did not pay any particular attention to the possibilities of the sea, represented by the Arctic Ocean with its many fjords cutting deeply into the rocky wilderness of the littoral. During World War I the German Supreme Command had considered the transport of supplies for the Russian armies from Great Britain and the USA through the White Sea to Arkhangelsk important enough to send submarines and a raider into these waters, where they laid mines and sank several ships. In the meantime, the Russians had finished the railway (begun in World War I) to the port of Murmansk on Kola Fjord, and created a naval base at Polyarnyy on a finger of the same fjord.

In contrast to Arkhangelsk, which was closed by ice for five to six months every winter, Murmansk and Polyarnyy were free from ice all year round because of the Gulf Stream, a branch of which flows along the coast of Norway and round the North Cape in the direction of the island of Novaya Zemlya. The temperature of this water is always above freezing even when the air temperature over land goes down to −50°C. It was obvious that Murmansk would play a far more important part than Arkhangelsk in supplying the Soviet Union with war material.

The Soviets had also increased the value of their northern naval bases by building the Stalin Canal from the Baltic to the White Sea. From Kronstadt/Leningrad, the canal route used the Neva River to

Lake Ladoga, then passed through Lake Onega and some smaller lakes. Of the 750 kilometers of the waterway, from the Gulf of Finland to the southwestern corner of the White Sea, only 227 kilometers had to be built as a canal. It had 19 locks for ships up to 3,000 tons, so that most types of smaller warships, including submarines, could use it.

The Stalin Canal was finished in 1933. At once some destroyers were transferred to the north by this route. On 21 July 1933, the Soviet Arctic Fleet was officially created in a ceremony attended by Stalin. The dictator was much interested in naval matters and in creating an efficient navy.

The build-up of the northern bases, including repair facilities and shipyards, took time, but in 1941, submarines were under construction in yards on Kola Fjord. When war began the Arctic Fleet was probably composed of:

 5 modern destroyers
 3 old destroyers
 3 torpedo boats
21 submarines
 4 minelayers
20 motor torpedo boats
 8 minesweepers
   a considerable number of patrol boats, icebreakers, and other auxiliary craft.

This fleet could be reinforced in several ways:

a) by ships from other theaters of war via inland waterways (closed during the winter months),

b) by ships based at the Soviet ports in the Far East, like Vladivostok. They could go through the Panama Canal, or around Asia and Africa, or use the Northern Seaway along the coast of Siberia. This route was only open for six to eight weeks in late summer. However, it was particularly used after Japan had attacked the USA and Great Britain,

c) by buying or borrowing warships from the Allies and sending them to the northern bases.

In the Norwegian campaign in April 1940 the Germans substituted surprise for seapower and succeeded, although with considerable losses. British seapower quickly made itself felt, and then continued to exert itself in raids on bases and traffic on the Norwegian coast, and in submarine operations. It was an ever-present threat and could not be neglected in the plans for the offensive that was to bring the

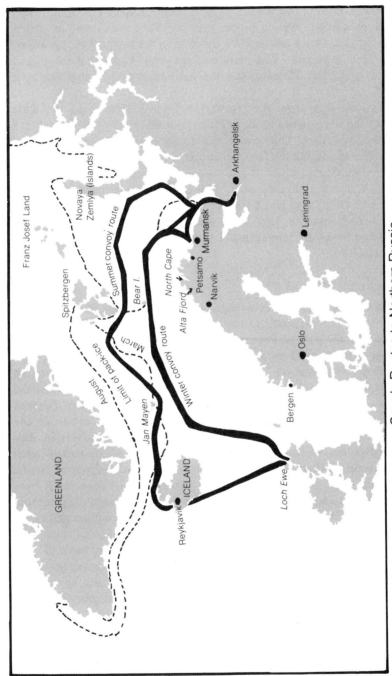

Supply Routes to Northern Russia

northern bases of the Soviets, at least those on Kola Fjord, into German possession. An operation that put these bases out of action quickly could have forestalled a move from the British side. However, the German Supreme Command and the Army Command, which had to carry out the offensive, saw the solution in a normal attack over land.

The distance from the Norwegian/Finnish frontier to the Kola Fjord did not amount to more than about 60 miles (100 kilometers) as the crow flies. The terrain was rocky wilderness without settlements or roads, but the German Supreme Command expected that the Mountain Corps, which it had selected for the operation, would be able to master these difficulties. This crack corps was commanded by General Dietl, who had been put ashore by destroyers in Narvik in northern Norway in April 1940 with some units of his mountaineers and had held out there against a superior British and French expeditionary force.

NORTHERN THEATER 1941

When the German campaign began on 22 June, the Mountain Corps at once secured the important nickel mines on Finnish territory near the port of Petsamo (now the Russian port of Pechenga). After bomb attacks by Soviet planes on several Finnish towns, Finland declared war on 26 June 1941. The mountain troops started their offensive into Soviet territory three days later. By that time the Russians had recovered from their first surprise. The two German battalions that had orders to occupy the Rybachiy (Fisher) Peninsula met with tough resistance when they tried to force their way in. The Russians landed troops from Motovski Bay east of the narrow neck connecting Rybachiy Peninsula with the mainland. Supported by the fire of three destroyers (probably *Uritzky*, *Kuibishev*, and *Gromyashchy*) and patrol boats, they defended the access to the peninsula so effectively that the German attack stalled. The frontline across the neck of the peninsula remained stationary until 1944.

The Rybachiy Peninsula, and with it the northern bank of Motovski Bay, remained in Soviet hands whilst the Germans advanced along its southern bank. As a consequence, their flank was always threatened from the sea. The Russians quickly recognized the opportunities afforded them by this situation, and made good use of them. Right from the beginning of the German advance, Soviet warships operated in Motovski Bay and shelled positions ashore. German

138

dive-bombers attacked them and reported a destroyer sunk (possibly *Gromyashchy*), but this could not be verified. In any case they were not able to neutralize the other destroyers and patrol boats in that area during the following weeks. Neither could they prevent an improvised Soviet landing operation. On 7 and 8 July, a squadron of minesweepers, subchasers, and patrol boats put ashore two battalions of marines behind the German flank on Motovski Bay. By that time, the mountain troops had reached the Liza River about halfway to Kola Bay and formed small bridgeheads on its east bank. To remove the threat posed by the Soviet beachhead, the advance had to be stopped and the troops regrouped.

After some days under increasing pressure the Russians evacuated their positions with the help of their ships. But when the Germans tried to resume their advance in the direction of Murmansk on 13 July, the Soviets again landed troops behind the German front, this time at least one regiment on the west bank of the Liza River near its mouth. Again the German advance had to be stopped. The Soviets reinforced their beachhead and defended it against all attacks, supported by the fire of their destroyers and patrol boats. On 3 August, they evacuated it again. This delayed the Germans so much that they did not begin their next offensive until 7 September. They did not succeed in making any headway, for the Russians had made good use of the time they had gained by their improvised amphibious operations. Their defenses had been strengthened so much that the Germans were unable to break through.

As a consequence, the Liza River, about halfway between Petsamo and Murmansk, remained the frontline until the German retreat in the fall of 1944. Murmansk and Polyarnyy remained fully operational for the Soviets, while their batteries on the Rybachiy Peninsula considerably hampered German traffic to and from Petsamo, which brought supplies for the front and took nickel ore back.

The attack launched by Finnish and German forces more to the south with the aim of cutting the Murmansk railway and reaching Kandalaksha, the westernmost port on the White Sea, did not succeed either. The difficulties of the terrain and stubborn Russian resistance stopped it halfway to the railway. A Finnish attack 200 kilometers to the south met with the same fate. Consequently, considerable German and Finnish forces were tied down for an indefinite time and had to be supplied.

General Dietl soon asked for direct support of his flank on Motovski Bay and near the mouth of the Liza River, but the German Navy was unable to provide it as long as the Rybachiy Peninsula remained in Russian hands. German plans to take it never matured because the Soviet defenders were supported by their Navy with gunfire, planes, and supplies.

In contrast to the "frozen" situation on land, a continuous and vigorous interplay of forces took place at sea in the northern theater. On the German side, a particularly weak point was the difficulty of getting sufficient supplies. On land, there was only one highway from the south which ended at Narvik, for all practical purposes. Sea transport was much more economical of fuel as well as of men. Therefore, a constant traffic of small convoys went along the Norwegian coast and around the North Cape to the ports near the front. There was no lack of targets for submarines and for planes.

On the side of the Allies, there developed a different kind of convoy traffic. First Great Britain, and soon the USA, sent large quantities of war material to Murmansk and Arkhangelsk. The first of the famous PQ-convoys left Iceland on 21 August 1941 and reached Arkhangelsk on 31 August without any losses. The Germans soon tried to intercept these convoys, which were protected mainly by British naval forces. Quite a number of actions ensued in which Soviet naval and air forces played only a minor part.

The stalled land campaign, the threat to the flank of the Mountain Corps, the dependence on supplies coming by sea, all quickly made it necessary to send German naval forces of some strength to northern Norway. The first unit to arrive was the 6th Destroyer Flotilla, a squadron of five ships, based at Kirkenes. Its task was to make offensive thrusts along the coast of Kola Peninsula and to attack shipping there. It was expected that this would compel the Soviets to draw warships from Motovski Bay in order to give their own traffic better protection.

On their first operation (12 to 13 July) the destroyers sighted a small convoy off Cape Teriberka 40 miles east of Kola Fjord. They sank the guardship *Passat* and one trawler; another trawler escaped. On their second raid (22 to 25 July) four destroyers proceeded to Cape Kanin at the entrance to the White Sea without meeting any traffic. They were repeatedly attacked by bombers but not hit. On their way back they sank the survey ship *Meridian*. (The two raids

Most of the supplies for the Germans fighting on the northern front were carried in ships which steamed along the Norwegian coast in convoys like this one.

did not influence events at the Liza River, where the attempt of the German Mountain Corps to advance in the direction of Murmansk was stopped by bombardments and landings from the sea.) Then two Soviet destroyers and a minelayer laid a minefield in the entrance to the White Sea. The mines had arrived with the first convoy from England. On 29 July, the German destroyers left Kirkenes again to attack shipping between the White Sea and Kara Sea but had to turn back because a British task force was reported in the Barents Sea north of Kola Fjord.

This force had assembled in an Icelandic fjord and consisted of two carriers, two heavy cruisers, and four destroyers. On 30 July it split up to attack Petsamo and Kirkenes. The carriers were sighted by reconnaissance planes before they launched their bombers. The bombers were met by all the fighters the Germans could scrape together, and suffered heavily without doing much damage. British reconnaissance did not discover the German destroyers, which succeeded in slipping into Varanger Fjord. On the way back the British force attacked Tromsø with a few planes, which caused little damage. Although no ships had been sunk, this operation clearly showed what might be expected in the future.

Three German destroyers remained in polar waters, and were used mostly for escorting convoys. On one short raid to Kola Bay they sank a Soviet patrol boat. How necessary it was to protect the convoys was shown on 7 September 1941 when the British cruisers *Nigeria* and *Aurora* made a dash to the entrance of Porsangen Fjord east of the North Cape. Here they surprised a convoy of two large transports with 1,500 men of the 6th Mountain Brigade on board, protected by the gunnery training ship *Bremse* (1,500 tons, 4 120-mm. guns) and some small craft. The *Bremse* at once attacked the British cruisers and was sunk after a hard fight. This enabled the convoy to escape into the interior of Porsangen Fjord.

All through this time no Soviet surface ships operated west of the Rybachiy Peninsula, but they continued to give effective support to their army. The German escorts were eventually reinforced by a squadron of minesweepers and one of motor minesweepers.

Soviet submarines in 1941

It is interesting to note that the Soviet Navy very quickly acted to cooperate with the Army. Of the nine submarines which began to operate on 22 June 1941, three took up defensive positions around Rybachiy Peninsula, two off Kola Fjord, and four were sent to attack shipping between Petsamo and the North Cape. They seem to have restricted their activities to observing traffic and conditions there, for the first Soviet submarine was reported on 7 July off Vardø, practically in sight of the Rybachiy Peninsula. It was another week before the first attempts were made to attack German ships. The German convoys were still very weakly protected because only a few escort vessels were available. In this first period of the war, the Soviet Navy may have missed a favorable opportunity for destroying supplies and hampering the German operations on land still more.

The German convoys generally consisted of two or three freighters protected by a few trawlers or whalers, weakly armed and inadequately equipped for antisubmarine warfare. As much as possible, these convoys used the passages between the skerries, rocky islands immediately off the coast. There they were protected against the sea and against submarine attack. But in some places the traffic had to go out to sea. This was the case from the North Cape all along the coast to Vardø, Kirkenes, and Petsamo.

Submarine operations in these areas were facilitated by the fact that there was deep water up to the coast, and that frequently the various thermal layers of the sea could be used to hide from the sonar of the submarine chasers. On the whole, it was not difficult for the submarines to find the German convoys. Of course, German air reconnaissance concentrated on the shipping lanes near the coast but the number of planes was always small. During the summer months it was difficult for the submarines to recharge their batteries because it never grew dark, and they had to go far out from the coast to surface. Light conditions when the sun was very low often made it difficult to distinguish the targets in their camouflage paint from the background of dark hills with patches of snow on them, and to estimate correctly the data for the attack.

In winter the long nights made it easier to recharge the batteries and to keep close to the shipping lanes. There were other difficulties, however. In very cold and stormy weather the water quickly froze on the upper deck and on the bridge. This was dangerous for the trim of the submarines and compelled them to dive often in order to get rid of the additional weight. Navigation near a rocky, much indented coast without lights, but with outlying rocks and rocky shoals, added to the difficulties. Incidentally, quite a number of the torpedoes launched by the Soviet submarines hit submerged rocks, and their detonations were taken by the submarine captains as hits on German ships.

This was the case in the very first attack, which took place at the entrance of Porsangen Fjord immediately east of the North Cape. On 14 July 1941 submarine ShCh–402 (585/700 tons) under Lieutenant Commander L. G. Stolgov launched two torpedoes against the German steamer *Hanau*, but they detonated on rocks near the ship. Stolgov had the impression that he had sunk his quarry. When he reached his base on Kola Fjord he announced his success with a salvo from his guns—a practice which became customary in the Soviet submarine arm.

On the same day Soviet submarine ShCh–401 attacked the submarine chasers UJ–177 and UJ–178 (converted trawlers) in the entrance to Varanger Fjord opposite Rybachiy Peninsula. Her torpedoes missed; she was hunted but escaped undamaged. There were no more submarine attacks during July 1941; occasionally submarines were sighted at great distances from the coast.

From July on a few German submarines operated in the Barents

Sea: generally two cruised off Kola Fjord, and sometimes they stood off the entrance to the White Sea. Soviet submarines repeatedly tried to torpedo German ones, and vice versa, but neither side hit anything.

On 21 August the Soviet submarine M–172 (200 tons) entered Petsamo Fjord submerged, undetected by a guardboat. After launching torpedoes against a steamer alongside a pier, M–172 gained the open sea again. This excellent performance was marred only by the fact that the torpedoes missed their target and damaged part of the pier. In the following night M–172 attacked another steamer, the hospital ship *Alexander von Humboldt*, but again her torpedoes missed.

In the second half of August, the British submarines *Tigris* and *Trident* (1,090/1,575 tons) began to operate from Murmansk, and succeeded in sinking four German steamers with an aggregate tonnage of 16,000 GRT within a few days.

At the end of August, the large Soviet submarines K–21, K–22, and K–23 (1,390/2,090 tons) reached the White Sea by way of the canal from the Baltic, which they had entered on 15 June. Soviet submarines now began to operate near the North Cape and even to the west of it. For example, K–1 cruised for 28 days near the Vest Fjord, without any success. On 10 September K–2 laid the first minefield near Vardø. It was swept without any difficulties. Two days later the same boat attacked the steamer *Lofoten* (1,500 GRT) with gunfire. There is a dramatic Russian report of this fight. The captain of the submarine estimated the steamer at 6,000 GRT and believed that he had destroyed her. In the German reports there is no mention of any damage. In any case the ship escaped although she was unescorted.

On the same day, ShCh–422 gained the first real success of the Soviet submarines in northern waters. Off Tana Fjord she torpedoed and sank the unescorted Norwegian steamer *Ottar Jarl* (1,460 GRT). On 15 September M–172 sank the Norwegian steamer *Renoy* (287 GRT), which was also unescorted. These small submarines of only 200 tons were well suited for operating in restricted waters: on 26 September M–174 penetrated deep into Petsamo Fjord and fired torpedoes at a steamer in the port of Liinihamaari; on 2 October M–171 repeated this performance. Again there are dramatic Russian reports and claims of scuttled steamers, but each time only the pier was hit. Attempting to get into Kirkenes, M–176 got entangled in a net and worked herself free with difficulty. M–176 and M–175 launched torpedoes against ships in Varanger Fjord but missed. Three more submarines, K–3, S–101, and S–102, arrived from the Baltic via the Stalin Canal.

Until the end of December 1941 there were always two British submarines stationed in Polyarnyy, which operated with considerable success against German shipping. Then they returned to England and were not replaced. The only British submarines which now entered the Soviet base had accompanied PQ-convoys to protect them against German surface ships. There does not seem to have been much official contact between British and Russian naval officers, mainly because the Soviet authorities and commissars, on the basis of their ideology, distrusted all capitalistic foreigners. But evidently there were unofficial meetings, and the performance of the Soviet submarines improved palpably.

In October 1941, few Soviet submarines were at sea—only a Norwegian fishing cutter was destroyed. Soviet submarine D–3 reported sinking three steamers and a tanker. However, it has been established that from 26 September to 11 October she undertook five attacks on German ships and convoys off Tana Fjord, and that not a single one of her torpedoes hit a ship. From the beginning of November on, the submarines were more active, laying mines and attacking convoys. On 5 November the German minesweeper M–22 was severely damaged by the explosion of a mine. A few days later, a Russian mine was recovered in the vicinity and examined.

Submarine M–172 again operated near the coast to the west of Varanger Fjord. On 18 November, she picked up a convoy with the help of her listening gear, and attacked it. The first torpedo missed; the second hit a ship which sank at once. The submarine captain estimated she was a tanker carrying 8,000 tons of cargo. She was a tanker, the *Vesco*, but her tonnage was only 331 GRT.

In the last days of November 1941 Soviet submarines for the first time attacked ships west of the North Cape, about 200 nautical miles from their bases. One sank two Norwegian fishing cutters not far from Hammerfest. It may have been K–3, which on 3 December attacked a steamer escorted by three subchasers near Hammerfest. K–3 launched two torpedoes and was noticed at once because she came to the surface. The steamer turned away and was not hit; the submarine dived again; the subchasers soon had good sonar contact and dropped depth charges. The submarine was damaged, and al-

Operating against the German supply traffic to northern Norway and Finland, M–172 was among the more successful of the small, mass-produced Soviet submarines, but did not survive the war.

though the subchasers lost contact the situation aboard the submarine became critical, as water came in through several leaks. The senior officer of the submarine division, Captain 2nd Rank M. I. Gadziev, was on board and decided to fight it out on the surface. The boat was armed with two 100-mm. guns whereas subchaser UJ–1708 had one 88-mm. gun and two 20-mm., the others only 20-mm. guns. The range was about 3,000 meters. After a few minutes a lucky hit caused the depth charges of UJ–1708 to detonate and the boat sank. The other two were hopelessly outgunned and retreated behind a smoke screen. K–3 reached the open sea and returned to Polyarnyy after the senior officer had been taken off by submarine K–23. This boat was sunk by German subchasers on 12 May 1942.

The Soviet submarines used their radio quite freely, so the German monitoring service generally knew how many were at sea. In November and December six Soviet and two British submarines operated off the coast of northern Norway. Most of the torpedoes of the Soviet boats missed their targets; some detonated on rocks. One success was the sinking of the steamer *Emshörn* (4,300 GRT) by M–174 off Vardø on 21 December 1941.

146

For the year 1941 the Soviet submarines in northern waters reported sinking 32 transport ships with 95,800 GRT, two minesweepers and three patrol boats, etc. In some Soviet publications these figures are still used, in others they have been reduced to 13 transports with 40,400 GRT and some patrol boats, etc. Actually, 12 ships with 28,000 GRT and three subchasers were lost to submarine activity. But only three ships with 6,400 GRT and one subchaser fell victim to Soviet submarines. The others were sunk by the British submarines operating from Polyarnyy.

Taken together, the activity of the Soviet and British submarines was developing into a threat to the German supply traffic, which was vital for holding the positions gained by the Mountain Corps. So far, the German escort forces were inadequate in numbers and equipment to protect the numerous convoys moving within easy reach of the Soviet bases. On 26 December 1941, Admiral Polar Coast wrote in his war diary:

I have to watch the activities of those submarines closely, for I do not have the means for taking effective countermeasures. Enemy submarines keep penetrating into the innermost reaches of the fjords nearly without opposition, and they are carrying out their attacks submerged or on the surface, just as they like. It is only due to the skillful handling of our few escort vessels that heavy losses have not yet been incurred. However, this situation is unacceptable for any length of time because heavy losses will be unavoidable. More antisubmarine forces have been requested several times already. They are now a vital necessity unless our traffic is to come to a complete standstill as soon as the enemy uses his submarines in a more systematic way.

It is remarkable that the Soviets made almost no use of their surface ships against the vulnerable convoys. Destroyers laid some minefields off the Rybachiy Peninsula, but not on the German shipping routes. Torpedo cutters (MTBs) attacked shipping near Petsamo on only two occasions. On 11/12 September, their target was a small convoy protected by a single patrol boat. Their torpedoes missed. On 5/6 October, they attacked several ships and sank the Norwegian cutter *Biörnungen* (163 GRT). Although on both occasions they met with very little resistance, they did not repeat their attacks.

The destroyers of the German 6th Flotilla all had to be sent home because of engine or other technical trouble. In December 1941 they were replaced by five destroyers of the 8th Flotilla. On 17 December these laid mines off Kola Bay. Then, at dusk and in snow squalls, they met two ships which they took for Russian destroyers. Actually, they were the British minesweepers *Speedy* and *Hazard*, waiting for the PQ–6 convoy. The German torpedoes missed; *Speedy* received four shells; then contact was lost. The British cruiser *Nigeria* and two Soviet destroyers tried to cut off the retreat of the German squadron but were too late.

The weakness of the German defense forces was underlined by British raids into Vest Fjord and Vags Fjord, i.e., into the Lofoten Islands. They were undertaken by cruisers, destroyers, and landing ships, in the last days of December 1941. Commandoes were landed and destroyed radio stations and fish processing plants. During this operation, the British sank three patrol boats and five steamers (14,000 GRT) and captured two small Norwegian mail steamers.

Hitler had always been obsessed by the threat of a large amphibious operation by the Allies on the Norwegian coast. He now pressed for more fortifications and better defenses. The regular British convoys to Murmansk were another problem, and it was decided to concentrate the surface forces of the German Navy in northern Norway. This meant that the patrol, escort, and guard forces had to be increased, too. So far, the Soviet Arctic Fleet had not made much use of the opportunities offered by a considerable enemy supply traffic that was insufficiently protected. Now better protection reduced these opportunities but not the number of targets.

NORTHERN THEATER 1942–1943

Surface forces

The activities of the Soviet surface ships remained almost exclusively defensive. The destroyers were used to lay defensive minefields and to help escort the convoys from and to England, but only near the Soviet bases. When Prime Minister Winston Churchill asked for more support, Stalin promised that his Navy would take over from 28° East (longitude of Cape Nordkinn east of the North Cape), but it is doubtful that Soviet participation was much improved, although the destroyers were reinforced from the Far East.

148

The Soviet destroyer *Kuibyshev*, ordered for the Baltic Fleet before the First World War, served as an escort in the Arctic Fleet during the entire Second World War.

On 15 July 1942 the flotilla leader *Baku* and destroyers *Razumny*, *Razyarenny*, and *Revnostny* left Vladivostok. *Revnostny* soon collided with a steamer and had to turn back. The others refueled in Petropavlovsk, passed the Bering Strait on 30 July and reached the port of Tiksi east of the delta of the River Lena, on 14 August. Here they had to wait for five weeks until ice conditions permitted them to pass Cape Chelyuskin. Constantly accompanied by an icebreaker, they reached Dikson on 24 September and entered Kola Fjord on 14 October.

From 11 to 30 August, the German pocket battleship *Admiral Scheer* operated against shipping in the Kara Sea, where she met much ice and fog but little traffic. She destroyed a large icebreaker and shelled Port Dikson on 27 August, then returned to Narvik. No Soviet attempts to intercept the ship by surface forces or to attack her with bombers are known.

In the spring and summer of 1942 the convoys from England to the Soviet ports were the target of strong attacks by German submarines and planes, and suffered considerably. PQ–16 (end of May) lost seven ships (43,000 GRT) of 35, PQ–17 (first days of July) lost 24 ships (144,000 GRT) of 36. However, there is no evidence that the Soviets took any steps to increase their share of the protection. PQ–18 was postponed to the middle of September in order to gain more protection with additional ships and the longer darkness, but it lost 13 ships (76,000 GRT) of 39. The British now announced that the next convoy would not sail before December, when it would be protected by darkness through practically its entire passage. However, the Soviets were in urgent need of supplies, and at their request, ships were sent singly, at intervals of 200 miles. Thirteen left England, seven reached Russian ports. No special measures seem to have been taken by the Soviets for increasing their safety. From the end of December 1942 on, convoys again were sent, one about every two months. Soviet destroyers and smaller ships escorted them on the last part of their run, as before.

In 1942 and 1943 German cruisers and destroyers attempted to attack these convoys several times. They had a number of encounters with British warships and there were losses on both sides. Only on one occasion (29 March 1942) was there a short exchange of shots between one Soviet and two German destroyers not far from Kola Fjord. German destroyers sank two Russian patrol boats not far from the Rybachiy Peninsula.

On 20 January 1943 the Soviet flotilla leader *Baku* (2,200/2,900 tons) and destroyer *Razumny* (1,700/2,100 tons), each armed with four 130-mm. guns, met the minelayer *Skagerrak* (1,300 GRT, some 105-mm. guns) off Syltefjord (60 miles west of Varanger Fjord), where she was to lay a field of mines. She was escorted by the minesweepers M–322 and M–303, each armed with two 105-mm. guns, and subchasers UJ–1104 and UJ–1105 (ex-trawlers). The speed of the German unit was at best half that of the Soviet destroyers; they were outgunned; there was no shelter nearby. According to the German war diaries, the Russian ships fired some salvoes at extreme range and then sheared off. No German ship was hit.

The Official History gives a somewhat different description of this engagement (abbreviated):

In January 1943, the C.-in-C. Fleet gave orders to attack a convoy which had left Tromsø with an easterly course. The blow was to be struck by the big destroyer *Baku* and the destroyer *Razumny*. They searched for the convoy in the arctic night and in bad visibility.

The enemy ships were sighted in the area of Cape Makkaur and could be made out as a destroyer, two transports, one motor minesweeper, and one escort vessel. *Baku* launched a salvo of torpedoes against the second transport and simultaneously opened fire with all guns. The defensive fire of the enemy ships and of 2 coastal batteries, which intervened in the fight, could not change the outcome of the engagement. The Soviet warships sank one of the transports and damaged the second, without being hit once themselves. In the year 1943 the destroyers undertook three attempts of this kind.[1]

None of them resulted in damage to a single German ship.

Operations of torpedo cutters and similar small craft were also few and far between, although they could have caused considerable damage to the German supply traffic. In November and December 1942, Soviet guard cutters laid several minefields near Vardø (14 mines), off Kirkenes (20 mines) and off Petsamo Fjord (34 mines). These caused the loss of four ships with an aggregate tonnage of 14,000 GRT, which sank or had to be beached. However, this kind of operation was not repeated for a long time, although the German losses cannot have remained unknown to the Russians.

Torpedo cutters (MTBs) were not active for a long time. Then on 21 September 1943, in the course of a repeated combined operation with submarines and planes, TKA–15 torpedoed and sank the steamer *Antje Fritzen* (4,330 GRT) in Varanger Fjord. But in November 1943, Admiral Polar Coast could still write in his war diary:

Russian MTBs were sighted in our coastal area only once (on 21 September 1943). The insignificant activity of the Russian MTBs is surprising. Despite the strong possibility that they would be successful attacking enemy shipping with mines and torpedoes from their nearby bases on the Fisher [Rybachiy] Peninsula, these promising craft are perhaps kept back because of weather and inadequate seaworthiness.

From that time on, they became more active, however, which was the best proof that they could operate in these waters.

Soviet air activity in 1942 and 1943

At the end of March 1942, magnetic ground mines, probably of British make, but dropped by Soviet planes, were encountered for the first time. A patrol boat struck such a mine in the entrance to Porsangen Fjord. In the following weeks three steamers totaling 8,000 GRT were also lost. German minesweepers dealt with this threat so well, however, that no further losses occurred until 21 September 1942, when a steamer of 4,800 GRT sank. From that date to the end of the war only one more steamer was mined (7 January 1944, 3,200 GRT).

151

In many places the Norwegian off-shore waters are too deep for ground mines, but there can be no doubt that a more intensive use of mines dropped from the air would have hampered German shipping considerably.

Air attacks on convoys increased in numbers but they were never particularly successful. All through the year 1942 only one steamer was lost to air attack (7 July, 1,900 GRT). Beginning in the fall of 1942, more planes attacked, using bombs, rockets, guns, and torpedoes, with or without parachute. Evidently, the Soviets had received new and more diverse material, but a short survey of Soviet air activity against the German convoys and a comparison with British attacks shows that their training was still insufficient.

In an attack on an eastbound convoy on 16 March 1942, seven torpedoes were dropped, but missed their targets, inflicting no damage. From April 1943 on, the attacks were carried out in greater numbers. A summary by Admiral Polar Coast for 16 to 30 April 1943 said: "Air attacks on convoys and single ships by up to 17 planes. A torpedo hit on steamer *Leesee* (2,600 GRT) which was lost. In the Kirkenes area 23 attacks with 82 planes, minor damage only."

In August 1943 (exact date not given), 40 planes in waves attacked the port of Petsamo and motor minesweepers leaving it. Ten planes were shot down by German fighters; no serious damage was done. Without suffering a single loss, German fighters shot down 26 Soviet planes that attacked convoys near Honningsvag at the entrance to Porsangen Fjord. On 28 August 1942 another convoy was attacked but suffered no damage; six planes were shot down by fighters. On 20 September, a small minelayer escorted by subchasers was attacked: three planes were shot down; five torpedoes missed their targets. A few days later, a large convoy was attacked by 55 planes when it approached Kirkenes. The escort vessels shot down four planes, fighters, 31. The convoy did not suffer any damage. The numbers of the planes that were shot down may be exaggerated, as was the case in many reports of fights. The Soviets do not give their plane losses in their publications, only details on single attacks, which often are exaggerated. They still claim to have sunk 12 transports with 35,000 GRT and one subchaser in 1942 in northern waters, and to have damaged three transports of 9,600 GRT.[2] Their actual success according to the German war diaries was no more than two ships of 2,000 GRT and one ferry barge, and some ships slightly damaged. There could be no mistake about whether a ship reached her destination or not.

The Soviet reports say that in the fall of 1942 their Arctic Fleet received more planes of newer types, and give the strength of their naval air arm as about 300 planes.

The difference in training between the Soviets and the British is shown by the outcome of an attack by British carrier-based planes on 4 October 1943 on two large convoys assembled in the entrance to Vest Fjord. With the loss of only three planes, 30 dive-bombers and 12 fighters sank four steamers of 12,700 GRT and damaged six more and a ferry barge so heavily that they had to be beached. Commanding Admiral Norway remarked in his war diary:

It can be assumed that the attack is the result of careful observation and the activity of a smoothly working underground organization. The enemy lost only 3 planes shot down by the AA guns of the ships. This is completely out of proportion to the success scored by the enemy. It shows how easily and at what relatively small risk the enemy can hit our vital convoy traffic in Norway during the temporary weakness of our Air Force.

For the Soviets careful observation was easy, at least in the Petsamo-Kirkenes area, which they could overlook from the Rybachiy Peninsula. In addition, they had a good underground organization with hidden observation posts put ashore by submarines in places inaccessible from land. But their successes remained modest. On 12 October 1943 a large convoy attacked by submarines and planes lost one steamer (5,400 GRT) to a submarine torpedo. On the following day the attacks continued but only a single ship was slightly damaged before reaching Kirkenes. On 19 October 15 of 35 attacking planes were shot down; the convoy, going west, did not suffer any damage.

Soviet submarines in 1942

Submarines were used continually by the Soviet Navy for offensive operations and for screening the convoys from Great Britain against German surface ships. At the beginning of the year 1942 the Soviets had about 30 submarines in the northern theater of war. Among them were six of the large K-class (1,390/2,090 tons) and 12 of the small M-class (205 and 256 tons). The others were of four types ranging in size between these. They operated off the coast of northern Norway from Varanger Fjord around the North Cape to the Lofoten Islands.

K–21 was the only one of the six large Soviet submarines in the northern theater to survive the war. Armed with two 100-mm. guns and two 47-mm. guns, she was fitted with ten torpedo tubes and could lay mines.

On 10 January, M–175 was torpedoed northwest of Rybachiy Peninsula by the German U–584. On 14 January, 15 miles northwest of Vardø, the Soviet submarine S–102 attacked a convoy of two steamers escorted by three subchasers. The tracks of the torpedoes were sighted but not soon enough for steamer *Türkheim* (1,900 GRT) to turn away. She was hit forward and sank slowly. The subchasers attacked with depth charges and damaged S–102. Her bow broke through the surface, she seemed to sink, but then she was heard again on the sonar, moving away slowly. She was hunted for more than 24 hours but finally succeeded in reaching the cover of the batteries on Rybachiy Peninsula where the subchasers could not follow. Soviet submarines often showed this kind of tenacity.

During the second half of the month K–22 and K–23 cruised off Porsangen and Tana Fjords and sank two small ships (500 and 100 GRT) by gunfire. An attack on a convoy failed because the torpedoes ran their course on the surface and could be avoided.

Submarines ShCh–422 and M–171, which were at sea at the same time, repeatedly attacked convoys but had no success. ShCh–421 (Lieutenant Commander N.A. Lunin) attacked a convoy in Porsangen Fjord on 5 February 1942. Two attempts were unsuccessful; at the third he torpedoed the steamer *Konsul Schulte* (3,000 GRT), which sank.

On 15 February submarine S–101 attacked a convoy off Tana Fjord and sank the Norwegian steamer *Mimona* (1,150 GRT) by torpedo. Three days later, the German minelayer *Brummer* (1,600/ 1,860 tons), leaving Porsangen Fjord in foggy weather in order to lay a protective minefield, suddenly sighted a submarine on the surface. The *Brummer* tried to ram but missed ShCh–403 by 50 yards.

When the ships passed, men on the deck of the submarine shouted "Russki," evidently thinking that they were being attacked by a British ship. Then the escorting minesweeper M–1503 rammed the submarine but struck only a glancing blow. The submarine crew rushed into the interior of the boat, but the hatch cover fell and caught the foot of her captain (Lieutenant Commander Kovalenko). A German petty officer threw him a line and pulled him aboard M–1503 while the submarine disappeared under the surface. Depth charges were dropped too late; ShCh–403 managed to return to her base.

On 19 February, M–171 attacked a convoy off Porsangen Fjord. Her torpedoes missed two steamers. Subchasers dropped depth charges, but missed, too. ShCh–402 then took up position off Porsangen Fjord. On 27 February, she sank patrol boat *Vandale* by torpedo, on 1 March 1942 attacked a convoy without success, and two days later was depth-charged and seriously damaged by subchasers UJ–1105 and UJ–1102. These had to break off the pursuit, however, because they escorted a valuable ship. ShCh–402 crept away and called for help. Submarine K–21 then assisted her on the way back to Polyarnyy.

From that time on a certain regularity characterized Soviet submarine operations, in connection with the Allied convoys sailing to and from Murmansk. When a convoy passed the North Cape, as far north of it as the ice situation permitted, four to five Soviet submarines would take up waiting positions between the convoy and the Norwegian coast. As soon as the convoy was safely out of reach of German surface forces, these submarines approached the coast and operated against traffic there. After PQ–12 and the return convoy QP–8 got through in the first week of March 1942, five submarines went into coastal waters but had no success.

After PQ–13 and QP–9 passed in the last week of March, four Soviet submarines operated on the coast. ShCh–402 torpedoed the steamer *Michael* (2,320 GRT) in the entrance to the Tana Fjord east of Nordkinn. Several attacks by boats of this group were not successful. ShCh–421 hit a mine in a protective field recently laid by German minelayers. She was damaged so seriously that she had to be scuttled after submarine K–22 had taken her crew on board.

In the middle of April 1942 the convoys PQ–14 and QP–10 set the same succession of events in motion. This time the Soviet Air Force bombed the German airfields at Kirkenes to prevent the German air squadrons from attacking the convoys, but the results were negligible. When the convoys had passed with the loss of five ships of 31,000 GRT, at least three Soviet submarines moved in to the coast. Here on 19 April ShCh–401 attacked a convoy near Tana Fjord, but the escorts, two minesweepers, located the submarine in time so that the ships of the convoy could turn away. On 24 April the same submarine torpedoed the steamer *Steensaas* (1,360 GRT). Two subchasers hunted her and dropped depth charges. ShCh–401 did not return to her base. There is a possibility that she was only damaged and that on the following day two Soviet torpedo cutters sank her. However, mistakes of this kind are hardly ever admitted in Soviet publications.

In the following weeks the small M-class submarines were particularly busy in and near Varanger Fjord. M–171 undertook four attacks and succeeded in torpedoing the steamer *Curityba* (4,970 GRT); M–171 tried her luck in five attacks, but in vain; M–176 had no better luck; M–173, which came into position for firing torpedoes five times, sank the steamer *Blankensee* (3,240 GRT). These boats were repeatedly hunted by German subchasers, for up to eight hours at a time, but always escaped, sometimes assisted by the batteries on Rybachiy Peninsula.

On 30 April 1942, the German subchaser UJ–1110 sighted a submarine when she surfaced in the middle of Varanger Fjord. UJ–1110, a converted trawler, opened fire. The submarine turned away. UJ–1110 could not catch up with her because she was faster. Commanding Admiral Norway remarked in his war diary:

The confident conduct of that submarine in the Varanger Fjord again proves that the enemy has detected our weakness in antisubmarine forces in Norway. Apparently, the submarines know that they will be pursued by submarine chasers and patrol boats only for a short time since they are indispensable for the important escort services. Therefore, submarines will withdraw submerged, or on the surface because of their superior speed, and a short time later, they will take up their attack positions again instead of being driven off or destroyed by depth charges by several subchasers.

However, these tactics did not always prove successful. In the first half of May, after PQ–15 and QP–11 had passed, four Soviet submarines operated on the coast and attacked several convoys, without success. On 12 May, off Nordkinn, submarine K–23 tried to torpedo two steamers which were protected not only by the usual three patrol boats, but also by a group of four subchasers. This arrangement was possible after the escort and antisubmarine forces

156

in northern Norway had been reinforced. It permitted a long submarine hunt without leaving the convoy unprotected. On this occasion the submarine attempted to escape or fight it out on the surface. It was about to succeed after a gun duel of two and a half hours when some planes arrived and forced the submarine to dive after bombing and probably damaging her. This permitted the subchasers to come up and take over. With their sonar gear they soon located their quarry. After several attacks with depth charges K–23 sank in a depth of 250 meters about 60 miles north of Nordkinn. Great pools of oil came up, as well as papers, among them a notebook with secret instructions in Russian and English. In K–23 was Captain M. I. Gadziev, who in December 1941 had been in K–3 when she destroyed the German subchaser UJ–1708 by gunfire. He was the chief of one of the five submarine divisions forming the submarine brigade stationed at Polyarnyy. Evidently, the division chiefs often took part in cruises of their submarines. In every boat, there was a commissar of the Communist Party.

Three days later another submarine tried to attack a convoy in Varanger Fjord, was pursued by subchasers for several hours, but then came to the surface and escaped into the shelter of the batteries on Rybachiy Peninsula. A lull in the activity of the Soviet submarines followed. Even after convoys PQ–16 and QP–12 had passed, with considerable losses, in the last days of May, no German convoys were attacked for four weeks, and almost no sightings of submarines were reported. Incidentally, a "sighting" did not always mean that a submarine had actually been there. As far as can be ascertained, no German ship was torpedoed in May, June, or July 1942.

The Allies had to postpone the next pair of convoys—PQ–17 and QP–13—because not enough destroyers were available. These were needed for a large convoy that was to bring supplies to Malta in the second week of June 1942. QP–13 started on 26 June from Arkhangelsk, PQ–17 on the following day from Iceland. A close escort group of cruisers and destroyers and a distant escort group, including the new U.S. battleship *Washington*, the British battleship *Duke of York*, and the British aircraft carrier *Victorious* (54 planes), were at sea to protect the convoys in case of attack by German surface ships, among which was the battleship *Tirpitz*, sister ship of the *Bismarck*. The usual submarine lines had been laid out in waiting positions.

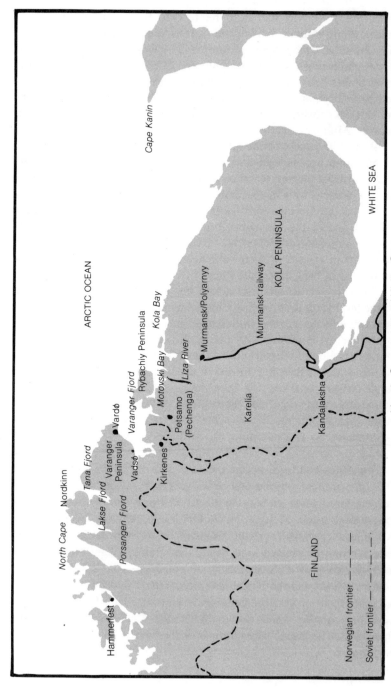

North Cape to the White Sea

In addition, Admiral Miles, Chief of the British Naval Mission in Moscow, and Rear Admiral Bevan, the British Senior Naval Officer in Murmansk, had been instructed to encourage the Soviets to participate as fully as possible, by a) bombarding German airfields in northern Norway, b) sending submarines to the Norwegian coast and to the east of Bear Island, c) protecting the convoys over the eastern part of the run with Soviet naval and air forces, d) permitting the use of Soviet bases by British reconnaissance seaplanes.

The Soviet sources do not comment on these requests.

The Soviets flew air attacks against four airfields and ports, but these caused only minor damage because the German fighters had been reinforced and were alerted in time. The attacks, carried out on 2 June 1942, had little, if any, influence on the outcome of the convoy operation.

Four of the large K-class submarines were stationed north and west of the North Cape. As usual, Soviet destroyers were kept in readiness in Kola Fjord, and two squadrons of Catalina planes of the Royal Air Force were transferred to the Kola area. The Germans had gathered the battleship *Tirpitz*, two pocket battleships, one heavy cruiser, and twelve destroyers in the fjords of northern Norway. Ten submarines were in waiting positions.

On 1 July PQ–17 was sighted for the first time by a plane. On 4 July, it passed north of Bear Island; four ships were hit by German planes. Late on 5 July, Admiral Pound, the First Sea Lord, gave the convoy the order to disperse because reports made it seem probable that German surface forces were approaching, and the Allied heavy ships were far away. Dispersal made it much easier for planes and submarines to attack, and the convoy lost 24 of its 36 ships. Actually, Admiral Pound was mistaken: the German staffs had no clear picture of the situation—the heavy ships left their anchorages in the course of 5 July, and could not have reached the convoy as quickly as the British Admiralty assumed.

On the afternoon of 5 July, the Soviet submarine K–21 (Lieutenant Commander N. A. Lunin) sighted the battleship *Tirpitz*, screened by destroyers. There is a dramatic and detailed Russian report of how Lieutenant Commander Lunin attacked the German ships and launched four torpedoes, which damaged the *Tirpitz* and sank one destroyer. For this feat he was named "Hero of the Soviet Union." Actually the *Tirpitz* was not hit; her captain did not even notice that his ship was attacked. Neither was there any damage to a destroyer, and the available war diaries are silent about this incident. Probably one of the destroyers dropped a few depth charges as a precautionary measure because there was an indistinct sonar echo.

On the German side there were no more losses during July, and nothing is known about the activities of the Soviet submarines after the convoys had passed. Submarines D–3 and M–176 did not return to their base and were probably lost in German defensive minefields between Nordkinn and Varanger Fjord.

On 4 and 11 August Soviet submarine ShCh–403 attacked German convoys near the entrance of Varanger Fjord. All her torpedoes missed; after the second attempt three subchasers hunted and probably damaged her, but she got away. On 14 August, an explosion in ShCh–402 killed her captain (Commander Stolgov) and 17 members of the crew, but the survivors managed to bring their boat from Tana Fjord back to Polyarnyy. West of the North Cape K–21 attacked a squadron of minesweepers but missed. On 22 and 23 August ShCh–422 attacked two convoys in Varanger Fjord without success. On 24 August another submarine—probably M–173— attacked a convoy in the entrance of Varanger Fjord, missed, was hunted and most likely was destroyed, for she did not return to her base.

In the middle of September 1942 the next pair of convoys (PQ–18 and QP–14) sailed, after the same operational preparations and under similar conditions as before, but the escort groups kept closer to the convoys. The German surface ships put to sea but were soon ordered back; the German Air Force did not succeed in eliminating the British carrier and suffered considerable losses to fighters. Thirteen transports out of 39 were sunk, with a loss of three German submarines and 20 planes.

Soviet submarines were not mentioned in the documents of either side but were probably in the usual positions. If they approached the coast afterwards they had no success, and there are no records of any intensive submarine hunting. The Soviet submarines still used their radio freely, and the German monitoring service was informed at least about the number of Soviet submarines at sea. Close observation often made it possible to distinguish the various submarines, so that they were given individual names.

In 1942, nine Soviet submarines were lost, six of them to mines. To replace them, six submarines of the Soviet Fleet in the Pacific were transferred, beginning at the end of September, to Polyarnyy

Built after the First World War, the Soviet submarine D–3 was rebuilt at the beginning of the Second World War, and claimed eight successes (none confirmed) before being lost, possibly in a German minefield, in July 1942.

via Dutch Harbor—San Francisco—Panama Canal—Halifax. The first arrived in Polyarnyy on 24 January 1943, the last in May. L–16 was torpedoed by the Japanese submarine I–25 on 11 October off the coast of Oregon.

In the last quarter of 1942 submarine activity was inconsiderable. Only two attacks on convoys were reported, on 25 October and 14 December in Varanger Fjord. Each time the torpedoes were sighted early enough to be avoided. Possibly submarines were sent to patrol the waters more to the east after the pocket battleship *Admiral Scheer* appeared in the Kara Sea. In December the Soviets shifted to minelaying; a number of minefields were discovered. The loss of three steamers in Varanger Fjord, which was attributed to submarines, was actually caused by mines laid by nine patrol cutters. The result was an order by the Commanding Admiral Norway barring steamers of 5,000 GRT or more from entering Varanger Fjord, because they were also endangered by the batteries on Rybachiy Peninsula. Fire from these batteries was well directed, they had ample ammunition, and their nuisance value was great, although they succeeded in sinking only two small steamers (860 and 990 GRT) in three years.

For the year 1942, the Soviet submarine brigade in the Arctic reported sinking 45 transports with 143,000 GRT, three mine-sweepers, one minelayer, and ten patrol boats. The actual figures (not including losses to mines) were 18 transports with 19,000 GRT and one patrol boat. Four submarines were promoted to "guard submarines," and four received the Red Banner Order. Of course, in the excitement of military action mistakes will always happen, and it is only human to be optimistic about one's successes. However, it seems noteworthy that in the Soviet armed forces this personal factor made itself felt to such an extent.

That the Soviet Fleet Command in the Arctic clearly recognized the potentialities of its submarines is confirmed by the Official History, which says:

For the operations on the sea communications of the enemy the Command of the Arctic Fleet principally used submarines. In the year 1942, submarines of the Arctic Fleet sank 17 German transports with an aggregate tonnage of 54,000 GRT and 3 warships. The most successful submarines were K–21 (Lunin), M–171, M–172, M–173, M–176, and D–3.[3]

No losses are given. Then the activities of the Naval Air Arm are mentioned. "The number of planes was increased more than three-fold."[4]

Naval activity in connection with the convoys from England is mentioned as follows:

The Arctic Fleet of the USSR reinforced the escorts of the convoys from the region of Bear Island near 20° East and created favorable conditions for shipping in its area of operations. But because it disposed neither of battleships nor of cruisers, the fight against the superior forces of the enemy was very difficult. Nevertheless, thanks to the good organization of the operations and to the mastership of the commanders and sailors the Fleet successfully executed its tasks.[5]

It should be mentioned that some of the light forces escorted traffic between Kola Fjord and Arkhangelsk and on the Northern Seaway around Siberia. In 1942, in the short shipping period, 247 transports and icebreakers passed along this route.

Soviet submarines in 1943

The British convoys to northern Russia started again in December 1942, now numbered from JW–51 on, and from RA–51 for the opposite direction. The first pair (15 to 25 December 1942) was not discovered by German reconnaissance, but it lost five ships out of 16 in Kola Fjord to air attacks and mines. On 1 January, submarine L–20 succeeded in sinking the steamer *Muansa* (5,480 GRT) off Kongsfjord. The ship was escorted by only one patrol vessel. Then L–20 laid a minefield off Tana Fjord and put spies ashore. L–22 also laid a minefield in Varanger Fjord. Both fields were cleared without loss.

JW–52 started from Iceland on 17 January 1943 and entered Kola Fjord on 27 January. Two days later RA–52 left Murmansk. Each lost only one steamer out of 14 and 11 ships respectively. Between and after the passages of these convoys Soviet submarines were busy.

At least six submarines were verified near the coast. After several unsuccessful attempts by three of them, M–171 damaged the transport *Ilona Siemers* (3,240 GRT) off Kongsfjord on 29 January, but the ship reached port under her own steam. She was escorted by only one vessel. On 1 February, ShCh–403 torpedoed patrol boat V–6115, M–172 torpedoed patrol boat V–5909, both in the Varanger area, and L–20 torpedoed the transport *Othmarschen* (7,000 GRT), which was escorted by two subchasers off Nordkinn.

A few days later another series of submarine attacks occurred. In the early morning of 5 February L–20 fired two torpedoes at the German minelayer *Brummer* and two destroyers which passed Nordkinn to lay mines off Kola Fjord. The ships were not hit. In the following night submarines K–3 (with Rear Admiral Vinogradov, in command of Submarine Brigade Arctic, aboard) and K–22 (with the commander of the 1st Submarine Division aboard) together attacked subchasers UJ–1101 and UJ–1108. These had put to sea in a gale force 8 in order to escort the minelaying group back into port. The submarines operated on the surface. A torpedo from K–3 missed UJ–1101, but hit UJ–1108, which sank. On the morning of 6 February K–22 and later L–20 launched torpedoes at the returning *Brummer* group but missed. Shortly afterwards, K–22 hit a mine in one of the protective fields and sank.

It is noteworthy that Soviet submarines often attacked patrol boats, subchasers, minesweepers, and similar small craft. For a long time German submarines were forbidden to do so because it was more important that they concentrate on the transport tonnage. It may be reasoned that the destruction of a small naval vessel means the loss of a better opportunity, but on the other hand it may open the way to a successful attack later on.

On 12 February a convoy of six ships bound for Kirkenes, protected by seven subchasers and similar craft, was attacked by K–3. Steamer *Fechenheim* (8,120 GRT) was hit by a torpedo but continued under her own power. One torpedo ran its course on the surface. This happened rather often to Soviet submarines.

During the passage of convoy JW–53 from 15 to 26 February 1943 the usual line of Soviet submarines was in waiting positions out at sea, but small submarines were busy in Varanger Fjord. Several times they appeared on the surface so near the shore that they were taken under fire by coastal batteries at Kiberg and Petsamo. Their torpedoes failed to hit anything. One at least was a surface runner.

The return convoy RA–53 started from Kola Fjord on 1 March. It met with very heavy weather, which on the German side was utilized to move the battleships *Tirpitz* and *Scharnhorst* and destroyers to northern Norway. This concentration of German ships (and the Allies' need to keep the greatest possible number of destroyers in the Atlantic to fight the submarines there) induced the British Admiralty to suspend the Murmansk convoys through spring and summer. The Soviet submarines were now available all the time for operations against the German supply traffic.

On 16 March, M–104 hit the steamer *Johannisberger* (4,530 GRT) with a torpedo and the ship had to be beached in Varanger Fjord. Near Nordkinn, K–3 undertook two attacks on convoys without hitting a ship, and then was destroyed by a group of subchasers. M–174 struck a mine in one of the defensive fields but succeeded in reaching her base. In the last days of March, three submarines attacked two convoys several times, but only S–55 scored a hit, sinking the steamer *Ajax* (2,300 GRT), out of a convoy of nine ships escorted by nine subchasers and similar craft.

In the following months the number of Soviet submarines operating near the coast increased. At the same time, air activity intensified, and sometimes Soviet torpedo cutters laid mines or tried to attack convoys. The batteries on Rybachiy Peninsula became more active, too, and their fire, always good, became extremely accurate. In April 1943, three steamers were hit, but were able to reach port.

A German convoy headed for Petsamo seeks cover behind a smoke screen from the Russian batteries on Rybachiy Peninsula.

There were heavy duels between the Soviet batteries and the Finnish guns near Petsamo, as well as the German batteries on the coast of Varanger Fjord. Then the Germans began taking the convoys past the Russian guns behind a dense smoke screen, and no more ships were hit for several months.

The submarines obviously used not only air reconnaissance reports but also coast watchers. With the help of the Norwegian resistance it was not difficult to find suitable hiding and watching places on the much-indented coast, which was thinly guarded by German units. These eventually combed through the most likely places and found a number of camps and gear of all kinds, including magnetic mines.

In the spring of 1943 small M-class submarines operated in Varanger Fjord and off Vardø, but did not make any hits in several attacks. The larger submarines laid mines or attacked convoys all along the coast from Varanger Fjord around the North Cape. Their successes were moderate: the steamer *Sturzsee* (708 GRT) sunk on 29 April, the tanker *Eurostadt* (1,118 GRT) sunk on 7 May. The steamer *Wartheland* (5,100 GRT) was hit by a dud and carried on.

In June and July 1943 a considerable number of Soviet submarines again operated in the waters near the northern coast of Norway. According to the observations of the German monitoring service, the trips of the individual boats were comparatively short. The small M-class submarines generally kept their positions for three to six days, the larger boats somewhat longer, but rarely over two weeks. Although they undertook quite a number of attacks on convoys they did not succeed in sinking a single transport all through the summer. But on 17 July submarine S–56 torpedoed and sank the minesweeper M–346, which escorted the minelayer *Brummer.* ShCh–403 fired at the *Brummer* but missed. Three days later S–56 sank the patrol boat *Alane.*

The Soviets had as many as 20 submarines at sea. They lost M–106 to depth charges and ramming on 5 July. ShCh–422 struck a mine in one of the German fields and sank. Air activity was lively, too. In June alone the Russians lost over one hundred planes without sinking a single ship. The batteries on the Rybachiy Peninsula tried to hit the convoys behind their smoke screens, probably after installing radar, but caused only minor damage with fragments. From May to October 1943, 47 convoys passed within reach of these batteries without losing a single ship.

In the following months the submarines made fewer attacks, possibly because the growing number of German minefields hampered their movements. On 1 September, M–104 torpedoed the steamer *Rüdesheimer* (2,036 GRT), which was brought in, however. On 3 September, S–51 sank the subchaser UJ–1202 off Kongsfjord, and on 11 September M–107 sank the subchaser UJ–1217 off Syltefjord.

In the second half of September 1943 Soviet submarines, torpedo cutters (MTBs), and planes suffered heavily, without significantly damaging any ships, although their machine guns caused some casualties. Attacks on ports and batteries resulted in some hits on the installations without affecting the supply transports. Torpedo cutter TKA–13 sank the steamer *Antje Fritzen* (4,330 GRT). On 12 October S–55 attacked a large convoy off Porsangen Fjord and sank the magnetic minesweeper *Ammerland* (5,380 GRT). The Official History still calls the ship "a transport with a valuable cargo of war material."[6]

S–55 did not return from her next cruise, and ShCh–403, M–173, and M–174 were also lost, probably on mines. The big submarine K–1 disappeared on the way back from the Kara Sea in a region where German mines had been laid. These losses are glossed over in the Soviet publications, but they explain why in the last part of the year 1943 the submarines ostensibly held back.

Boston planes appeared for the first time in larger numbers, but the increasing darkness of the Arctic winter cut the time available for the attacks almost to nil. Soviet air reconnaissance now covered the coast west of the North Cape to Hammerfest. At the end of October, the large icebreakers *Stalin* and *Fedor Lidke* returned from the Siberian route to the White Sea, escorted by six destroyers and at least four minesweepers. According to Soviet account, from Kara Strait to Gorlo Strait the escorts fought heroic battles against German submarines, sinking two and seriously damaging three more. Actually, only U–636 was in that vicinity, returning from laying a minefield off Yugor Strait. Her captain noted in his war diary: "Many far distant detonations, probably of depth charges." He did not sight any Soviet ships.

To some extent MTBs took over the mission of attacking the convoys. In an attack by five of them on 12 December in Varanger Fjord, the torpedoes missed, so they used their guns. Three MTBs were sunk; five survivors were rescued. Another group attacked and sank patrol boat Vp–6106 in the same area.

On 21 December a commando detachment was put ashore deep inside Varanger Fjord, probably by small surface craft. The commandoes made a surprise attack on an air force truck column and then disappeared again.

According to their reports, Soviet submarines in the year 1943 sank 45 transports with 149,225 GRT, one submarine, one destroyer, one minelayer, and 12 smaller warships. Actually, their torpedoes sank eight transports with 26,700 GRT, one submarine, and seven smaller warships. In addition, five transports with 27,100 GRT were hit but reached port.

According to the war diary of Admiral Polar Coast who was responsible for the convoys and their protection, in 1943 shipping with an aggregate tonnage of over six million GRT (6,333,000) was escorted in the Narvik—Petsamo area, i.e., around the North Cape. Losses through enemy action amounted to 0.46% (29,200 GRT), from other sources 0.15% (9,500 GRT), less than in 1942 when all losses came to 0.82%. (Evidently he did not count unescorted ships.) These figures show that Soviet naval and air activity did not cause vital damage to German supply shipping, although it made a large escort apparatus necessary.

From December 1943 to April 1944, the British sent four convoys to northern Russia, JW–55 to JW–58, with only small losses to submarines and planes because the escorts had been reinforced and improved. On 26 December the German battleship *Scharnhorst* was intercepted north of the North Cape and sunk. Of the German large ships, only the battleship *Tirpitz* remained ready for action in northern Norway. As a result of British superiority in the air she never succeeded in operating against any of the Murmansk convoys. Repeatedly, the Allies attempted to eliminate her with massive bomb attacks. These did not put her out of action, however, until on 12 November 1944 a large British bomber formation caught the German fighters napping and hit the large ship with several bombs of 5.4 tons. She foundered in her berth in a roadstead near the town of Tromsø.

Large concentrations of German submarines suffered heavy losses and sank few ships. The Germans recognized rather late that a new, promising weapon, the acoustic homing torpedo, was being outwitted by the "foxer," a buoy towed by the escort vessels and emitting a noise which attracted the acoustic torpedoes. Dozens of "hits" reported by the submarines only destroyed foxers, which were easy to replace.

As the convoys resumed their rhythm, Soviet naval activity continued as before, improved by a kind of "combined operation" and characterized by increased use of MTBs and aircraft. The submarines were less active, perhaps because of heavy losses.

January to April, 1944

Convoy JW–56 and return convoy RA–56 were at sea between 12 January and 11 February 1944. Before they joined the escorts of JW–56, four Soviet destroyers approached the Norwegian coast. This was part of RV–1, the first combined operation of Soviet forces under the command of Admiral Golovko. Besides the destroyers, seven submarines as well as torpedo cutters and naval planes operated against German coastal traffic in the second half of January 1944, with meager results.

On the German side, the number of the escorts had been increased, and the convoys were larger: eight to twelve steamers were protected by at least as many small warships. Torpedo cutters tried to attack several times in the Varanger Fjord, but were beaten off; no ship

Ten American minesweepers of the Admirable class were transferred to the Soviet Arctic Fleet in 1943 and designated T–111 through T–120. Three were sunk in the Kara Sea in 1944 by German submarines.

was hit. The Soviet Naval Air Arm was active mainly with single planes (probably reconnaissance), which did not get through to the convoys at sea, and which, in a number of attacks on the ports, damaged one steamer slightly.

The Soviet submarines attacked at least six times, but had only one success. On 28 January, S–56 hit the steamer *Henriette Schulte* (5,056 GRT) with a torpedo launched outside the escort perimeter of a large convoy near Tana Fjord. The ship had to be abandoned. The small motor tanker *Mil* (244 GRT) was lost on a mine in Varanger Fjord on 25 January.

On 11 February 15 Soviet bombers tried to attack the battleship *Tirpitz* in Alta Fjord, where she had been damaged by British midget submarines. Repairs were almost finished; it was important to cripple the ship again. However, only four bombers found the target. All bombs (1,000 kg.) missed; only one detonated close enough to the ship to cause slight damage. Three nights later Soviet bombers attacked the port of Hammerfest and succeeded in sinking two small Norwegian mail steamers (316 and 336 GRT).

On 20 February 1944 convoy JW–57 started from England; the return convoy RA–57 reached there on 10 March. When JW–57 left its home ports the High Command of the Soviet Arctic Fleet began RV–2, the second combined operation against German supply shipping. Submarine L–20 landed a raiding party near Makkaur

(Bats Fjord), which searched several isolated houses and took four Norwegians prisoner.

Soviet planes dropped mines in several places in the Varanger Fjord but were observed by the newly installed radar. The mines were swept before they could do any damage to shipping. At least six submarines operated near the German convoy routes but had no success, although Soviet reports claim that on 4 March submarine S–56 torpedoed and sank a steamer of 6,000 GRT. A later report stated that on that day S–56 carried out the first Soviet attack ever made without showing the periscope, utilizing acoustic data exclusively. It is very probable that the captain did not observe a hit on the steamer but heard an explosion and took it for a hit. According to the German documents no ship was lost on that day. Torpedo cutters had no luck when they tried to intercept a convoy.

On 17 March Soviet air reconnaissance discovered a German convoy off Syltefjord on an easterly course. Submarine M–201 and torpedo cutters tried to attack it and claimed to have sunk or damaged several ships. Actually, they were unsuccessful. Then the Soviets sent 50 bombers and torpedo planes, but these were intercepted by German fighters and suffered some losses. They did not hit a single ship, although they reported several sunk or damaged. In this period the only success of the Soviet Air Force was the sinking of patrol boat V–6109 (ex-trawler, 378 GRT) by torpedo planes on 23 March.

Convoy JW–58 left Iceland on 27 March and reached Kola Fjord on 5 April. It consisted of 49 transports and the U.S. cruiser *Milwaukee*, which was to be handed over to the Soviets. The convoy was protected so strongly that not a single ship was damaged, whereas the Germans lost three of 17 attacking submarines and a number of reconnaissance planes. On the last part of the route the Soviets reinforced the escorting forces with four destroyers, four minesweepers, and four subchasers, which left Polyarnyy on 3 April.

On the same day, two British carriers, which had taken part in the operation, launched 41 bombers, protected by the same number of fighters, to attack the battleship *Tirpitz*. With a loss of four planes they succeeded in hitting their target with 15 bombs which killed 122 members of the crew, wounded 316, and put the ship out of action for three months.

The return convoy RA–58 (36 steamers) left Kola Fjord on 7 April 1944. Because of the heavy losses of reconnaissance planes, the German Air Force could search for the convoy only at night, with radar-equipped planes, and found it so late that only four of ten submarines could attack. They used acoustic homing torpedoes exclusively, which all detonated prematurely.

The Soviet Arctic Fleet started its combined operation RV–3 immediately after RA–58 had left Kola Fjord. On 10 April, Ground Attack Air Regiment 46 operated against a German convoy. Fifty-five planes arrived in three waves but hit not a single ship. Then low-flying planes attacked the port of Kirkenes and damaged two steamers with near misses. Off the same port, torpedo cutters sank the collier *Stoer* (665 GRT) by torpedo. On 22 April, torpedo cutters again attacked a convoy near the entrance to Petsamo Fjord. Discovered early, they launched their torpedoes at too great a distance. All the ships turned away, unharmed. On the following day, Air Regiment 46 again attacked a convoy unsuccessfully and lost its commanding officer (Captain Katunin) when his plane was shot down.

The Soviet submarines were not very active. Only once or twice were attacks on German convoys attempted, and no ships were sunk or damaged. Submarine S–54 did not return to her base from one operation. She probably struck a mine.

April to July, 1944

For the winter and spring of 1944, the main task of the Soviet Arctic Fleet, according to the Official History, was "to safeguard the Allied convoys in the operational zone of the Soviet Fleet." But "at the same time the northern fleet was to persevere in its war on the naval communications of the enemy." For the summer and fall of 1944 the task was "systematically to interrupt the sea communications of the enemy along the northern coast of Norway and in the Varanger Fjord." Moreover "powerful blows were to be struck by bombers and ground-attack planes against the bases and airfields of the enemy."[7] Protection of convoy traffic took third place.

For these tasks the northern fleet was reinforced during spring and summer 1944 by 6 submarines, 2 minesweepers, 32 MTBs, and 62 subchasers. This brought the fleet to a strength of 29 submarines, 9 destroyers, 19 coastal defense vessels, 47 MTBs, and 132 subchasers (losses not deducted). The fleet air arm was increased to more than 600 planes.

The next move of the Allies was to bring a great number of

transport ships back to England from the White Sea and from the Kola Fjord as convoy RA–59. The Soviets used this convoy to send 2,300 sailors under Admiral Levchenko to England. There they were to take over the British battleship *Royal Sovereign*, nine destroyers, and four submarines, which the Soviet government received as compensation for its share in the Italian warships handed over to the Allies.

RA–59 also carried the crew of the cruiser *Milwaukee* (now Soviet *Murmansk*), which was returning to the USA. The convoy started from Kola on 28 April. At first, it was escorted by three Soviet destroyers, three minesweepers, and six subchasers, as well as British escorts. These sank three of twelve attacking German submarines, while the convoy lost only one steamer. Before it put to sea, planes from the British task force providing distant cover attempted to bomb the *Tirpitz* in Alta Fjord. Bad weather prevented them from finding their target, and they struck at a German convoy, sinking three ships (15,000 GRT) and losing six planes.

In May, the British repeated this kind of operation against the *Tirpitz* three times. They did not get through to the battleship (which had special fighter protection) but they sank at least four steamers of 20,000 GRT and damaged many more. There were no more planes in these attacks than in the similar Soviet operations east of the North Cape which were much less effective. However, the Soviet performance improved, and their means increased.

When convoy RA–59 had left the Soviet area, combined operation RV–4 started. On 6 May, three Soviet motor torpedo boats stopped the small Norwegian steamer *Moder* (124 GRT) plying between the ports on the Varanger Fjord. The 14 Norwegians on board were taken prisoner; the ship was set on fire. In vain, a German artillery ferry barge tried to save her.

Admiral Polar Coast remarked in his war diary: "A surprise daytime attack of this kind by enemy motor torpedo boats on this coast without any defense on our part demonstrates the weakness of our naval and air forces."

Two days later three Soviet MTBs attacked two German patrol boats in the same vicinity with torpedoes and gunfire. But the German ships were ready for action: soon one of the MTBs was hit and began to burn; another was damaged. The burning boat sank; the others retreated behind an artificial smoke screen. Four Germans were wounded.

On 11 May, bombers and torpedo planes attacked two convoys, one near Makkaur and the other off Kongsfjord, but succeeded in sinking only the patrol boat V–6115. On 13 and 14 May, Soviet air squadrons undertook ten attacks (with an average of 22 planes) against the port and shipping in Kirkenes. The steamers *Pernambuco* (4,120 GRT) and *Patagonia* (5,900 GRT) caught fire and were severely damaged, as was subchaser UJ–1210. At least six planes were shot down.

On 25 May, Soviet planes, well-protected by fighters, attacked a convoy in ten waves, sank the steamer *Solviken* (3,500 GRT) with torpedoes and damaged another with a bomb. Five Soviet submarines waited for the same convoy near Makkaur, but missed it, although they had for the first time formed a regular patrol line.

In the second half of May 1944, planes of the Coastal Command of the Royal Air Force sank six of fourteen submarines that tried to reach the North Atlantic from Norwegian bases.

After the failure of the German offensive at Kursk in Central Russia in July 1943, the Russian armies (well-equipped, largely with material from the USA) had successfully undertaken a series of massive attacks and were moving inexorably westwards all along the front between the Baltic and the Black Sea. Only in the Arctic area (North Karelia) had there been no change: everything remained quiet on the front along the Liza River.

At sea, Soviet activity continued to follow the same pattern. Attacks by planes and MTBs on the shipping bringing vital supplies for the German army increased somewhat. The reason probably was that more material was available. However, the British carrier planes destroyed more shipping in a few raids than the Soviet Air Force did in the whole year. With the submarines it was not much different: their aggressiveness had diminished distinctly.

On 6 June 1944, American and British forces landed in Normandy, quickly formed a large beachhead and created the third front, the diversion for which Stalin had clamored since 1942. But even now, no change became noticeable in the naval activities of the Soviet Fleet in northern waters.

The first half of June 1944 was quiet, even in the Varanger Fjord. Then the Soviets launched their combined operation RV–5. Torpedo cutters (MTBs) started it by laying mines off Kirkenes; submarine L–20 laid mines more to the west. At least four submarines took up waiting positions. On 15 June a convoy bound for Petsamo entered the Varanger Fjord. The batteries on the Rybachiy Peninsula fired 1,100 rounds at the German ships but these were protected so effectively by smoke screens that no ship was hit. Then at least 25 planes and some MTBs attacked but were beaten off by strong defense forces on the water and in the air. With the exception of some scratches caused by fragments, the convoy was not harmed: all its ships reached Petsamo.

On the same day, Soviet air reconnaissance sighted a convoy of ten transports, heavily escorted, after it left Hammerfest for the Varanger Fjord. On the following day, it was sighted and reported after it rounded the North Cape and proceeded on the normal shipping route. By this stage of the war, Soviet submarines had direct radio contact with their reconnaissance planes. Therefore it seems strange that only submarine M–200 tried to approach. She was headed off by a submarine-hunting group. The others may have been stationed too far from the coast and perhaps could not approach because of German planes.

On the morning of 17 June, several air squadrons repeatedly attacked the convoy. They had good cloud cover and used smoke bombs to hamper the antiaircraft fire. The steamer *Florianopolis* (7,420 GRT) was hit by a bomb far forward and had a fire in the hold. The ship was brought into the port of Kirkenes, however. At least two Soviet planes were shot down by the escorts, more by fighters. One of the torpedoes dropped with a parachute hit the stern of the steamer *Dixie* (1,610 GRT), which sank after her crew had been taken off. The minesweepers preceding the convoy had no difficulty sweeping the small minefield laid by torpedo cutters in the approaches to Kirkenes.

When the convoy entered this port and in the hours following, the Soviets undertook massive air attacks on port and town, with 100 to 150 planes. They caused considerable destruction in the port installations and damaged the steamer *Marga Cordes* (1,112 GRT). After unloading quickly, five steamers left during the evening of 19 June for the return trip, with thirteen small warships. They were soon reported by Soviet planes and repeatedly attacked by submarines, which evidently had closed up to the coastal route in the meantime. However, the submarines were located early enough to prevent damage to the ships of the convoy, three of which entered Tana Fjord. The other two proceeded westwards. Submarine S–104 sighted them and launched four torpedoes when the ships were in such a bearing that the submarine captain expected to hit several targets with one salvo. He reported that he struck three targets and destroyed one steamer and two escort vessels. Actually, two torpedoes hit subchaser UJ–1209 (ex-trawler) forward and aft and caused her to sink after a quarter of an hour. While two of the escorts kept the submarine down with depth charges, the rest of the convoy proceeded and reached its port of destination unharmed. Evidently the submarine captain relied on acoustic observation exclusively and overestimated his success, not unlike his opposite numbers on the German side.

On 22 June a considerable number of Soviet planes twice attacked a small westbound convoy near Vardø, damaging an artillery ferry barge, which continued with the convoy, however. Four planes were shot down. In the last week of the month the Soviets undertook strong air attacks on Kirkenes. Again the harbor installations suffered considerably. The steamer *Herta* (717 GRT) caught fire and was left a wreck; the damaged steamer *Florianopolis* (7,420 GRT) was hit again and had to be beached.

On 28 June, a small convoy bound for Petsamo was shelled by the batteries on Rybachiy Peninsula. The steamer *Vulkan* (989 GRT) was hit and had to be set aground. When the convoy left Petsamo again, torpedo cutters attacked it and sank the steamer *Nerissa* (992 GRT). Air attacks failed; the other ships got through.

In July 1944, the Soviets again undertook a combined operation (probably RV–6) against the German convoy traffic. On 4 July, 80 to 100 planes attacked Kirkenes and damaged some shore installations but did not hit any ships. During daylight Soviet planes attacked Norwegian fishing cutters and again torpedoed the wreck of the steamer *Natal*, which had been beached and abandoned. In the course of time, it took at least ten torpedoes.

Submarine L–15 laid mines off Rolvsøya. Beginning on 13 July four more submarines took up waiting positions; the MTB brigade was kept in readiness. On 13 July a German convoy was reported coming from the west, probably destined for ports on the Varanger Fjord. On the following day, it was sighted at Porsangen Fjord, and the next morning its twelve ships entered Varanger Fjord, protected by numerous small warships. Here submarines S–56 and M–200 tried to attack. M–200 launched four torpedoes and reported the sinking of a steamer of 5,000 GRT. Actually, no ship was hit. Nine torpedo cutters sent to intercept the convoy missed it at first, but then were directed to it by air reconnaissance. They did not succeed in penetrating the ring of escorts, however. Torpedo cutter TKA–239 was put out of action by subchaser UJ–1211, which took two prisoners. Her attempt to take the burning ship in tow failed. The other torpedo cutters scuttled two Norwegian fishing vessels. Air attacks on the convoy followed but caused only slight damage. All the German ships reached their destinations.

In the second half of July four massive air attacks on installations and ships in Vardø and Kirkenes resulted mainly in destruction ashore. The small Dutch vessel *Roerdamp* (289 GRT) had to be beached. No larger ships were hit. Patrol vessel V–6307 (trawler-type) was lost during this time.

August to October, 1944

At the end of July 1944, the four submarines taken over by the Russians from the Royal Navy were ready for sea. They were of the U-class, with a displacement of 540/750 tons. One of the captains, Lieutenant Commander Yaroslav Josseliani, has described his impressions. They are interesting inasmuch as they show how heavily influenced he was by Soviet propaganda. For instance, he ascribes the collapse of the German submarine campaign in the Atlantic to the battle of Stalingrad, "because after that event Germany was no longer able to build submarines in the same numbers as before."[8] Actually, the output of German industry in general and of the shipyards in particular reached its peak in September 1944. As a submarine specialist, Josseliani should have appreciated the importance of the improved means for locating submarines, both on and under the surface. The reason for the breakdown of the submarine war was the fact that German submarine design and tactics had not kept up with these new developments, particularly the use of radar by planes. The technical solutions existed before the war but they were not utilized in time.

The first of the ex-British submarines evidently left the prescribed route and was sunk by a British bomber on 27 July 1944. The other three reached Polyarnyy early in August.

At that time the first of a group of six German submarines were on their way from their base at Hammerfest to operate against Soviet shipping in the Kara Sea. This they did till October, some in two trips, others by taking fuel from boats which had to return.

On 8 August, U–365 torpedoed the steamer *Marina Raskova* (5,685 GRT) en route from Arkhangelsk to Pork Dikson. The three escorting minesweepers stopped because they had the impression that the steamer had struck a mine. This gave the submarine the chance to sink two of them. The third got away.

This remained the only major success of the whole operation. The submarines sank only two more patrol vessels, although they attacked several convoys. The failure of most of their torpedoes to detonate they attributed to the low temperature of the water. Near Cape Chelyuskin they encountered much ice. U–362 was sunk by a Soviet subchaser. As far as can be ascertained there was no Soviet reaction to this operation. Nothing is known about the results of six minefields of twelve mines each laid by the submarines.

On 15 August, convoy JW–59 (33 transports and 11 subchasers intended for the Soviet Arctic Fleet) left for Murmansk, protected directly and indirectly by strong forces. Two days later, the battleship *Arkhangelsk* (ex *Royal Sovereign*) and five destroyers (ex U.S. flushdeckers) with Russian crews under Admiral Levchenko put to sea and overtook convoy JW–59, passing it to the north. From 20 August on both groups were under air observation and then under submarine attack. U–711 launched torpedoes against the *Arkhangelsk* and the destroyer *Zarsky* but they detonated before reaching their targets. The escort carrier *Nabob* was torpedoed but was towed to safety. The destroyer-escort *Bickerton* and sloop *Kite* were sunk by submarines. U–344 and U–354 were destroyed by escort forces. Four air attacks on the battleship *Tirpitz*, with 247 planes in all, caused insignificant damage.

During these events the Soviet Arctic Fleet undertook another combined operation, with planes, torpedo cutters, and submarines. It started on 17 August with a heavy bombardment of Kirkenes by 80 to 100 planes. In spite of strong reaction by German fighters, the steamer *Peter Bornhofen* (1,349 GRT) was sunk; the steamer *Zebu* (1,894 GRT) was damaged and had to be beached. According to German reports the Soviets lost 37 planes.

The next objective was a German convoy of six steamers escorted by 18 minesweepers and patrol boats, approaching from the west. Of four submarines in waiting positions only M–201 reached the convoy. On 18 August shortly before midnight she attacked and sank patrol boat V–6112.

Now it was the turn of the torpedo cutters. Three of them laid mines ahead of the convoy, but minesweepers formed the van, and no ship struck a mine. Early in the morning of 19 August, about ten torpedo cutters attacked from several directions, utilizing smoke screens very cleverly. They sank the steamer *Colmar* (3,946 GRT) with one torpedo and escort V–6102 with two. The German records acknowledged the skillful tactics of these attacks. Two torpedo cutters were sunk by M-boats.

On 23 August the towns and ports of Vardø and Vadsø were attacked by 70 to 80 and by 120 planes, respectively, and suffered considerable damage. An artillery ferry barge was sunk, but no transports. On this occasion a westbound German convoy of five steamers, two hospital ships, and eleven escort ships was reported, but not attacked. The submarines in waiting positions were alerted; S–103 made contact and reported hitting a steamer, but no ship was touched, and the torpedoes were not even observed. On 24 August, when the convoy passed Cape Nordkinn, submarine S–15 torpedoed the steamer *Dessau* (5,983 GRT), which was towed into port, however. Four days later, an attack by submarine S–103 on an eastbound convoy failed.

The return convoy from Murmansk, RA–59A, nine steamers protected by the escorts of JW–59, left Kola Fjord on 28 August. Neither German reconnaissance planes nor submarines got through to the transports. U–394 was sunk by planes and escorts. On 6 September, the convoy reached Scotland and entered Loch Ewe. As usual, Russian participation was limited to the first part of the trip.

The increase in Soviet activity on and over the Barents Sea was probably a consequence of successes in the Baltic area, and was facilitated by the increase of material available, especially planes and torpedo cutters. The Finns were at the end of their strength and could no longer defend themselves against the Soviet superiority. On 4 September, they concluded an armistice with the Soviet Union, and the German forces had to leave the country by 15 September. In northern Finland they actually stayed longer because the road from central Finland to the Baltic was already barred, and the troops there had to march via Kirkenes to northern Norway. Besides, the German Supreme Command wanted to keep the nickel mines east of Petsamo working as long as possible. Therefore the situation on the Liza front did not change for some weeks, and the war at sea still followed the old pattern, whilst on the west coast of Norway the British intensified their attacks on German supply traffic.

Again a British convoy to Murmansk and a Soviet combined operation coincided. On 14 September, the Soviets started another series of air attacks on ports and ships; torpedo cutters were active; submarines took up waiting positions. On 15 September, convoy JW–60 left Loch Ewe with 30 transports. It was so well protected and conducted that neither German planes nor submarines succeeded in attacking it. On 25 September, it arrived in Kola Fjord, and some of the ships proceeded to the White Sea with Soviet escorts.

From 14 to 16 September, ports and ships in the southern part of the Varanger Fjord were heavily attacked from the air. In Kirkenes, the steamer *Wolsum* (3,668 GRT), with a cargo of ammunition, blew up; subchaser UJ–1224 was sunk; artillery ferry barge F–223 was damaged. An attack by four torpedo cutters and fifteen fighter-bombers on a westbound convoy near Petsamo was beaten off without damage to the ships. One cutter was sunk; eleven members of the crew were captured. On 21 September, off the North Cape, two torpedo planes attacked the auxiliary *Friesenland* (5,434 GRT), a ship specially equipped with catapults for launching seaplanes. She was hit by a torpedo and had to be beached.

After an interval of nearly four weeks Soviet submarines appeared again. On 24 September, S–56 attacked a convoy off Cape Nordkinn with torpedoes but missed. Two days later, she attacked a group of minesweepers, again without success. Other submarines were at sea but did not make contact. An attack by nine torpedo cutters in two groups on 25 September was foiled by the escorts; one torpedo cutter was sunk. Simultaneous attacks by nearly 100 planes sank patrol boat V–6101 and damaged four small warships.

The return convoy RA–60 left Kola Fjord the night of 27/28 September, evaded two groups of submarines, but lost two ships (14,400 GRT) to the torpedoes of U–310, which proceeded singly. About that time, the snorkel-equipped submarines U–315 and U–313 attempted to penetrate to the berth of the battleship *Arkhangelsk* in Kola Fjord. A torpedo net prevented them from getting near their target, and they had to turn back. Even if they had succeeded they would not have affected the naval operations, for the big ship did not take part in any bombardment or action. Stalin, who was fascinated by the large warships, probably acquired her for her prestige and propaganda value.

During the second half of September 1944, two German army corps retreated through central Finland on their way to northern

Norway. They were pressed more and more by Soviet and finally also by Finnish forces. Yet Hitler wanted to hold a large beachhead from the Liza front to Petsamo and Kirkenes. This proved impossible, however, when a strong Soviet army (five army corps and the 7th Air Army) threatened to cut off the German Mountain Corps which still held the front along the Liza River. To support this offensive, the Red Fleet intensified its activities, undertook a number of operations, concentrated its submarines and torpedo cutters in the area, and even used destroyers for coast bombardments.

The Soviet land offensive started on 7 October 1944 and soon succeeded in breaking through the thin German defenses south of the Liza front, which now had to be given up. To hamper the German retreat, the Red Fleet landed nearly 3,000 marines with minesweepers and torpedo cutters in Maatsuono Bay opposite the Rybachiy Peninsula on 10 October. Two days later, 660 men were put ashore at the entrance of Petsamo Fjord. These amphibious operations made the German retreat more difficult but eventually all the German units succeeded in extricating themselves, even those which had been cut off temporarily.

On 16 October 1944 Hitler consented to give the order for the evacuation of Finnish Lapland. The two army corps in the interior marched through empty country, harassed by rearguard attacks, and reached northern Norway in full fighting trim. On the coast Petsamo was evacuated on 18 October 1944, after the nickel mines had been put out of action. On the same day, 500 Soviet marines were put ashore west of Petsamo; landings of a similar size followed on 23 and 25 October nearer to Kirkenes. None of these operations met with much resistance because the Germans were evacuating this part of the coastal area. They left Kirkenes on 25 October after they had carried away 30,000 tons of material in ships. About the same time 10,000 tons were shipped from Porsangen Fjord because the northernmost part of Norway was to be given up, too.

On 26 October Soviet forces occupied Kirkenes, and four destroyers shelled the ports of Vadsø and Vardø, without any noticeable effect. By that time, the evacuation of the Varanger Peninsula had already begun: Vadsø was given up on 28 October; the last troops left Vardø on 30 October by sea, unhampered by Soviet naval forces.

For evacuating the men from the ports, batteries, radar positions, and defense installations around the Varanger Fjord, the Germans had to use sea transport on a large scale, directly under the eyes of the Soviets. Consequently these concentrated their submarines, torpedo cutters, and air forces against the German convoys. They held their larger ships back, however.

Eleven Soviet submarines operated in the Barents Sea near the Norwegian coast. Two were minelayers and laid several fields, but no transport or warship struck a mine, only a Norwegian cutter. On 11 October 1944, the Arctic Fleet was particularly active, obviously in connection with the offensive on land. At first, about 30 fighter-bombers attacked a convoy leaving Petsamo, and hit the steamer *Olsa* (4,016 GRT), which was towed into Kirkenes, however. Before she arrived this port was bombarded by 70 planes, which sank the steamer *Botha* (908 GRT) and damaged a coal barge. In other attacks some small, local craft were damaged.

On the same day MTBs (torpedo cutters) attacked an eastbound convoy off Kiberg and torpedoed the leading minesweeper M–303, which sank. The other escorts destroyed one MTB and damaged another.

Shortly afterwards an eastbound convoy was attacked first from the air, then by a submarine, again from the air, and then by another submarine. The first three attacks were countered without any damage to the German ships (two steamers, one barge, and seven escorts). The second underwater attack was carried out by submarine S–104. It launched a torpedo salvo and sank a steamer and subchaser UJ–1220. The steamer did not displace 7,000 GRT, as the submarine captain assumed. It was the *Lumme*, of 1,730 GRT. From the air, this convoy was attacked five times, last off Nordkinn, each time unsuccessfully. Some planes were hit by the ships which almost exhausted their ammunition.

On 13 October 1944, a group of torpedo cutters tried to attack a westbound convoy but the heavy fire of the escorts prevented them from approaching close enough to launch their torpedoes. On the following day, after the convoy passed Cape Nordkinn, it was attacked by torpedo planes, which scored two hits on the tanker *Sudmeer* (8,133 GRT). This was a particularly serious loss, for tankers were needed urgently, and the ship was carrying back much valuable equipment.

Torpedo cutters also tried to attack shipping in the inner part of the Varanger Fjord but were not successful because the fire of the ships and escorts was too heavy. On 15 October, patrol boat Vp–

6704 was sunk by a bomb and reported by the Soviet planes as a destroyer.

On the following day, there was much activity again. First torpedo cutters, called in by air reconnaissance, tried to find a westbound convoy but missed it. It was then attacked by 23 planes. A torpedo sank the motor minesweeper R–301; four planes were shot down. Off Nordkinn, a submarine attack on another convoy failed. Near Kirkenes, three torpedo cutters made a dash at the slow artillery ferry barge F–24, but the fire of the well-armed little ship proved too strong for them. When two were damaged, the group turned back.

On 17 October, patrol boat Vp–6107 (trawler type, 475 GRT) was attacked by 20 planes and so damaged that she had to be abandoned.

Another series of attacks followed from 20 to 22 October. A westbound convoy (one steamer, two tugs, eight escorts) was attacked north of Vardø by torpedo cutters, but they turned away after several of them had been hit by gunfire. Only the motor minesweeper R–151 was damaged slightly. On the following day torpedo cutters attacked again and succeeded in torpedoing the minesweeper M–31, which sank. Then fighter-bombers attacked and sank a tug and the already damaged R–151.

On the same day, about 50 Boston bombers, protected by the same number of fighters, attacked Kirkenes in four waves. The only ship hit was the artillery ferry F–6. German fighters claimed they shot down 21 of the attacking Soviet planes.

On 22 October, another westbound convoy was the target of fighter-bombers, which severely damaged the patrol boats Vp–6308 and Vp–6311. Then four torpedo cutters tried to attack but heavy fire forced them to retreat. On 27 October, 24 planes attacked MRS–26, a steamer converted to carry motor launches for sweeping shallow mines. They sank her with several bomb hits. This incident ended the Soviet air activity against German shipping in northern waters.

November to December, 1944

The submarines did not carry on much longer. Apparently the last attacks were undertaken in the first days of November 1944 by the ex-British submarine B–2 under Commander Josseliani.

According to his report he operated in the vicinity of Cape Nordkinn. There, at noon on 1 November 1944, he sighted what he calls "an unescorted tanker of 3–4,000 GRT. Apparently this was a ship which had become separated when other submarines attacked another convoy." Twice he launched one or two torpedoes against this ship but missed each time. At the third attempt the ship was hit and "went up in a sheet of flame and sank stern first."[9]

On the German side, no submarine attacks were noticed on that day, and no ship disappeared. Only the small Norwegian steamer *Stortind* (168 GRT), proceeding independently, was lost on that day. If this was Josseliani's target, the small size of the ship would explain his misses.

Two days later, submarine B–2 sighted a convoy of four transports escorted by two "torpedo boats" (none were in the Barents Sea) and a dozen other escort vessels. Josseliani attacked at once and launched torpedoes at a transport of 10,000 GRT (no ships of that size were used there) and another slightly smaller transport. Both ships burned: the largest broke in two, the other sank stern first.

In the German documents nothing could be found about these attacks and losses. Of course, during retreat and defeat, not all war diaries were kept well, and not all reached the higher staffs and the archives. However, the loss of two big ships with valuable cargoes in plain sight of a dozen warships would not have gone unnoticed, especially since things had calmed down by that time all along the Norwegian polar coast.

The three German army corps were in orderly retreat, aided by the late beginning of the Arctic winter. Soviet pressure decreased— no Soviet forces followed into Norwegian territory. The Mountain Corps took up positions forward of Narvik, with the Lyngen Fjord as the main defense line, keeping Hammerfest occupied as forward base. The other two corps were transported back to Germany.

In this last phase of Soviet operations against the retreating Germans, Soviet submarines reported sinking eighteen German ships, but after careful research it can be stated that they actually sank only one steamer and two subchasers. The torpedo cutters claimed to have sunk ten ships, but two minesweepers were their actual score. The air arm was more successful: in fourteen major attacks, it sank four steamers, one tug, and seven escort vessels of different types.

Taken together, these attacks and the ensuing losses made the German retreat more difficult, but they were not at all decisive. Most of the convoys got through unharmed; most of the men and the bulk of the material were saved; the defense of northern Norway on Norwegian soil could be organized with ample means.

From 20 October to the end of November, a Soviet unit of one destroyer, five minesweepers (ex U.S.), and five subchasers (also ex U.S.) protected the big icebreakers *Josef Stalin* and *Severny Veter* on their way back from the eastern part of the North-Siberian route to Kola Fjord. This operation is interesting because in the Kara Sea the escorts reported beating off ten attacks by German submarines and sinking quite a few of them, although from 2 October on, not a single German submarine operated in the Kara Sea.

From November 1944 to the end of the war Soviet naval forces in northern waters played a defensive part only, protecting their own shipping and the Allied convoys, which still carried great quantities of war material to northern Russia. The Germans had concentrated a considerable number of submarines in this theater of war, where conditions were more favorable than in the Atlantic for the submarines, which had been outdated by technical developments.

Convoys JW–61 (35 steamers and six lend-lease subchasers for the Soviet Navy) left Loch Ewe on 20 October and reached Kola Fjord on 28 October without losing a ship, although nineteen submarines operated against it and some came near enough to launch acoustic homing torpedoes. No submarine was sunk, either. Soviet escorts then took part of the convoy to the White Sea.

From 29 October to 6 November special convoy JW–61A (two big transports) carried 11,000 Soviet soldiers, who had been prisoners of war, back to their country.

On 2 November return convoy RA–61 (33 steamers) left Kola Fjord for England. Soviet escorts had brought part of it as convoy DB–10 from the White Sea. Submarines U–310 and U–295 attacked it without success. The Soviet minesweepers T–111 and T–113 then hunted them, also without success. When RA–61 was outside Kola Fjord U–295 torpedoed the British destroyer-escort *Mounsey*. Other attacks failed; the convoy suffered no further damage; no submarine was sunk.

On 27 November 1944 air reconnaissance sighted the convoy JW–62 (30 ships). Seventeen submarines attempted to attack it but did not get near enough to launch torpedoes. The convoy reached Kola Fjord unharmed. By that time, in addition to their convoys between the Kola Fjord and the White Sea, the Soviets had instituted convoys to Petsamo and Kirkenes. Against these, the German submarines had more luck. In several attacks they sank the steamers *Proletary* (1,123 GRT) and *Revoluziya* (435 GRT) as well as two ex-American subchasers. Attempts to torpedo two Soviet destroyers failed.

Before the return convoy RA–62 (28 ships) left Kola Fjord on 9 December, Soviet destroyers and several Allied and Soviet submarine hunting groups undertook an intensive search for submarines along the course the convoy was to take. U–387 was destroyed, according to British reports, by the depth charges of the corvette *Marlborough Castle*; according to Soviet reports, the submarine was rammed by the destroyer *Chvuchiy*. U–997 missed two Soviet destroyers with acoustic homing torpedoes.

This submarine hunt was so effective that only U–365 was able to get near the convoy. On 10 December, she missed a tanker; on the following day, she torpedoed the destroyer *Cassandra*. The boat continued to keep contact and was sunk by a plane on 12 December. RA–62 encountered no more difficulties before reaching Loch Ewe.

In the last days of December, U–995 and U–956 made several attacks on Soviet convoys on the Kola coast. U–956 torpedoed the steamer *Tbilisi* (7,176 GRT), which had to be beached; U–995 sank a small steamer.

NORTHERN THEATER 1945

At the beginning of the year 1945 the Soviet Arctic Fleet consisted of 1 battleship, 1 heavy cruiser, 18 destroyers, 22 submarines, 12 coastal defense ships, 64 minesweepers and motor minesweepers, 30 large subchasers, 40 MTBs, and 721 airplanes, among them 129 torpedo planes and bombers.

Its main task was protection of the naval communications for the convoys, of fishery, and of the communications with northern Norway. . . . The area held by the enemy receded farther and farther from the Soviet bases and shipping routes.[10]

It is stressed that the sea routes of the enemy were now outside the operational zone of the Soviet Arctic Fleet.[11] Nowhere is the idea expressed that it would have been possible to follow the enemy.

As a consequence, activities in the Barents Sea continued as before, with the Soviets doing part of the escort service on the eastern part of the route used by the Allied convoys. In addition, they ran their own convoys from Kola to Varanger Fjord and into the White Sea. German submarines were always present between Bear Island and

Kola; the German Air Force was very weak and rarely penetrated to the transports. There was no noticeable Soviet air or submarine activity against German bases and shipping in northern Norway.

Convoy JW–63 (35 ships) reached Kola Fjord unnoticed on 8 January 1945. The return convoy RA–63 left on 11 January and also passed the danger zone without being sighted. In the first days of January, three submarines carried six midget submarines to Kola Fjord, where they were to attack the battleship *Arkhangelsk* and escort vessels. Technical breakdowns in the hastily designed and constructed midgets made it necessary to break off the operation.

In the second half of January, six German submarines operated near the Kola coast. On 16 January, Soviet convoy KB–1 (six freighters, two tankers) left for the White Sea, escorted by nine destroyers and six bombing planes. U–997 succeeded in torpedoing the destroyer *Deyatelny* (ex-British *Churchill*), which sank. On 20 January two heavily protected steamers left Kola for Varanger Fjord. U–293 torpedoed the destroyer *Raz-Jarenny* which was towed in by the minesweeper T–117 with considerable difficulty. This rescue is described in detail in the Official History, but the loss of the other destroyer is not reported.

Convoy JW–64 (26 ships) was sighted on 6 February but was so well protected that neither a group of twelve submarines nor air attacks by 48 and 30 bombers had any success. On 13 February, off Kola Fjord, U–992 (in a group of four submarines) torpedoed the British corvette *Denbigh Castle*, which was towed in by the Soviet salvage vessel *Burevestnik*. On the following day the same group attacked the Soviet convoy BK–3, coming from the White Sea with ships for the return convoy RA–64. Although it had a strong escort of Soviet destroyers, tanker *Norfjell* (8,129 GRT) and freighter *Horace Gray* (7,200 GRT) were sunk. Now strong groups of Allied and Soviet destroyers, escort vessels and subchasers tried to drive the German submarines from the entrance to Kola Fjord. British ships succeeded in sinking U–425. But when RA–64 (34 ships) left, the sloop *Lark* and freighter *Thomas Scott* (7,177 GRT) were torpedoed. A Soviet subchaser saved some of the crew of *Lark*; the destroyer *Zestky* towed the freighter into Kola Fjord but she could not be repaired. Near Bear Island German bombers attacked the convoy. At first they suffered losses and were not successful. But on 23 February they sank the straggler *Henry Bacon* (1,177 GRT), the last ship destroyed by German planes in World War II.

Convoy JW–65 (24 ships) left the Clyde on 11 March 1945. Thirteen submarines awaited it in two lines outside Kola Fjord. They sank the steamers *Horace Bushnell* (7,176 GRT) and *Thomas Donaldson* (7,217 GRT), the sloop *Lapwing* and a Soviet subchaser. No submarine was destroyed. After an intensive search, return convoy RA–65 left on 23 March. The submarines had been ordered to attack shipping along the coast to the east (they sank two trawlers), so RA–65 reached Scapa Flow unmolested on 31 March.

About half of the German submarines in the Barents Sea were equipped by this time with snorkels, which made operating easier. The Soviets evidently had increased their patrol forces and also used their torpedo cutters for that purpose. Some of the submarines were heavily attacked with depth charges, and U–716 was rammed by a patrol vessel, but none were sunk.

JW–66, the last convoy, left the Clyde on 16 April. After it was detected by the German monitoring service, six submarines were sent to intercept it, but air reconnaissance was unable to locate the convoy. The submarines were ordered to the area off the Kola Fjord with the snorkel boats on the innermost positions. Ten more submarines were sent there directly. On their way, they attacked several Soviet coastal convoys, sank the steamer *Onega* (1,603 GRT) and a patrol boat, and torpedoed the steamer *Idefiord* (4,287 GRT), which was towed into port. JW–66 was sighted by only one submarine which tried to attack, in vain.

With Soviet permission a British force laid a deep minefield off the Kola Fjord on 22 April 1945. In the short time before the armistice it does not seem to have sunk any ships. The submarine hunt before RA–66 left was more successful. Of fourteen boats present, U–307 and U–286 were sunk by British groups, although the Soviets credit the sinking of U–286 to their destroyer *Karl Liebknecht*. U–986 sank the frigate *Goodall*; U–427 missed two Canadian destroyers and escaped after a long pursuit during which some 678 depth-charge detonations were registered. U–313 had a fight with Soviet subchasers, but also got away. This energetic anti-submarine activity permitted RA–66 to pass the danger zone and to reach its destination unharmed.

This was the last operation in northern waters. British submarines and planes continued to attack bases and shipping on the Norwegian coast south of Hammerfest until the end of the hostilities.

In the northern theater Soviet strategy remained defensive throughout the war. After stopping the German land offensive on the Liza River the Soviet Army did not undertake a counteroffensive until the Germans had to retreat from Finland in the fall of 1944. In conformity with this strategy the Soviet naval forces divided their activities between protecting the Allied convoys from the West, as well as their own traffic from Murmansk to Arkhangelsk and the North-Siberian route, and attacking the German supply traffic between the North Cape and Petsamo. They never seriously attempted to interrupt the German supply traffic, for this would have made sense only in direct connection with a Soviet offensive on land.

Conclusions

An examination of the events in the three theaters of war—Baltic, Black Sea, and Barents Sea—makes it clear that the abrupt beginning of the war in June 1941 can have surprised the Red Navy only in the Baltic, if anywhere. Only there were forces of both opponents at sea and within each other's reach right from the start. The Red Baltic Fleet had been put into a state of alert three days before, but the available sources do not say what measures were taken, or how the higher commands presented the situation to the forces at sea and to the defenders of the threatened bases, particularly of Libau. In any case, the ships were held back despite evident German violations of the neutrality, such as the minelaying up to the entrance of the Gulf of Finland.

In the other two theaters of war the Soviet naval forces had time to mobilize undisturbed by the enemy. In the Black Sea, where only a few Rumanian ships were to be encountered, reaction was quick. As early as 26 June destroyers shelled the Rumanian naval base of Constanta. The loss of the *Moskva* on this occasion when she hit a mine may have been the reason that the operation was not repeated. Somewhat later the importance of blocking the enemy advance on land by holding the town and port of Odessa became evident. In this imperative and clear task the Red Fleet in the Black Sea showed its best side. There can be no doubt that the long defense—supported by an effective supply traffic, frequent bombardments of the enemy positions and a bold counterattack from the sea—followed by the highly successful evacuation, helped determine later events in southern Russia.

The time gained by the long resistance of Odessa made it possible to prepare the defense of the Crimea, and of the great base of Sevastopol in particular. A whole army, transported from Odessa to Sevastopol intact and fully armed, was decisive for holding this fortress till the summer of 1942. The Red Fleet carried its full share of the burden in this defense also. The German offensive along the east coast of the Black Sea was delayed approximately a year, which favored the defense there, of course. The German army got stuck halfway, without being able to occupy the few remaining Black Sea ports, and without gaining Georgia and access to the main oil fields of the Soviets. By a number of amphibious operations, by transporting strong army units and large amounts of supplies, by shelling and bombing German-held positions and ports, the Red Fleet and its air arm exerted a decisive influence on the operations on land.

In the Barents Sea, Soviet submarines left for offensive operations on the very day of the German attack. The Soviet High Command quickly realized that the Germans planned to gain Murmansk by advancing across the land wilderness and were completely neglecting the possibilities of the sea. The Soviets took successful counter-measures by utilizing the sea for amphibious operations. Small as their forces were in numbers, they succeeded so well in hampering the German advance, that eventually it stopped halfway to Murmansk. Possession of this ice-free port made it possible for the Soviets to receive large amounts of war material from their western Allies. By helping to stop the enemy advance on land and robbing it of the success it expected and needed, the Soviet Arctic Fleet influenced the course of the war.

In the Baltic, a strange situation developed initially, in which both navies operated defensively. They laid strong minefields to protect their own movements. Neither side undertook offensive thrusts, apart from some not very effective submarine cruises in enemy waters. For the attitude of the Red Baltic Fleet, the incident in Irbe Strait, the entrance to the Gulf of Riga, on 6 July 1941, is particularly illuminating, insignificant as it appears. Nobody would have thought it possible that the slow and unwieldy MRS–26 (carrying twelve motor launches) and minesweeper M–23, with their inferior speed of about 15 knots and inferior armament of a few 105-mm. guns, could have forced their way into the Gulf of Riga and to Ust-Dwinsk against four far superior Soviet destroyers. The only explanation that seems applicable is that the destroyers were on

190

a mission to lay defensive minefields inside the Gulf of Riga, and that in their orders nothing was to be found about meeting enemy ships. Now, the importance of orders, and of obeying them to the letter, is one of the fundamental tenets of the Soviet system. Over and over again, it is stressed that orders must be executed literally. No doubts are permitted; orders are always accurate and have to be followed accordingly. Therefore it seems quite possible that in this situation the captains of the destroyers carried out their mine-laying tasks and then could not find any guidance in their orders for dealing with the German ships. Strange as this seems, there is no better explanation for this and similar incidents.

In any case, the Red Fleet in the Baltic concentrated on defense all through the campaign of the year 1941. Although its submarines were able to gain the open sea until ice closed the Gulf of Finland, they were hardly in evidence: their successes were minimal. The retreat of the surface forces from their base at Reval and then from Hangö was carried out stubbornly, but with heavy losses, caused mainly by mines. In the first world war, Russian minelaying and minesweeping had been excellent. But evidently, the large amount of experience gained in this branch of naval warfare, important in these comparatively shallow waters, had not been evaluated sufficiently. Otherwise, losses to mines during the retreats might have been kept down.

However, a considerable part of the Red Fleet had remained in and near Kronstadt, the main naval base. Reinforced by the ships that succeeded in retreating from the outer ports, it now supported the Soviet Army and played an important part in the defense of Leningrad and of the Oranienbaum beachhead. This support would not have been possible but for the mistakes of the German Supreme Command, which overlooked the strategic possibilities of the Baltic for the 1941 campaign, and did not realize the importance of a fleet in the innermost part of the Gulf of Finland.

In all three theaters of war, the Red fleets did good work in supporting their armies. They executed a great many amphibious operations, often without regard to the sacrifices of men who were thrown ashore ruthlessly, without sufficient preparation or equipment.

By these supporting operations the Red fleets acted as a kind of off-shore "fleet in being" and evidently liked this task. Again and again, the official publications underline its importance and place the offensive operations second. These were by no means neglected

—the supply traffic and the bases of the enemy were attacked, but never with the energy shown in the cooperation with the land forces. Submarines, planes, and motor torpedo boats were the main offensive weapons; the larger ships were usually held back. The light forces operated with varying intensity and success, but never in such a way as to cut off the life lines of the enemy completely. Soviet publications do not explain why such regular and easy targets as the convoy traffic to Kirkenes and Petsamo on the Varanger Fjord or the 190 Anapa convoys to the Taman Peninsula were not attacked with stronger means and greater energy. Larger surface ships were hardly ever committed against these tempting objects, quite in contrast to their activity in the defense of Leningrad or in the support of Sevastopol. Necessarily, events like the loss of the flotilla leader *Moskva* in June 1941 and of the three destroyers in October 1943 must have influenced the local high command and the Supreme Command to hold back the larger ships. However, there were situations in which they could have greatly assisted the army without undue risk, for instance, during the evacuation of the Kuban bridgehead or the Eltigen blockade, or during the Germans' last days in Sevastopol. In the Black Sea, the scarcity of repair facilities may have been a factor, but in the other regions the repair situation seems to have been better.

In 1945, the Baltic Red Banner Fleet was far less active than the situation warranted. The Official History tries to explain the reasons but contradicts itself. At first, it says:

Since only a limited number of submarines and MTBs was available, and since operations of the heavy surface ships were not possible, the Fleet could not fully blockade the Courland Group and other besieged beachheads from the sea, and neither could it interrupt the sea communications of the enemy for any longer period.[1]

But two pages later, we read:

The active operations of the Fleet did not leave any possibility of the enemy supporting the sea flanks of his land forces from the sea efficiently . . . The operations of the Fleet substantially contributed to batter the German troops in the Baltic republics, in East Prussia, and in eastern Pomerania.

This is what they undoubtedly did *not* do. The German armies were beaten on land, large parts retreated to the coast, formed bridgeheads, and were evacuated over sea. Although the Soviet air forces were far superior in numbers to the few remaining planes on the

German side, the larger German surface ships were able to support and evacuate these bridgeheads practically to the end of the hostilities. Most of their losses were caused by British bombs and mines. Indubitably, the Soviet Fleet missed quite a series of favorable opportunities in the Baltic during the last months of the war.

In the German naval forces it was common knowledge that the Soviets generally reacted slowly to changes in the tactical situation at sea. Even in 1944–45 the larger German ships could count on being able to bombard Russian positions on the coast for four days before they had to expect massive air attacks. This lack of quick response had been noticed during the previous years in the Gulf of Finland, where German patrols were attacked from the air with increasing vehemence as long as they kept guard close behind the minefields. Attacks ceased, however, as soon as the boats retreated a few miles. The same happened at Sõrve Peninsula and at other places. Destroyers were bombarded when they entered the port of Reval, but not Paldiski some miles to the west.

The Soviet sources do not mention details of this kind. It is very probable that the main reason for this behavior is to be found in the rigid Soviet system of command and control. This system goes back to the institution of the "war commissars," which replaced the "workers' and soldiers' councils" in 1918, shortly after the Communists had seized power. It was created by the Soviet Communist Party in order to keep the military commanders under close control. From 1925 on, General Tukhachevsky worked tenaciously at improving the status of the military commanders and at restoring their right to give orders without fear of interference by party officials. However, in the Great Purge of 1937, the commissars were fully reinstated. Hundreds of high officers were executed, among them Tukhachevsky. It took a considerable time to reestablish the inner order of the Soviet armed forces.

This may be an explanation for the unexpected difficulties which the Soviet forces encountered in the war against the numerically far inferior Finns. It seems that they had not fully recovered from the consequences of the Purge even in 1941 when the Germans attacked. After the serious reverses in the initial phase of the war, Party control was strengthened by officially instituting commissars again in the armed forces on 16 July 1941. But this measure does not seem to have worked out as Stalin and his men expected. The commissars held the same rank as the corresponding military commanders, and they reported independently and without having to inform their military counterparts. For these, it was safest to obey orders strictly and literally. Acting in a way not mentioned in the orders could be dangerous if it was not completely successful.

A number of examples from the experiences of other navies indicate that the higher commands tried to regulate all the details of an operation beforehand, instead of giving freedom of decision and action to the officers who were responsible on the spot. These have to follow general directions, of course, but otherwise should be able to act according to the development of the situation. It is very probable that supervision by the representatives of the Communist Party made it particularly difficult to act quickly and resolutely in the fast changing situations at sea.

The system had to be changed in the following year. Without giving any reasons, the *Great Soviet Encyclopedia* says in its article on the Great Patriotic War: "On 10 October 1942, individual freedom of action and personal responsibility were restored in Army and Navy, and the institution of commissars, which had been created on 16 July 1941, was abolished again."[2]

How much independence and freedom for decision and action this change of the system actually gave to the commanding officers is not explained. The title of "commissar" disappeared, but the Party members remained. They wore uniforms and were officially under the orders of the commanding officers. Nevertheless, they were Party officials as before, and they retained their ability to report through Party channels, whether officially or unofficially.

That the Party apparatus remained in existence within the armed forces and played an important part, is shown by the following passage from the Official History concerning the reoccupation of the Taman Peninsula in September 1943:

Since the fate of the operation depended to a high degree on the successful performance of the landing forces, the Chief of the Political Administration of the 18th Army, Colonel L. J. Brezhnev, together with a group of political workers, visited the units of the landing forces, conferred with their commanding officers, and personally presented membership books of the Communist Party.[3]

It would be interesting to know if on these occasions Comrade Brezhnev met Admiral Gorshkov, and what their mutual impressions were. But personal particulars of this kind, which give color to the picture of leading men, are hardly ever mentioned in Soviet historiography. Memoirs of officers in high positions are rare and those existing are noncommittal on the subject of personal experiences and ideas.

Postwar publications discuss relations between the Communist Party and the armed forces quite openly and show clearly that the Party keeps the military under tight control, whatever the name of the current form of organization may be. To give one of many examples: On 12 June 1971, the Party paper *Kommunist vooruzhennykh sil* reported: "The principle of one-man command is strictly observed in the Army and Navy. But as a rule, commanders and chiefs at all levels actively rely for support on Party organizations . . . consult with their deputies (for political affairs) and assistants and with political workers and other communists."[4]

Things were certainly not different during the war when over 100,000 activists had been sent into the armed forces to keep the spirit up and to watch over ideology. Numerous reports pointed out how many Party and Komsomol members served, for example, in the crews of successful submarines. The Communist Party was present everywhere, and every commander had to take this circumstance into account in his decisions. This cannot always have been an advantage, although the shared mission of fighting an aggressor must have made cooperation easier.

In certain cases the reason for the lack of initiative may have been that the higher command levels, up to the Supreme Command, underestimated the remaining German naval strength because the Soviet forces invariably exaggerated their successes when they drew up their reports. Exaggeration is not uncommon in the armed forces of most countries, for it is human nature to overestimate oneself occasionally, quite apart from the excitement in battle. In the war experience of other navies there are a number of counterparts to the Soviet "battles of the underwater pips" against imagined submarines.

However, in the Soviet naval forces this tendency was so pronounced, and the successes so exaggerated, that it seems justifiable to look for the reasons somewhere else. They might lie in the Soviet system of education, particularly in the armed forces, which emphasizes all kinds of gradations, rewards, commendations, orders, medals, etc., leading up to membership in the Communist Party. As a consequence, everybody was out for "good marks" and reported accordingly in a most optimistic way, encouraged by the fact that it was rarely possible during the war to verify these assertions, and higher up everybody was pleased when he could report successes. But these exaggerated results should have been corrected in official publications that appeared ten or twenty years after the war, for the archives of the other side were accessible immediately after the end of the hostilities. It seems a certain sign of weakness that this has not been done in so many cases.

Critical evaluation of operations or tactics is very rare in the Soviet publications. They narrate "heroic deeds" of sailors and pilots and submarine captains in great detail; "heavy blows" are always given, but never received; and practically nothing is said about leadership and its problems higher up. The senior officers are only represented by photographs with many rows of medals: it is "the Party" which commands and decides, and which is always right.

As to training and tactics, the impression on the German side, gained in many fights, was that the Soviet crews fought bravely and stubbornly on the defense, but that their performance in offensive tasks was rarely above average, and often indifferent. To judge gunnery (which had been excellent in the Russian Navy in World War I) too few fights happened between ships carrying guns of a caliber of 100 mm. or more. The performance of naval aviation improved in the course of the war, but the results against warships—mostly small ones—were more often obtained by tenacious repetition of the attacks than by the skill of individual pilots. Submarines sometimes boldly attacked small steamers and patrol craft on the surface, relying on their larger guns and higher speed. In passages through minefields, for example, in 1942 in the Gulf of Finland, they showed ingenuity and great courage. Many times submarines damaged by depth charges or mines were brought safely to port by their crews with remarkable perseverance. But their underwater tactics were not good enough to yield more than mediocre results. The skill of the motor torpedo boats increased during the war; they often attacked bravely, but they were at a disadvantage because they caught fire easily when they were hit by shells. The most successful part of Soviet naval activity was landing operations, a great number of which were carried out in all three theaters of war. The actual landing generally succeeded: the success of the entire operation often was jeopardized in the next phase by insufficient follow-up. Cooperation with the Army improved greatly in the course of time.

In a long war, sailors develop an intuitive feeling for the qualities of their adversaries. The German crews fully acknowledged the courage and tenacity of the Russians, but they held their Western opponents at sea in greater respect.

196

Sources

A) The war diaries of the German naval staffs and units, almost complete with the exception of the last months of the war, are stored in the German Military Archives in Freiburg, West Germany (Militärachiv, Wiesentalstrasse 10, D7800 Freiburg); microfilms are in the U.S. Naval Archives in Washington, D.C. Many, but not all, of the excerpts used in this book have been translated by the author.

B) Soviet publications (most translated into German in East Berlin).

OFFICIAL:

The Great Soviet Encyclopedia, 2nd edition, Moscow, 1951; German edition, 1953.

The Great Patriotic War, Moscow, 1965; German edition, 1965, six volumes, quoted as the Official History.

SEMI-OFFICIAL:

Isakov, I. S., *The Red Fleet in the Second World War*, English edition, London, about 1950.

Piterski, N. A., *The Soviet Fleet in the Second World War*, Moscow, 1964; German edition, Stalling/Oldenburg, 1966.

Savateev, P. N., *Blows from the Depths of the Seas* (reports on submarine operations), Moscow, 1961.

Telpukhovsky, B. S., *The Soviet History of the Great Patriotic War 1941–1945*, Moscow, 1959.

These sources, as well as many books and articles dealing with single theaters of war, operations, types of ships, etc., stories of submarines and their cruises, etc., have been evaluated for facts by Professor J. Rohwer and Dr. G. Hümmelchen for their *Chronology of the War at Sea 1939–1945*, London: Jan Allen, 1972/4, two volumes.

C) Historical studies.

GENERAL:

Meister, J., *Der Seekrieg in den osteuropäischen Gewässern* (The Naval War in East-European Waters) *1941–1945*, Munich, 1958.

Mitchell, D. W., *A History of Russian and Soviet Sea Power*, New York, 1974.

Saunders, M. G., *The Soviet Navy*, London, 1958.

Woodward, D., *The Russians at Sea*, London, 1965.

SPECIAL SUBJECT:

Forstmeier, F., *Odessa 1941*, Freiburg, 1967.

Forstmeier, F., *Die Räumung des Kuban-Brückenkopfes im Herbst 1943* (Evacuating the Kuban Bridgehead in Fall 1943), Darmstadt, 1964.

MGFA, *Operationsgebiet östliche Ostsee* (Operational Area Eastern Baltic), Stuttgart, 1961.

Rohwer, J., *Die Versenkung der jüdischen Flüchtlingstransporter* Struma *und* Mefkure *im Schwarzen Meer* (Sinking of the Jewish Refugee Transports *Struma* and *Mefkure* in the Black Sea), Frankfurt, 1965.

D) Articles in the U.S. Naval Institute *Proceedings*, in *Marinerundschau* and in other periodicals.

Notes

(References are to books listen in Sources.)

Historical Background

1. Gorshkov, S. G., *The Sea Power of the State*, Moscow, 1976.
2. Gorshkov, S. G., *Navies in War and Peace*, U.S.N.I. *Proceedings*, February 1974, p. 36.
3. *Ibid.*, April 1974, p. 54.

The Baltic

1. For source of all extracts from war diaries, see Sources.
2. *The Great Patriotic War, vol. II*, p. 52.
3. *Ibid., vol. II*, pp. 100–101.
4. Meister, p. 43.
5. Piterski, p. 525.
6. *The Great Patriotic War, vol. III*, p. 556.
7. Isakov, p. 31.
8. Piterski, p. 253.
9. *The Great Patriotic War, vol. III*, p. 496.
10. *Ibid., vol. III*, p. 501.
11. *Ibid., vol. IV*, p. 520
12. Piterski, pp. 278–279.
13. *Ibid.*, p. 279.
14. *The Great Patriotic War, vol. IV*, p. 523.
15. *Ibid., vol. V*, p. 263.
16. *Ibid., vol. V*, pp. 258–263.
17. Piterski, p. 292.
18. *The Great Patriotic War, vol. IV*, p. 522.
19. *Ibid.*, p. 523.
20. Piterski, p. 294.
21. *Ibid.*
22. *The Fighting Road of the Soviet Sea War Fleet*, Moscow, 1974; German ed., East Berlin, 1976, p. 377.
23. *The Great Patriotic War, vol. V*, p. 274.
24. Ruge, F., *Der Seekrieg*, U.S. Naval Institute, 1956, p. 198.

The Black Sea

1. *The Great Patriotic War, vol. II*, p. 52.
2. Forstmeier, F., *Odessa 1941*, Freiburg, 1967, pp. 83ff.
3. *The Great Patriotic War, vol. II*, p. 370.
4. *Ibid., vol. III*.
5. *Ibid., vol. III*, p. 538.
6. Savateev, pp. 21–22.
7. *The Great Patriotic War, vol. III*, pp. 306–307.
8. *Ibid., vol. III*, p. 511.
9. *Ibid., vol. III*, p. 513.
10. *Ibid., vol. III*, p. 513.
11. *Ibid., vol. III*, p. 423.
12. *Ibid., vol. III*, p. 425.
13. *Ibid., vol. III*, p. 425.
14. NHT papers, German Miltary Archives, Freiburg.
15. *Ibid*.
16. *The Great Patriotic War, vol. III*, p. 430.
17. Piterski, p. 347.
18. Basov, "The actual losses of the German fleet . . . ," in Berewjanko, *Portiv falsifikatarov istorii vtoroj Mirovoj vrj*, Moscow, 1959, pp. 232–260.
19. *The Great Patriotic War, vol. IV*, p. 512.
20. *Ibid., vol. IV*, p. 513.
21. Piterski, p. 360.
22. *The Great Patriotic War, vol. IV*, p. 514.
23. *Ibid., vol. IV*, p. 514.

The Northern Theater

1. *The Great Patriotic War, vol. III*, p. 487.
2. Piterski, p. 261.
3. *The Great Patriotic War, vol. II*, p. 554.
4. *Ibid., vol. II*, p. 714.
5. *Ibid., vol. II*, p. 552.
6. *Ibid., vol. III*.
7. *Ibid., vol. IV*, p. 524.
8. Josseliani, *Notes of a Submariner*, Moscow, 1951, from unpublished contribution by J. Rohwer to NHT papers, p. 152.
9. *Ibid.*, p. 165.
10. *The Great Patriotic War, vol. V*, p. 276.
11. *Ibid., vol. V*, p. 260.

Conclusions

1. *The Great Patriotic War, vol. V*, p. 274.
2. *The Great Soviet Encyclopedia, vol. VII*, p. 99.
3. *The Great Patriotic War, vol. III*, p. 423.
4. Quoted in H. Goldhamer, *The Soviet Soldier*, London: Leo Cooper, 1975, p. 297.

Index